St. Louis Community College

Forest Park
Florissant Valley
Meramec

Instructional Resources
St. Louis, Missouri

Literary Authority

and the Modern Chinese Writer

Literary Authority

and the Modern Chinese Writer

Ambivalence and Autobiography

Wendy Larson

Duke University Press   *Durham and London 1991*

© 1991 Duke University Press
All rights reserved
Printed in the United States of America
on acid-free paper ∞
Typeset in Sabon.
Library of Congress Cataloging-in-Publication information
appear on the last printed page of this book.

To My Mother, Iola J. Larson

Contents

Acknowledgments xi

Introduction 1

1 Referentiality and Authority 11

Sima Qian: The Prototypical Circumstantial Autobiography 13
Liu Yuxi: Rank, Status, Official Life 17
Tao Yuanming and the Alternate Orthodoxy 19
The Recluse-Literatus and Modern Ideology 24
Bo Juyi: Wine, Poetry, and the Literatus 26
Summary 28

2 Autobiographies of the Late Qing Dynasty and Political
Implication 31

The Examination System 31
Literary Value and Status 35
Mystification and Economic or Political Power 40
Education and Textual Value 44
Affairs and Intellectual Involvement 46
Writing as Indicator: Intellectual Definition and the Nation 47
Late Qing Autobiography and Political Signification 47
Lin Shu and the Impressionistic Stance 48
Yi Shunding 50

Qing Circumstantial Autobiographies and Political Ideology:
Wang Tao   51
Liang Qichao   55
Self-Narrative at Thirty   56
Toward May Fourth   59

3 Shen Congwen and Ba Jin: Literary Authority Against the
"World"   61

Shen Congwen: The Military Against the Literary   65
Military Order and Utopian Consciousness   66
The Material: Desire and Attainment   67
From Freedom to Entrapment: Learning the Codes   69
Books Against the World: Books as World   70
Wen Against *Wu*   72
The "World" and Sensual Experience   72
From Military to Textual   73
Passivity and Textual Authority   74
Ba Jin and the Alternative of Labor   76
Conflicting Ideologies: Oppression Revealed   76
Writing in the Real World: Hazardous Work   78
Reinventing the Tradition   79
Ai Wu: Social Involvement or Writing   80
The Literary as a Category: Effete and Ineffectual   81

4 Hu Shi and Lu Xun: Writing, Identity, and Race   87

Lu Xun and the *Zhengren junzi*   88
Revolution Against Literature   89
Forced Out of "China"   93
Japan: An Alternate to "China"   98
Return, Race, and Nation   99
Hu Shi: Piles of Rotten Paper   101
Chinese Scholarship and Literature: Overdetermined
Textuality   109
The "Hu Shi" of the PRC: An Antitextual Ideology   110

5 Guo Moruo: "China" versus China   113

Social Relevance: A Solution to Textuality   114
Guo Moruo: Ultimate Litterateur   117

Nation, Race, Writer   119
Myth and the Orthodoxy   119
Destruction of Orthodoxy and the Childhood World   121
Education and the Bankruptcy of the Orthodox   124
The Rejection of "China"   127
Internalization of the Nation   131
Literary Authority   137
Position, Rank, and the Intellectual   139
Alternatives   141
Toward a New Writing   144
Resolution   146

Conclusion: Writers and Modern China   153

Notes   161

Works Cited   195

Index   203

Acknowledgments

There are many people and organizations who deserve thanks for their role in the process of this study. The Committee for Scholarly Communication with the People's Republic of China funded me for two years of study and research at Beijing University during 1979–1981, when much of the research for this manuscript was completed. The University of California at Berkeley provided a great deal of support in the form of graduate fellowships and expertise. The University of Oregon provided summer research support, and the finishing touches were put on this book when I was a research fellow at the Oregon Humanities Center.

At the University of California at Berkeley, Cyril Birch was very generous in allowing me to investigate what must have seemed, at times, like an odd and disorganized study, and he helped immensely in encouraging me to go forward and in providing illuminating comments. The terms "circumstantial" and "impressionistic" are his suggestions, and I feel they accurately depict the contradiction that is the basis of my study. Samuel Cheung also gave me valuable advice in my interpretation of the autobiographies of some premodern writers and encouraged me to seek out other texts to corroborate my findings in modern autobiography. D. A. Miller guided me through a maze of contemporary theoretical writings and always seemed to know exactly what I should be reading. At Beijing University, Sun Yushi pointed out several modern studies and autobiographies I should be aware of, and Yue Daiyun helped me sustain the belief that this study was worthwhile and introduced me to material both in modern Chinese literature and contemporary theory. Others have read the manuscript and provided critical comments. Tani Barlow gave me an invaluable detailed reading that provided the basis for substantial revision, and Angela Zito reorganized my essay on Hu Shi into a much more compelling narrative. Mary Erbaugh read the manuscript with great care and pointed out my many repetitions and confusing use of language. Ted Huters has provided a very productive combination of encouragement and constructive criticism, both in his own work, which I regard as extremely thought-provoking, and in his willingness to read and reread, criticize and recriticize the manuscript. I also want to thank Reynolds Smith, senior editor at Duke University Press, for his interest, patience, and very useful suggestions.

Final thanks goes to Xu Luo, Marty, and Alisa, who had to put up with enough weekend work to try the patience of the most supportive families.

Literary Authority

and the Modern Chinese Writer

Introduction

Throughout the twentieth century Chinese writers have wrestled with the problem of how to create a new literary tradition that both maintains some of the culturally unique aspects of a very rich pre-twentieth-century tradition and succeeds in promoting a new modernity. Although it can be argued that the search for literary modernity began in the last half of the Qing dynasty, it is clear that for most scholars the May Fourth movement marks a radical break with the past. The movement itself is demarcated by the date May 4, 1919, but the May Fourth era—a time when ideas of realism, romanticism, feminism, science, democracy, anarchism, liberalism, socialism, liberation, and communism ran through the pages of intellectual journals—begins before this date and continues after it. It is impossible to determine the exact end of the May Fourth era, but it must be sometime between the May 30 Incident of 1925 and the Nationalist/Communist split of 1927. Certainly by the last half of the 1920s the political circumstances of China had altered to the extent that scholars began to refer to the period as "post-May Fourth."

By 1925 the May Fourth movement was waning or over, but the writers who were central to the cultural aspect of the movement continued to work into the 1930s, the 1940s, and in some cases up through the contemporary period. This study began with the question of how these writers, through autobiography, defined the "self" and "work" of a writer in the period immediately following May Fourth, approximately from 1925 to 1935. The problem of authority in literature immediately became central to locating and analyzing the ways in which Chinese writers theorized their selves, their work, and their texts.[1]

Thus my study of the problem of literary authority began with the reading of Chinese autobiographies, which I initially approached as a subset within the genre of *zhuanji,* or biography.[2] Reading in modern (as opposed to premodern) autobiographies alerted me to an inexplicable paradox informing many manuscripts, which later became central to my developing thesis on writers of the May Fourth generation and their discourse on text and the writer.[3] The first and most obvious clue to this paradox was that *in autobiographies written by writers and scholars* the authors frequently expressed doubt and anxiety about their profession, and sometimes a passion bordering on hatred emerged. The "themes" or content of the autobiographies contained considerable questioning directed at the ideologies of self and work which the writer or scholar was constructing. On a structural level these texts presented even more evidence that writers and scholars were negatively reinscribing the textual labor that was the work of the writing intellectual. The autobiographies were structured in such a way that a binary contrast between something literary—the writer, the text, scholarship—and another alternative was established. In each case the work that was defined by its relationship to writing—textual work—was negatively constructed as passive and degrading and the alternative as positive and active. Writing was established within the text as something distinctly different from material production, existing "outside" the socioeconomic world. In terms of the identity or self of the writer or scholar the result of this reinscription was that, because of his affiliation with textual labor, the writer appeared burdened by lack of involvement in material production and insignificant influence on social progress and was stymied in his attempt to redefine himself as one constituted through productive, actively engaged work.[4] Thus the writer, the scholar, and textual work were constituted negatively, and the negative/positive comparison between textual work and its alternatives became a source of contradiction for the modern writer.

This contradiction, between what I later called "literary authority" and "socio-material authority," became the center of my research on autobiography. I relinquished my study of autobiography as a genre or a subgenre and began to investigate the textual authority invested in premodern texts and its constitution as a negative or positive orientation. I could not find any such contradiction nor, despite the existence of premodern debates on the value of textual work (discussed in chapter two), any text that demeaned textual work to the extent I had found in modern texts. However, I determined that within the limited number of pre-modern "autobiographies" that I considered, texts could be arranged along a continuum depending on the type of references used to define the self of the author. At one end of the continuum were the *circumstantial* texts, in which the *context of referentiality* was the socio-material world of kinship, ancestry, "real" time and place, proper names, and official position.[5] At the other end were the *impressionistic* autobiographies, which suppressed reference to kinship, "real" time and place, proper name, and official position and substituted reference to aspects of the life of a detached literatus. This system of references, which I termed a "literary code," included allusion to reading and writing for pleasure, drinking, solitary and nonsocial activities, and figural nomination as opposed to the use of "real" socially and genealogically determined names. It is important to note here that both circumstantial and impressionistic systems of reference are textual strategies and traditions; even though circumstantial texts utilize references to specifically social ties, names, and positions, this nonetheless constitutes a type of textual organization. The opposition is not between a type of text that is somehow more "material" against one that is more "literary," but rather between two differing types of representation within texts.

Most premodern autobiographies fell somewhere between these two poles, but a few were excellent prototypes of the differing referentiality of these two extremes. Even though many texts contained a combination, clear differences in authority for premodern autobiographies did exist; some made use of the more orthodox social authority of kinship, ancestry, and position in the textual construction of an identity, and others favored suppression of this earlier tradition, instead promoting a "self" through reference to a more literary code. The circumstantial texts created a self within the confines of orthodox social existence, whereas the textually constructed identity of the authors of impressionistic texts emerged through denial of this existence and replacement by another. However, in contrast to the modern texts the premodern autobiographies did not privilege one type of authority while dismissing another. There were few overt signs within the text that authors who chose the "impressionistic" type of self-portrayal devalued this "literary code" or felt it inferior to any other alternative.

Two questions were left by these investigations. First, when did textual work begin to be conceived of as negative and passive, and how did that process take place? Second, why were modern texts almost all circumstantial, and what had happened to impressionistic authorization?

Outside autobiography there was ample evidence that by early Republican times texts and textual work were problematic.[6] That textual work frequently was formulated as negative, passive, and degrading *within autobiography* was an indication that not only textual work, but also the identity of the writer and scholar were in question. The intellectual creation of modern ideology was working to redefine those whose primary work was textual, the meaning of their work, and the function of the text within society. In order to answer questions concerning the negative inscription of textual labor, my research evolved into a wider investigation into the status, function, and position of writing and the writer in China in the first half of the twentieth century and incorporated materials from texts other than autobiographies.

Through textual analysis of the autobiographies written by writers and scholars, and additional investigation of historical sources, political documents, popular opinion, and background information on the lives of the writers and scholars in question, I was able to substantiate my central thesis: by the late 1920s, at the latest, writers of the May Fourth generation were constituting textual work and specifically literary work negatively. Despite this deleterious characterization, writers and scholars continued their work and thus suffered under a contradiction between the socio-material authority which they ostensibly desired and the reality of their textually determined careers. It is this contradiction which is clearly indicated in the autobiographies of writers and scholars of this era.

The contradiction in authority that I have located exists on the level of content and thematic expression—the author actually complains about the dehabilitating effects of being a writer and claims he does not want to continue or did not want to work as a writer in the first place—and in various subtexts of the autobiographies. In numerous texts I located not only a negative reinscription of textual labor, but also an underlying contradiction between textual work and other work that, despite all claims to the contrary, privileges textual work. In other words although textual labor was attacked, it was also structurally present in the writer's attempts to demean it and thus was overdetermined, or represented in the work many times over and in different strata. Sometimes the level of transparent communication is at odds with the meaning of one or more subtexts. Shen Congwen's text, for example, is structured in the form of a metaphor that works against the professed desires of the author, privileging the literary over the socio-material. Although the author directly states his aversion for textual work, the structure of his autobiography indicates an overlying textual authority that undermines his protestations. Guo Moruo and Ba Jin present themselves as drawn into a life of literary writing against their will, almost by default; although these writers claim a desire to establish themselves as soldiers or workers, *others* insist on their skill with words and force them to take up or resume literary endeavors. Lu Xun attacks the way in which texts are studied, or imposed on students in Chinese education, and establishes literature in opposition to revolution; however, he then presents his decision to become a writer as something he is pushed toward when increasing patriotic awareness reshapes his conception of medical work. Hu Shi contrasts negative textual work with what he sees as the more material and valuable work of science but organizes his own work on principles taken from textual work.

When I investigated late Qing autobiographies, I found the same continuum and poles of referentiality that existed in the premodern texts. My focus on May Fourth texts and the problem of authority did not allow me time or space to make a representative study of pre-Qing and Qing autobiographies, but within the small number of texts I studied impressionistic texts were a better indicator of conservatism than circumstantial texts, which could signify either conservatism or progressivism. The circumstantial autobiography appeared to be a tool that could be utilized by writers in their own internal production of modernity, while the impressionistic autobiography became a premodern form that could not indicate modernity. Rather, reference to the premodern "code" of literary concepts, entities, and behavior that was the trademark of the impressionistic autobiography became one way for an author to display a relatively oldstyle intellectual stance, as opposed to the newly emerging "modernity" of the reformers. My investigations into Republican autobiographies proved this tendency to be accurate, and as the impressionistic autobiography disappeared entirely in the modern era, when older writers had long since taken and maintained a distinctive posture, there was a diminishing number of new writers willing to adopt a similar antireform pose. Nonetheless, although the form was gone, a preoccupation with textual authority characteristic of impressionistic texts remained.

I interpreted the elimination of the impressionistic autobiography as part of the redefinition of textual work which occurred at the end of the Qing dynasty and into the Republican era. Of course, changes in the concept of the text, scholar, and writer were occurring much earlier, but the end of the Qing represents a radical break with parts of earlier tradition.[7] The examination system, which was a major ideological unifier and determined the content and form of education and the formulation of textual value, was abolished in 1905. Part of the redefinition process involved a devaluing of the corpus of the Chinese literary tradition, or the "Chinese learning" which was the basis of the exam. Documents from the late Qing period make it clear that to many reformers this tradition was seen as empty and useless against vital Western traditions and was implicated in China's military defeats.

Thus another paradox appears: while Liang Qichao and others are promoting new-style fiction as a means toward national salvation, intellectuals are thoroughly repudiating the Chinese literary tradition and attacking overemphasis on study of texts (as opposed to material phenomena investigated by science and the technology of engineering) by students and textual work by scholars. Late Qing and early Republican years find critics elevating literature as essential to China's modernization and defending literature against the "attacks" of those who were saying it was worthless. For example, in a 1923 lecture at Shanghai University, Guo Moruo said: "Art and literature have these great missions: to unify the emotions of humanity and to elevate the human spirit, beautifying life. This is already enough to affirm the eternal value of literature and art, even though some mindless people are blindly attacking them, saying they are useless ornamentation. But art and literature will develop more and more every day." Guo makes it clear that literature as a social institution is under assault, but as a writer he defends literary work and even construes it as the repository of the good and the beautiful.[8] During the late Qing and early Republican years the status and function of literature was in transition, and viewpoints ranged from the demotion of literary writing as ornamentation to its elevation as the only true abstract good and beautiful. Furthermore, however, I believe the elevation of literature that is common in theoretical documents from approximately 1900 to 1925 (and to some extent to the present time) is partially an attempt by writers and other intellectuals to recoup the value of textual work which had been under attack in the last thirty or forty years of the nineteenth century and which was dealt a decisive blow in the abolition of the examination system.

Writing in 1922, Hu Shi gives an evaluation of the examination system that shows to what extent he feels the system is indicative of past textual traditions:

China's national language (*guoyu*) was formed long ago, and used widely long ago. It has long since produced many first rate literary works. But the national language was not recognized by everyone, nor was literature written in the national language: what is the reason behind this? There are two reasons: one is that the examination system was not abolished, and the other is that there was not a systematic promotion of the national language.

For every day that the examination system continued, the prestige of the classical language increased. The reason that under the examination system so many vernacular works could appear is that the temptations of wealth and fame could not buy off Shi Naiyan, Cao Xueqin, and Wu Jingci, so political power could not suppress the production and widespread availability of *Shuihu zhuan* [Men of the marshes], *Xiyou ji* [Journey to the west], and *Honglou meng* [Dream of the red chamber]. This alone is the most fortunate and glorious aspect of Chinese literature. But the examination system could force most literati to pass their time delving into piles of old writing, so they never discovered what kinds of literature exist outside their classical writing. If the examination system was still functioning, vernacular literature never would have had such an easy victory.

Hu describes the examination system as a literary deterrent that prevented *wenren* from studying and creating a living literature.[9] From the late Qing reformers' point of view China's defeats at the hands of Japan and Western countries was not only or even primarily a result of undeveloped military strength, but rather came from hundreds of years of emphasis on the wrong kinds of study and scholarship—cultural traditions which produced an intellectual elite who were masters of a body of texts but ignorant of what was in the process of becoming identified as "modern" skills. Long before the Qing, but with increasing intensity by the late 1800s, the examination and its accompanying education were criticized as excessively literary. As long as the examination system was intact, "Chinese learning" was useful, in that mastery of it opened the opportunity for success not only in the exam itself, but also in service to the government through eventual official appointment. The ratification of "Chinese learning" through its connection to political power that had been operative through the examination system for several centuries disappeared when the examination was abolished and education was reformed in the late Qing dynasty. Thus the impressionistic autobiography, which established the literary essence of "Chinese learning" as its context of referentiality and subsequent authority, could not be used to indicate modernity.

Although I have used autobiographies as my primary documents, this study is not a history or study of autobiography. It is an investigation of the authority invested in writing and writers in the late 1920s and early 1930s, and the changes in this authority at the time. Because in an autobiography the proposed subject and object of the text is the same, they are excellent source materials to use in a study of authority.[10] Since my central concern is textual work and the way it is reinscribed in the early modern period, I have used only those autobiographies written by scholars or writers, whose basic self-definition comes from their affiliation with textual labor. It is in looking at this modern ideology of text that the premodern circumstantial/impressionistic dichotomy becomes significant. There are no modern impressionistic texts—autobiographies that avoid reference to ancestry, social ties, socially sanctioned names. Nonetheless, the contradiction that exists within modern texts—a privileging of literary structures against a more openly professed set of social or material references and desires—replicates the division of "literary" references in the impressionistic autobiography and "socio-material" references in the circumstantial autobiography. This suggests two things. First, as previously discussed, the categories of "literary" and "socio-material" are not only modern ideologies. Second, the conscious elevation of anti-textual work and the unconscious or implied privileging of textual work is pronounced only in the modern era. Thus while the form of the dialectic comes from Chinese intellectual discourse, the relative and hierarchical arrangement of its parts is an attempt not only to continue to deal with premodern categories, but also to establish a modern ideology that distinguishes itself from the past.

Once I had established the negative apprehension of textual labor that took place among writers in the late 1920s and early 1930s, another important question was raised. What are the alternatives that writers and authors offer against textual labor, and what characteristics make them attractive as nontextual options? As positive alternatives to the negative work of a writer or scholar, authors writing in the late 1920s and early 1930s propose four basic areas: manual labor, physical revolutionary work, physical military work, and finally a redefinition of writing that reorients it as a part of, rather than differentiated from, activity in the socio-material world. The first three options are most widely implied or discussed and involve the writer/scholar altering his identity away from constitution as an "intellectual" (*zhishifenzi*) and into constitution as a "worker" (*gongren*), "revolutionary" (*gemingzhe*), or "soldier" (*junren*).[11] The last option maintains the writer in his role as intellectual. It involves the reconceptualization of *literature* as socialist or realist and of *scholarship* as *yanjiu* (research) rather than *kaozheng* (evidential research). It is probable that realism, and especially socialist realism, were attractive to May Fourth writers and later writers because they solved the problem of the text by realigning writing and the writer as very close to, if not actually part of, the forces of material production.

It is important to note that in investigating the *construction* of a modern textual ideology, I have made use of all kinds of texts, including some that other scholars may ignore or even find offensive. For example, in my discussion of the twentieth-century appropriation of Tao Yuanming as an overly literary poet who has no inkling of reality for the true peasant or farmer and who romanticizes farm life, I have utilized the criticisms of leftist theorists who are using Tao as a negative example. In discussing Hu Shi, I pulled out documents from the 1950s which attacked Hu Shi as an overly textual scholar and tried to thoroughly demolish his scholarly reputation. In neither case am I trying to prove that Tao Yuanming and Hu Shi are as their detractors claim; I neither accept nor reject their arguments. In evaluating twentieth-century formulations it is impossible to avoid the study of modern forms, including the reinscription of the past.

This being said, I must admit that my own analysis of the autobiographies of Tao Yuanming and Hu Shi contributes to modern attempts to recast them and their work as overly textual. In the case of Tao Yuanming, I have tried to point out that many twentieth-century critics have been positive about Tao's historical reputation as a "field and garden poet" but nonetheless have had to deal with the problems of reinterpreting that phrase within the context of modern society. Even though Tao may have been quite revolutionary in his time as he solidified a tradition of intellectual eremitism, by the twentieth century he was the orthodox representative of this kind of writing and intellectual life. It is only by looking backward, seeing Tao from the point of view of modern concerns about the role of the text and the intellectual, that I can interpret and make sense of his autobiography as a kind of literati code.

The case of Hu Shi is even more difficult because Hu's long and multifaceted career makes him one of the most problematic figures I discuss. In his essays of the 1920s Hu was working on the problem of textual versus nontextual work; with this background in mind my analysis of his auto-

biography as expressing ambivalence on this issue is convincing. However, the attacks on Hu Shi in the 1950s were motivated by politics and by
Hu's affiliation with the Nationalist government more than by a serious
appraisal of his scholarship or career. Nonetheless, the fact that leftist
critics wanted to attack Hu does not stipulate a certain approach or topic
in their attacks; in that critics sometimes focus on a certain theory and
practice of textual work, they are at least concentrating on something Hu
Shi himself much earlier had identified as an area of concern. From the
point of view of this manuscript their criticism is not so much a critique of
Hu Shi as it is testimony to the continuing significance of evaluating
textual versus other kinds of work in contemporary China.[12]

I have tried to focus on texts that approach the life of the author in its
entirety rather than in one temporally defined segment; I have avoided
autobiographies that deal with only a few years of the author's life. This
criteria is evident in the author's stance and does not privilege a long text
over a short one.

I have used *pinyin* throughout the text, changing names cited within
quotes in the text to *pinyin* but retaining bibliographic references in the
original Romanization.

1

Referentiality and Authority

Referentiality and culturally determined signification within a text or other system of discourse has been a longstanding topic of research in semiotics and sociological anthropology, areas of study that have spanned many decades and volumes. My approach to the four texts analyzed in this chapter is basically semiotic; in each text I collect incidences of certain types of signification whose meaning depends on reference within a particular textual code. Although the texts I have chosen are all "autobiographies" according to the guidelines established in the preface, they should not be taken as representative of premodern Chinese autobiographies or as attempts to indicate and discuss the history of Chinese autobiography. Even though there is no classification for autobiographies in the *Siku quanshu* nor any body of literature Chinese scholars regard as autobiography, there are hundreds of texts—*zizhuan, zishu,* and *zixu* as well as diaries, journals, travelogues, poetry, confessions, and self-admonishments—which should be discussed in a comprehensive or even preliminary history of autobiography.[1] My thesis in this chapter is that among premodern autobiographies there are a number of texts which, if categorized according to signifying referents, fall into my two main categories of "circumstantial," in which the author refers primarily to his social and material circumstances, defining the self by its relationship to institutions and structures that signify status and power and locating the self physically within places identified with common, socially accepted names; and "impressionistic," in which the writer attempts definition through identification with an atemporal, intertextual tradition that suppresses reference to the temporally and spatially organized world of ancestry and position, substituting instead references to the leisured life of the literati.[2] Within the text the writer is positing a definition of the intellectual self and its role in society which will differ radically depending on the type of autobiography he chooses to employ.[3] The following examples, two of which are clearly circumstantial and two of which are equally as clearly impressionistic, indicate that whereas the denigration of textual labor common in modern writer's autobiographies does not exist in these premodern works, the self of the intellectual has been constructed in at least two very dissimilar ways.[4] The individual intellectual in the circumstantial autobiography is formed through textual affiliation with society's present and past affairs, whereas the intellectual of the impressionistic autobiography is distinguished through a textual construction of a life of withdrawal from affairs and association with literary pursuits. Thus the split between an intellectual determined through affiliation with textual work as opposed to social (or, in modern times, physical) labor, which is so plainly displayed in the modern autobiography, is not solely a modern ideology.

The circumstantial autobiography is a textual construction that relies on reference to ancestry, position, locale, and status, creating an intellectual figure that is firmly entrenched within the signifying institutions of society. This is the bulk of the orthodox tradition of official biography, although many early biographies contain a brief character appraisal at the end. The impressionistic autobiography eschews this orientation, instead substituting for it the figure of the somewhat reclused, leisured literatus who spends his time reading and writing poetry and discussing literature with his friends over a bottle of wine.[5] This also becomes an orthodox tradition, although it is not common in official biography. Both are *wenren*, but each draws on a specific aspect of the *wenren* tradition in self-definition.

Although the impressionistic autobiography refers to a more exclusively literary code of poetry, discussion of writing, and the general existence of an intellectual whose time is taken up with literary endeavors, it is not in itself a more "literary" document than the circumstantial text. Only the referents, which are the only segment of the text relevant to this study, are more exclusively literary, not the style or even the author. Thus the "literary code" is not just writing or literary writing, but includes reference to various components of the life-style of a nonsocially engaged literatus.

Sima Qian: The Prototypical Circumstantial Autobiography

One of the earliest known autobiographies in China, that of the historian Sima Qian, consists of the seventieth chapter of his *Shiji* (Records of the grand historian). Like many autobiographical essays that follow, this text is appended to or included in the main text as an explanation of the questions which surround the text itself: the author's reasons for writing it and the circumstances of its existence.[6] A reason not given in the text yet discernible in its progression is Sima Qian's desire to defend himself and his actions in a story well-known to Chinese historians. When he championed the cause of the general Li Ling, who surrendered to the Xiongnu rather than follow the established practice of fighting to the death, Emperor Wu of the Han ordered Sima to chose between castration or death; in order to finish the work of the *Shiji*, he chose castration.[7] Thus the autobiography is a vindication of the self and an attempt to validate his text even though historical record has called into question his authority both as representative and transmitter of orthodox morality. As such the text is an attempt to fix or define the identity of the self with relation to what the writer regards as the context of its emergence.

At the beginning of his translation of the *Shiji*, Burton Watson inserts this note: "Following custom, Sima Qian begins his account with a genealogy of his family, tracing it back, as is the wont of Chinese writers, to the golden ages of the legendary past" [42]. The custom to which he refers is that of biography, which begins the life of the individual in the distant past, placing him in a temporal sequence in which his life appears as simply a moment along the way. Sima Qian conforms with this tradition by reciting a brief genealogy which becomes somewhat lengthier as it arrives at the life of his father, Sima Tan, who was the Grand Historian before him. The "Discussion of the Essentials of the Six Schools" is an essay by his father that details his father's ideas on the various philosophic schools of the time.

When he arrives at his own life, Sima Qian deals with the time from his birth up until his entry into government service in one short section:

> He had a son named Qian. Qian was born at Longmen. He plowed and pastured on the sunny side of the hills along the River. At the age of ten he could read the old writings. When he was twenty he traveled south to the Yangzi and Huai rivers (Jiangsu), he climbed Huiji and looked for the cave of Yu (Zhejiang), and he saw the Nine Peaks (Henan). He sailed down the Yuan and Xiang rivers and in the north

forded the Wen and Si rivers (Shandong). He studied the learning of the cities of Qi and Lu. He observed the customs and practices inherited from Confucius and took part in the archery contest at Mount Yi in Zou. He met with danger and trouble in Po and Xue and Bengcheng. Then he passed through Liang and Chu and returned home. After this Qian entered government service as a Langzhong. [48]

This section uses names that in actual social usage correspond to commonly identifiable locales, and the language is referential to the context of the phenomenal world and orthodox ideology. Through reference to the physical world this section of the essay situates the identity of the writer in a spatial context, whereas the previous section situated the identity of the writer in a temporal context. The self or identity of the writer is defined temporally through its lineage and spatially through the physical sites of its existence. Both the temporal and spatial aspects of this definition of the self take material phenomena as the framework of their reference.

Sima Qian mentions his participation in a large military expedition that was sent to the southwest in 111 A.D. in an attempt to conquer new territory for Han rule, and his father's resentment at being unable to attend the ceremony of the Feng Sacrifice at Mt. Tai. As a "symbol of the divine election of the ruling house," the Feng Sacrifice contains and indicates the cosmology of the assumption and continuation of the abstracted power that allows the emperor to continue his rule. The military expedition is a symbol for the physical manifestation of power which the emperor can exert to extend and maintain his rule. In that they are indications of the existence and extension of powerful political and moral institutions, both the Feng Sacrifices and the military expedition are linked to the phenomenal world which was defined spatially and temporally in the last two segments of the text.

Sima Qian quotes his father as he implores his son to take over the duty of Grand Historian when he dies:

> The Grand Historian grasped his hand and said, weeping, "Our ancestors were Grand Historians for the House of Zhou. From the most ancient times they were eminent and renowned when in the days of Yu and Xia they were in charge of astronomical affairs. In later ages our family declined. Will this tradition end with me? . . .
>
> I have been Grand Historian, and yet I have failed to set forth a record of all the enlightened rulers and wise lords, the faithful minis-

ters and gentlemen who were ready to die for duty. I am fearful that the historical materials will be neglected and lost. You must remember and think of this!" [49]

Significantly, the transfer of the power to record and preserve the exemplary lives and deeds of enlightened men is put into a monologue (with a short acceptance by Sima Qian attached) spoken by his father. Sima Qian's embodiment as one in a conceived chain of historical recorders who maintain morality and even, through their records, create the morality of the past comes out of the mouth of a previous holder of this power whose temporal and spatial existence is important in establishing his and his son's authority.

The moment of Sima Qian's assumption of the position of Grand Historian comes immediately after this speech: "Three years after the death of his father, Qian became Grand Historian" [50]. After the reading of the available records the first act he records is the rectification of time: "Five years after this was the first year of the era Taizhu. At dawn on the first day of the eleventh month, the day *jiazi* [December 25, 102], the zenith of winter, the calendar of heavens was first corrected and set up in the Illustrious Hall. All the spirits received the chronology" [50]. Sima Qian then repeats a slightly altered version of his father's words and expresses his determination to carry out his father's will.

The self which Sima Qian constructs is partially based on the act of rectification. This is most obvious in Sima Qian's attempt to rectify the physical self, which has been mutilated through castration, by defending his acts and by privileging his role as Grand Historian. Similar to the rectification of time, which is accomplished through the reordering of the calendar, the rectification of the self is accomplished through the individual assumption of a moral role which is passed through time and through the persona of a moral figure of authority. The rectification of the self is effected through transmission, a duty of the Grand Historian which Sima Qian emphasizes when he explains his responsibilities to his friend Hu Sui. Self-definition is accomplished through appeal to transmission, first through the father and then through the work to which this autobiography is attached. The authenticity of the self and the text is linked to and proven by their value in assisting transmission. Thus the act of transmission is vital in its ability to authorize the act of writing as well as the author's identity, or in authorizing both the self and the text.

Transmission implies both information, or content, and position, which must define the role of the transmitter and perhaps the implied role of the receiver. Sima Qian situates his discourse in relation to the seminal power structures of elite Chinese society: rites and calendar time, which indicate the power of the emperor as the proper representative of the will of heaven, the emperor's appearance (the color of his vestments), and the books which are his sacred texts. The self as he writes it takes its being only in relation to these elements, all of which are external to the characteristics of the self (appearance, personality traits, likes and dislikes, etc.) or any essentialized vision of the self that would accentuate individual traits. Rather, the self emerges through situation within and juxtaposition against this social context.[8] The identity of the writer becomes evident only through the defining power of phenomena such as the Feng Sacrifice, the emperor's vestments, and the military expedition to the southwest.[9]

In the last section of this chapter Siam Qian refers to his castration and claims that misfortune often inspires writing, lists the contents of the *Shiji* chapter by chapter, and reviews his purpose and accomplishments in the writing of the *Shiji*. Although he does not directly defend himself in the Li Ling case, reference to it in conjunction with his examples of writers who were inspired to write through misfortune establish this section as a defense and validation of his own writing (the *Shiji*). The self has been invalidated through castration, yet it can revalidate itself through its position as inheritor of the right to preserve and transmit records and as the rectifier of morality, or as a narrator of orthodoxy.[10] The loss of his self through castration can be rectified by writing, and the self can be regained.[11]

Thus although the motivation behind the writing, validation and rectification, springs from personal circumstances, Sima Qian still deals with his life only in its official capacity and only in its relation to external phenomena, social structures and institutions, and political ideology. He is the tool through which historical records and the historical identity (ancestry and line) will be transmitted. In his own self-rectification he can rectify future transmissions as well; his mutilation and humiliation will disappear through his assumption of the role of transmitter of records, and the name that will be transmitted to future generations will not be connected to his disfigurement, but to the morality he seeks to hand down and to his own role as transmitter of that morality. By attaching the autobiography to another text as an explication, Sima Qian can avoid potential criticism that he is attempting to write his own biography.

In identifying Sima Qian's autobiography as the prototype of a circumstantial type of text, I am focusing only on the kind of referents he uses to construct a textual self. This interpretation says nothing about the style of Sima's writing or his character, which some critics have identified as extremely emotive and romantic, or about the fictionality or factualness of his historical account.[12]

Liu Yuxi: Rank, Status, Official Life

Another example of a circumstantial autobiography is "Zi Liuzi zizhuan" [The autobiography of Zi Liuzi] by Liu Yuxi (772?–842). He begins:

> Zi Liuzi's name is Mengde. The son Sheng of his ancestor the Emperor Jing of the Han along with his wife Jia was given the rank of the King of Zhongshan (*Zhongshan wang*), and posthumously called Jing; so his grandchildren are enfeoffed as people of Zhongshan. For seven generations his ancestors Liang served the northern dynasty and often served as councillor for the provincial governor. When the capitol was moved to Luoyang, they became northerners of Duchangli.
>
> They have always served as Confucians. Their graves are at the north mountain of Luoyang. [240]

About one-third of the text traces Liu Yuxi's ancestry, listing the occupations of his great grandfather, his grandfather, and his father. The family's whereabouts are also clearly delineated. Liu discusses his own success in the government's civil service examinations, his teaching duties, his illness, and his subsequent official positions. He identifies the times of occurrences and refers to specific historical events and the names of people involved. The entire narrative is basically little more than a recitation of the names of the posts he held, the names of the cities in which he lived, and at the end the epitaph he wrote to be put on his tombstone. He wrote this autobiography at the age of seventy-one, not long before he died.

In this text the name the author uses is his socially and culturally sanctioned name, which is also the name of the author's ancestors. This name functions as a link of a chain that places him in line with official history, which consists of ancestors and close relatives who held official positions and whose names and titles could contribute to the status of the author, giving him definition in his relation to other people and to holders of political power. Through referential language which takes these elements as its context, the autobiography of Liu Yuxi aligns itself with structures of political power. Ancestors appear not as multifaceted people who perform in numerous capacities but as progenitors—those who give the author lineage and establish his name in time. The author's works are also listed by name, establishing his identity as inheritor of the public role of officeholder.

The authority of the text derives from an alignment of the self within political configurations which influence and control social intercourse in the material world. Thus the textual creation of self is accomplished through juxtaposition with a common recognized and acknowledged structure which also exists temporally, in the manifestation of ancestry, and spatially, in official position and location. As in the text of Sima Qian, these defining elements exist outside any essentially determined self that is individual in focus.

In this autobiography friends are mentioned by name, yet only when they are related to the author's official persona or to their own identity as a public figure. For example, Liu Yuxi's friend Wang Shuwen, who for a time was powerful enough to help him obtain a post, is mentioned several times.[13]

Another feature of Liu Yuxi's autobiography which is similar to Sima Qian's text is the motivation behind its writing. Both authors have a desire to vindicate the self. After his friend Wang Shuwen fell out of favor, Liu Yuxi spent his life in banishment, continually transferred from one far-away place to another. He wrote his autobiography only when he knew death was approaching; by this time he had been exonerated and honored once again with new titles. He recounts his life, each position he held, and the reason he held it, but he does little in the way of direct self-justification. At the end of the autobiography he adds on his own self-epitaph, which proclaims his innocence. Liu's implied self-justification requires a minimal recording of process at least in reference to past events and implies an orientation toward social events and phenomena. In this text nowhere does Liu Yuxi describe his own personality or emphasize his relationship to literature, even though he was a well-known poet who wrote voluminously during his old age.

The autobiographies of Sima Qian and Liu Yuxi are excellent examples of the circumstantial pole of autobiographies, texts in which the author defines himself through reference to physical and social circumstances, including those which existed before his birth but now contribute to his societal makeup. In this short essay as much as in a longer work, the self is a textual construct that emerges out of a referential context of social status, political position, and other orthodox manifestations of society. Since this type of text is similar to biography not only in form but also in content, it is also an attractive means of self-definition for a writer who has been criticized and may not have a favorable biography written by another writer. In this capacity within the Chinese tradition it is a true auto-biography, or a biography written by the self, that attempts to define the self in a context identical to that of orthodox biography.

Tao Yuanming and the Alternate Orthodoxy

In approximately 420 A.D., when Tao Yuanming (365–427) was fifty-six years old, he wrote a short autobiography, *Wuliu xiansheng zhuan* (The autobiography of Mr. Five Willows).[14] As the name suggests, it is written in biography form, and references to the author are in the third person. It is one of the earliest texts of its kind and is very short:

> No one knows where he comes from, or is clear about his name. Next to his dwelling are five willow trees, from which he gets his nickname. He is quiet and seldom speaks, and does not envy glory or profit. He loves to read, but does not seek deep understanding; whenever he comprehends meaning, he is so happy he forgets to eat. It is his nature to like wine, but his family is poor and he cannot often obtain it. His relatives and friends long since knew of this, so they sometimes prepare wine and have him over. Together they finish the wine, and eventually he will surely be drunk; when drunk, he retires, but no one ever takes offence if he leaves or stays. The surrounding walls [of his house] are broken down, and do not provide shelter from the wind and sun. His short cloth jacket is worn and patched, his baskets and gourds always empty. But his life is peaceful. He often writes to amuse himself; here he can express himself, and he forgets loss and gain. He will end his life in this way. People praise him, saying: "[The wife of] Qian Lou once said [of her recluse husband]: 'He was not anxious about poverty and lowliness, and did not wildly seek riches.'" If we plumb to the depths of these words, cannot we see that he is just this kind of person? When drunk, he writes poetry with great exhilaration, and takes pleasure in this. Is he a subject of Wu Huai or Ge Tian?[15]

In his very illuminating discussion of this short text, A. R. Davis provides commentary tracing the use of certain terms in previous texts and comments:

> This very brief self-portrait, written according to the conventions of a biography in Ban Gu's *Han shu* with a character appraisal at the end, is one of the most celebrated and most influential pieces of Chinese prose. . . . It was certainly one of the most successful attempts at creating a self-image in the history of Chinese literature and was probably a prime means by which Tao built his own legend within his own lifetime. . . . This at once self-depreciating, self-assuring description had its peculiar appeal for the Chinese writer-official whose social position was so often in the last resort insecure. [208–9]

Davis also notes that "this piece is almost completely unoriginal, being a pastiche of quotations or near quotations from the corpus of literature of hermitage, which by Tao's time was considerable" [209], pointing out the literary referentiality of the piece and its implicit opposition against the textual self-creation of a writer-official whose social position is secure or who wishes to secure it through reference to social orthodoxy [146–47]. However, although Davis mentions that the character appraisal at the end to some extent gives the autobiography the form of biography, in terms of referents, the text is remarkably distinct.

Thus Davis implies either that Tao Yuanming is consciously constructing an alternative to the employed writer-official or that in scholarship Tao and his work have come to represent an alternative life-style, work ethic, and social or political orientation. This viewpoint is supported by Xiao Wangqing, who claims that most critics have regarded Tao as an enlightened recluse who loves to read, especially "heterodox books," and that Tao has become a positive alternative to the official that most scholars looked forward to becoming.[16] Another modern critic, Guo Bogong, places Tao and his work in direct opposition to "government official," not only in the influence of future criticism, but in Tao's mentality itself: "From the viewpoint of the ordinary person, becoming an official naturally is a glorious thing. But he thought it was despicable, so after he left his post, he forever cut relations with politics. Life as a farmer was very harsh, but he still had leisure time to go sightseeing at Lu Mountain."[17]

Another modern critic, Gao Dapeng, traces the three elements—*shi, nong,* and *yin* [gentry, peasant, and recluse]—that constitute the building blocks in the mythification of Tao Yuanming from ancient to modern texts.[18] Gao claims that, at least according to his poetry, Tao did indeed work in the fields, but more important is his elevation of agricultural labor and the peasant life-style into a type of "agricultural philosophy" that functions as an "ideal foundation" in his writings [30]. Thus not only is Tao not isolated, as are most literati, from actual agricultural work, but in fact he identifies with it and is the first poet to take pride in it [31]. In this romanticization and beautification of farm and village life (also mentioned by Liang Qichao), Tao is able to become a prototype for future field and garden poets.

For Peng Dagao the *yin* aspect of Tao's persona is even more appealing to future intellectuals. Much as he elevates farm work, Tao takes pride in his isolation and removal from social and political affairs, putting into practice a form of existence latently ideal in the hearts and minds of literati:

> Whether it is in terms of nature, society, culture, or religion, the term *yin* has a traditional historical usage, so we can say it has become the "collective unconscious mind" of Chinese literati. It has become internalized as one aspect of the intellectual character. This is its most basic definition and foundation; simply put, it is the most fundamental, most common, and even highest value. . . . From this we can see that *yin* is a moral ideal for Chinese literati, and also an aesthetic ideal as well as ideology of supremacy—in the long-term progress of history, it has become the common dream of the literati. Tao Qian bravely did what they did not dare to do. His appearance gave reality to their dream in the most beautiful and powerful form. Therefore he provided a substitute satisfaction in the "unconscious minds" of the literati, and brought out a collective cry from their personalities, thinking, and morality. Their dreams were realized in his poetry, and thus Tao Qian became a hero-like idol. The creation of this hero was most influenced by *yin*. [43–44]

Gao feels the glorification of Tao's poetry as a repository of literati value continued until the Song, when it reached its highest peak [79–80].

The works of Tao Yuanming were not as much appreciated during his time as they came to be later during the Tang and Song dynasties. Very little of his poetry was included in the literary anthology *Wenxuan* [An anthology of selected writings], and in *Shipin* [Poetry rating] his work was rated as average (*zhongpin*). He was not even mentioned in *Wenxin diaolong* [The literary mind and the carving of dragons]. Criticism of Tao Yuanming contains complaints that he refers too frequently to wine and its pleasures and that he takes an attitude that detaches him from others and sets him above them. Tao was and still is called a "poet of fields and gardens" who had no connection to reality [Lu Xinli, 1979:3].[19]

In comparison to the circumstantial text Tao Yuanming's text presents a radically different context of referentiality. The most striking feature of this kind of autobiography is atemporality. Even though the form of biography is clear, the pre-present, the lives of the author's ancestors or even the existence of his father, is suppressed, nor is there mention of his own childhood or any incident of his life before the time of writing. Tao Yuanming disassociates himself with progression of time and places himself squarely in the middle of a temporal vacuum. His first line, "No one knows where he came from, or is clear about his name," effectively cuts off two aspects of the self that extend into the past to exploit the organizational power of ancestry: their circumstances in space, or the locale in which they lived and worked, and their name, which is the social classification of their existence in time.[20] His closing line makes a reference to two mythical emperors and questions his figurative relationship to them. Thus the author brings out his connection to the world of literary, verbal structures—these emperors are legendary, mythical figures—while denying or invalidating his own connection with those of the actual past and present. The author is placing himself in a vast temporal context that implies timelessness.

In suppressing the name of his ancestors and his own name, Tao Yuanming is suppressing the links to the social world that such names would imply. On top of this implied denial, however, Tao Yuanming also attempts to interpret his fanciful name, "Mr. Five Willows," as generating from the five willow trees planted near his home, causing name to refer back not to immediate society and its historical past, but to arbitrary phenomena. In this mocking of the orthodox value of nomination as the means by which the individual is associated with official history, the writer denies his relationship to this plane of existence. Instead, the name is empty, tying him to phenomena that have no meaning in the established social world.

In contrast to Sima Qian and Liu Yuxi, Tao Yuanming states his personality traits in a straightforward manner and does not link them to any incident or development. The affectations he lists are nonsocial: he is quiet and seldom speaks, and he detaches himself from envy of glory or profit, two attributes associated with excessive attachment to the material world or political power. Tao's next step—his statement that he loves to read—situates him within the dimension of writing. Although his connection with literature is profound in one sense, as it causes him to forget his sensual existence, he repudiates any rational search for understanding of literature, claiming to seek emotional gratification, not intellectual illumination. This denial works to sever any link which may associate him with literature as an institution and to emphasize personal gratification, a quality which has limited social significance.

In his reference to wine, which Tao Yuanming likes even though poverty keeps him from frequent indulgence, the author begins the construction of an alternate aesthetics and ideology which will take the place of the orthodox constitution of a scholar-official in his self-definition. Poverty and a simple life-style are alluded to again in his reference to his broken-down house, his worn-out clothing, and his empty food baskets. The only instance in the autobiography that shows him in social interaction with other people is when he drinks with them; even so, he often retires without anyone taking notice. Once again, he stresses his affinity for literature and writing and then ends his text with an allusion.

The elements of this autobiography in order of their appearance are an unknown place, an unknown name, a quiet personality, rejected worldliness, writing, wine, poverty, friends in wine, and a repetition of the last three elements, ending in reference to a myth. The narrative goes from an unknown to a myth, and the middle section is almost entirely references to writing, wine, and poverty.[21] In contrast with the autobiography of Sima Qian, there is no awareness of time, place is denied, name is rejected or perverted, and history does not exist. Tao Yuanming's narration is atemporal and the self is shaped through a context of reference composed of nonexistent or mythical figures, names and places, and qualities. The self is not rooted in either the past of known "history" or in the immediate political present, but rather in a literary or mythical time, locating identity entirely within a whimsical individual present.[22] The only link with the past is the rhetorical question referring to mythical figures at the end of the autobiography.

In this text the author is reclaiming the autonomy of the self from the orthodoxy of place, political power, and social structure and positioning it in another context which eventually developed into an orthodoxy of its own. The authorizing context of the autobiography of Sima Qian, the writer's position in the historical and immediate social world, does not even exist in Tao Yuanming's autobiography. The authority for self-definition is located entirely in the image of the detached, self-sufficient literatus who lives in and for the pleasure of reading poetry, discussing literature, and drinking.

Tao Yuanming is giving the reader very little information in his autobiography; the length of the text alone belies any attempt to transmit information. The text does not attempt to pass on information but to define the self first without reference to the official world of position and status and second with reference to another, alternative tradition. Thus the true name of the author cannot be used, for it is tied to the outside world through its inherent relationship to ancestors and status.[23]

It is through this opposing, suppressing set of alternative references that the impressionistic autobiography creates a totally unique textual identity. This text is a crafting of the self through its relation to a code which implies essentially literary as opposed to social and historical phenomena, and a denial of any position in the material world which consists of history, status, and official position. Thus although the language is and must be referential, the object of reference is the set of qualities appropriate to a disengaged literati. Poetry, wine, poverty, and self-indulgence are the characteristic elements of the myth in which the author participates and the existence of which he perpetuates. Poverty is one of the most basic factors, for it lessens the likelihood of status in the official world. Poetic literature is an integral constituent, yet its significance as a segment of the literary code lies in the author's interpretation of literature as a means of personal gratification and delight as opposed to literature's position as a social phenomenon delineating status or historical progression.

Impressionistic autobiographies challenge the significance of history, ancestry, and memory in constructing a textual self. Memory is the mind of the present remembering, and through this process altering, the past and bringing out the parts of it which inform the present self. Memory does not imply chronology, but it does indicate a time structure in that a past which forms a collective pool of information is available to be ferreted out and employed by the conscious or unconscious mind. However, as Tao Yuanming effectively denies time, and past in both time and place, he does not make use of memory as a device the self can employ in its own definition.[24] Because the autobiography resists specificity in a social or material context, it imparts a "floating" sense of detachment from familiar conceptual landmarks.

The Recluse-Literatus and Modern Ideology

In the mid and late 1920s and early 1930s it is the excessively literary context of referentiality which comes to connote a negative authority for poets and, more generally, writers.[25] Although it may be argued that modern critics tell us little about Tao's writing and the way in which it has functioned in Chinese literary history, through their comments we can evaluate the modern reinscription of ancient texts and thus the creation of a modern ideology of literature.[26] Within Tao Yuanming's text the literary code as defined above, although lucidly and unambiguously delineated against an alternative, is a positive form. Therefore although the appropriation of the literary code as adverse may be a late 1920s occurrence with roots in the early modern or late Qing period, the development of a differentiating conceptualization of one who does textual labor (the "scholar" in "scholar-official" or "writer" in "writer-official")—the splitting of the term and actuality of the *wenren* into two distinct zones—apparently occurs much earlier.

A brief look at some of the interpretations of Tao Yuanming's poetry during the 1920s and 1930s gives some indications of the deleterious implications which had become associated with his work by that time and which are related to the general reconceptualization of literary work as deficient.[27] In many descriptions Tao's work is identified with a reality-denying, escapist mentality that pretends to take farm life as a topic, but in actuality has nothing to do with the true life of a peasant.[28] Critics complain that his work is hampered by literary considerations at the expense of "real life" and even displays a deceptively attractive literary quality that could beguile an unwary reader into believing he or she is dealing with a utopic reality.

In the book *Wenxin* [Literary mind], first published in 1933 by Ye Shaojun (1893–1988) and Xia Mianzun (1885–1946), the student Lehua, who later is forced through economic need to become an iron worker, is enamored of Tao's writing. Lehua's father and his uncle also enjoy Tao's work, and since they have collected many volumes of his writing, Lehua has ample opportunity to pursue his interests when they are not at home. He especially enjoys Tao's descriptions of fields and gardens, so when his mother informs him that poverty may force their family to return to the countryside to live, he is delighted. The prospect of living a leisurely life planting and reading in the country appeals to him tremendously: "How dignified and noble!" [54].

The romantic vision Lehua has built up in his mind is broken when his father takes him to task for his interest in Tao's poetry: "Don't dream. This is for his era, not yours. Country life is not like that now; the peasants must buy expensive food from others just to survive. Our interest in these field and garden poets is just to enliven our brains. We are just city people taking a trip to the country" [55].

The issue of Tao's identity and the problem of intellectuals taking up residence in the country, trying to write about peasant life, or otherwise altering their essential relationship to work progresses one step further in the much later (1956) collection of essays *Wensi* [Literary thoughts] by the now well-known social scientist Cao Juren (1903–1972). Whereas Lehua's father points out the difference between Tao's era and the present time, in the essay "Literary Fabrications" Cao shows that it is not merely a matter of different eras. Tao Yuanming did not incorporate the reality of the peasant life of his own era into his poetry at all, and he should not be considered a "farmer's poet" [105]. The "reality" of the times, a peasant life of poverty and chaos, had been documented in many places, and yet Tao made no mention of it in his poetry. According to Cao, most of China's "field and garden poets," such as Tao Yuanming or Lu Fangweng of the Southern Song, are removed from actual working life and do not have peasant friends.[29] In their poetry these authors merely take a slice of farm life and turn it into a picture [102]. Cao suggests that Tao has a desire to hide from reality, a tendency which is also shown in his utopic *Taohua yuanji* [Peach blossom spring]; like most poets of the times, he escapes into Daoism and Buddhism and writes from an illusion of actual farm life.[30]

What Cao Juren identifies as the excessively literary context of referentiality of Tao's self-portrayal corresponds to the removal from "reality" which other twentieth-century critics formulate as the essential quality of his work; in the modern reconstruction Tao has specified the ingredients of a literary code which will now take on a new and negative implication. The image of the detached, leisurely poet who lives for the sensual delight of which literary appreciation is a major part came to be associated with Tao and his work. The criticism that Tao is removed from reality can refer not only to the context of his poetry, but also to the entire set of literary referents which isolate his intellectual identity.

Bo Juyi: Wine, Poetry, and the Literatus

Another somewhat longer (and more circumstantial) example of the impressionistic autobiography is Bo Juyi's *Zuiyin xiansheng zhuan* [The Biography of Master Singing Drunk], written when he was sixty-seven.[31] It begins typically: "Master Singing Drunk has forgotten his name, birthplace, and office, and does not know who he is" [256]. Bo Juyi identifies the place where he lives at the present time as Luo Xia, and mentions the basic elements in a stereotypical definition of a poet: his dwelling has a pond, trees, land, an open-air pavilion and bridge; he is at peace, he is poor and old; his nature is to love wine, music, and poetry; his guests come to drink, write, and listen to music.

As he mentions his attraction to Buddhism, the author names four friends and their home towns. Each person is a friend "in" some interest or pursuit: Ru Man is his "monk" friend or friend in Buddhism; Wei Chu is his friend in appreciation of scenery (*shanshui you*); Liu Meng is his friend in poetry, and his friend in wine is Huangbu Langzhi [257]. These associates do not represent a section of those Bo Juyi deals with in his day-to-day affairs, but perform as attributes of certain desired projections of the author's identity: Buddhism, scenery, poetry, and wine. Just as Tao Yuanming's social intercourse is described in terms of the projected image he desires, so are Bo Juyi's friends generated only as embodiments of his slightly more extended projection.

The other people mentioned in the autobiography are his wife, to whose reprimands he refers only in order to vindicate his own dubious qualities, and a series of people near the end of the essay. These people, however, are only invoked in their typicality and in their ability to function as back-drops to his self-construction, and not in their qualities as actual historical personages: "I was born between heaven and earth, my skills and be-havior are not nearly as good as those of the ancients; but I am richer than Qian Lou, have lived a life longer than that of Yan Yuan, and have eaten more than Bo Yi; and I am happier than Rong Qiqi and healthier than Wei Shubao. How fortunate! What else do I need!"[32] From this point on wine, writing, and music are the only referents of the essay.

Like Tao Yuanming, Bo Juyi attempts an explanation of his fanci-ful name, Master Singing Drunk. In replacing his socially sanctioned name, this name functions much as that of Tao Yuanming: it disassoci-ates the author from his functional name and at the same time from his position in material society. The reference is not quite as "floating," however, as "singing" and "drunk" are two of the attributes Bo Juyi wishes to associate with his textually formed self. Nonetheless, the sever-ance of the name from its historical and functional sign effects the same result: nomination as a socially significant act is undermined, and the self is cut free of its specific relation with the society that determines signifying names and from the limitation to produce meaning through these names alone.

Figural nomination and its explanation is a frequent means of establishing separation from "affairs" in impressionistic autobiographies. In Tao Yuanming's text the name is an indicator of arbitrariness in connection to the material and social world, or a denial of meaningful connection with that segment of reality. In the autobiography of Bo Juyi it is also a creation and confirmation of the mythical self he desires to portray and a superimposition of the value of that myth over the known name; at the same time the figural name also functions as a rejection of the material historicity of the name that carries an ancestry and a past. The self in the impressionistic text does not gain its authenticity from the proper and correct use of names, but from this seemingly frivolous perversion of the socially sanctioned meaning of a name. What is a denial of the true name becomes an affirmation of a new figure of the self, which incorporates the concept of a false or unrectified name.

Summary

The above analysis proposes two radically discrete contexts of referentiality for the textual self-definition of the writer. In terms of referentiality these two poles of autobiographies could be distinguished by words such as "literary" and "non-literary"; the fact that poets such as Liu Yuxi wrote circumstantial ("non-literary") texts would not alter the accuracy of this categorization.[33] Although this differentiation may be correct, it focuses on style and thus obscures my emphasis on the codes of referentiality central to my argument and meaningful in explaining the contradiction of authority of modern autobiographies. Nonetheless, it is likely that the impressionistic text did come to be associated with a more "literary" personality, someone like the fictional Jia Baoyu, who had rejected the traditional road through the examination system to position and power and sought to mold himself in a literary context.[34] After the time of Tao Yuanming, however, this literary context, or the persona of the detached literatus, was certainly as stereotypical as the official with his Confucian orthodoxy; although adherence to this position represented rejection of the main role society had delineated for its intellectuals, it was not only a stance of alienation.[35] The tradition of the detached literatus who refused to take the examination and insisted on an artistic aesthetic that varied from the norm was highly developed well before the Qing dynasty. On one hand, then, the context of referentiality of the impressionistic text should be regarded as a rejection of the orthodox Confucian tradition, but on the other it must also be viewed as the embracing of a well-established alternative in which the author takes on an acceptable role of litterateur, in the process establishing belles lettres in an oppositional relationship against history and officialdom.[36]

2

Autobiographies of the Late Qing Dynasty and Political Implication

To enrich your family, no need to buy good land:
Books hold a thousand measures of grain.
For an easy life, no need to build a mansion:
In books are found houses of gold.
Going out, be not vexed at absence of followers:
In books, carriages and horses form a crown.
Marrying, be not vexed by lack of a good go-between:
In books there are girls with faces of jade.
A boy who wants to become a somebody
Devotes himself to the classics, faces the window, and reads.
—Song Emperor Zhenzong

The examination that places individuals in a field of surveillance also situates them in a network of writing; it engages them in a whole mass of documents that capture and fix them.—Michel Foucault, *Discipline and Punish*

The Examination System

The examination system as it existed in the Qing dynasty had evolved over hundreds of years, beginning with a kind of recommendatory examination system in the Western Han and developing through the Tang, Song, and Ming into an examination which underscored "knowledge of classics, stereotyped theories of administration, and literary attainments" [Ho, 111]. Although the examination system was used during the reign of Empress Wu (r. 690–705), most officials during Tang times were not chosen through the examination [Elman, 1989:379–81]. In early Tang times the examination had covered up to six fields, including classics, law, and mathematics, but it was later narrowed down to only one examination, the *jinshi* exam, which emphasized creative writing [Ho, 12–14]. The eventual literary focus of the examination may have been a side product of its rationale for existence:

> As part of the process of developing a broad range of new institutional mechanisms by which to govern more than 100 million subjects, Northern Song rulers chose civil service examinations to limit the development of alternative military and aristocratic power centers and to draw into their government the sons of elites from newly emerging regions in South China. Deftly appropriating the civilian values of Confucianism to legitimate the institution of fair and impartial bureaucratic channels to select officials, which were open theoretically to almost all Chinese regardless of social background, Song emperors put in place an examination system that would occupy a central institutional position in Chinese government and society until 1905, when the civil service examinations were abolished. [Elman, 1989:380]

By selectively manipulating content authorities could increasingly cause the examination not only to open the door to elites, but to exclude material outside their training.[1] The tie between orthodox Confucianism and the examination system was strengthened in 736 when the authority over the exams was transferred from the Board of Civil Appointments to the Board of Rites [Franke, 5].

The content of the examination system was revised and altered many times over the centuries, and scholars frequently attacked or defended the system. In the 1043 memorial to the throne of Fan Zhongyan (989–1052), for example, the exams were criticized for their excessive emphasis on literary criteria: "The state selects the presented scholars, however, only according to [their ability to write] poems and poetic description, and the candidates in the other categories of the examination according to their written elucidation of passages from the classics. The literati discard the important trends and run along petty ways" [Franke, 16]. This criticism of the exam as being unrelated to actual, practical matters of society was echoed by Wang Anshi, Gu Yanwu, and Huang Zongxi, the latter suggesting that the examination should include specialized tests in mathematics, music, astronomy, weather forecasting, fire arms, and water conservation [Franke, 17–22].[2]

The status and significance that Confucian society attached to book learning was challenged even more strongly during the Qing dynasty. Since the late eighteenth century the examination focused on philological issues at the expense of moral philosophy or current affairs; this and the earlier addition of the *bagu* writing style divorced the examination even further from practical matters [Ayers, 32]. Although it may be true that by 1850 money was at least as important as academic degrees in determining status, the economic-oriented fields of industry and finance were not represented on the examination [Ho, 256]. The fields of science and technology, which are less ideological and more oriented toward outside phenomena than traditional fields, likewise were not covered.

One of the most forceful attacks on the examination system was engineered by Qing reformer Zhang Zhidong, who felt the exam was too literary and did not test candidates in a sufficient scope of affairs. His suggestion, similar to that of Ouyang Xiu in 1044, was to emphasize the dissertation and discussion in essays on the *shi* and *fu* poetry and to abandon the *bagu* writing style. He also petitioned to have the test of small formal calligraphy eliminated [Ayers, 35, 186–87].[3] Symbolic of an interpretation of writing as form equal to or more important than content, calligraphy is often mentioned by critics of the examination as one type of uselessly applied textual effort.

Some stronger critics of the examination demanded the abolition of the system, claiming it was the actual cause of what they perceived as China's lack of development in comparison to foreign countries:

> In China, since the prevalence of the examination essay, the ancient learning has become neglected and uncultivated. The reason for establishing this society is our genuine desire to sweep away the practice up until now of such limited and narrow [scholarship], and to collect the talents of our time to aid in reform. Along with our study of Chinese moral principles we will blend the occidental art of enriching [the country] and strengthening [the army].[4]

When the abolition of the examination system was announced and took place in 1905, however, Zhang Zhidong began to develop plans to establish a School for the Preservation of Antiquity; he petitioned the throne to establish this school on July 9, 1907, and it was opened August 28 of the same year. The school was to concentrate on Chinese subjects, emphasizing national literature, both prose and poetry, as well as the spoken and written language [Ayers, 249].

Zhang obviously perceived the value of the examination system as a unifying influence in the spiritual and conceptual realm of Chinese thought and realized that while its abolition would allow China to progress in previously undeveloped ways, a chaotic spiritual gap may result from the lack of a guiding and unifying ideology. Those who were traditionally the rulers of China "were masters of writing in a culture where the written word had almost magic potency, and now the main authority of writing in this culture was gone" [Johnson, 58]. By the Qing era the powerful in government were those "with skill in writing and familiarity with the literary tradition" [Johnson, 48].[5] As previously mentioned, only toward the end of the nineteenth century did other elements, such as money, begin to be as important an element as official degree in determining status.[6]

It would be difficult to underestimate the importance of the examination system in determining the consciousness and ideology of the elite in Chinese society. The abolition of a system which had been such an important factor in determining consciousness can only have been a serious disruption in the identity of the intellectual and a significant element in the destruction of the "spiritual authority" which defined this ideology [Borthwick, 85]. The extremely literary nature of the examination content, eventually identified as "empty learning" (*xuxue*) by Zhang Zhidong and others, also represented a unified vision of a uniquely Chinese ideology and intellectual framework. It was inevitable that the disappearance of this long-term unifier would result in further questioning of a textual corpus that was already under attack in the same social environs that demanded the abolition of the examination. With a change in the status of this textual corpus would come a readjustment in the position of its representative and progenitor, the writer.[7]

Even so, it is important to realize that changes were not immediate. Writing in 1915, Ping Wen Kuo, a member of the Jiangsu Provincial Educational Commission to Europe and America, discusses the "separation of the civil service examination system from the educational system":

> The abolishing of the system of granting official degrees by the government to graduates of colleges marks the separation of the civil service examination system from the educational system proper, and is of great significance in the history of education in China. . . . In spite of this fact, entrance to official life continued to be regarded as the goal of all higher intellectual training. When China first introduced the modern educational system, she followed the practice of the old examination system in conferring upon graduates of colleges official

degrees, giving them a right to enter official life. But since the number of college graduates far exceeded the number of vacant public offices, many college graduates, though possessing official rank, necessarily failed to receive appointment in the government service. Aside from this state of affairs, which was in itself undesirable, this custom made the student class continue to look upon official life as the goal of education, while those who had no ambition to enter public service regarded as unnecessary all intellectual training beyond the mere rudimentary knowledge necessary for daily life and business. Indeed, so deeply imbedded in the constitution of the Chinese mind is this conception of education that even the abolishment of the system did not entirely succeed in removing it.[8]

Kuo indicates that while the structural basis for linking book learning to political position was gone with the abolition of the examination system, force of habit and lack of well-developed alternatives allowed students to continue to behave as if the system was in force.

Literary Value and Status

During the latter half of the Qing Dynasty, literati views toward the status and function of writing and of those who wrote were undergoing rapid change. There have been many useful studies of this period, but in terms of those attempting to evaluate literary theory and its position in intellectual discourse, Theodore Huters's work on late Qing writing is most enlightening and to the point.[9] In his 1987 article Huters attempts to elucidate "the process by which advocacy of the centrality of prose to contemporary learning came to the fore" [52]. Huters discusses an early separation of substance (*ti*), function (*yong*), and written expression (*wen*) by Liu Yi (1017–86), and Cheng Yi's (1033–1107) "willingness to at least accord writing a position as one of the prime constituents of learning" [55].[10] These references are part of Huters's evidence for what he calls the "increasing contemporary [Qing] regard for letters" [67], which occurred despite the fact that some major scholars, notably Dai Zhen (1724–77), Duan Yucai (1735–1815), and Jiao Xun (1763–1818) "have in common the relegation of letters to a subsidiary position" [61] *within* the triad of letters, moral philosophy, and evidential research. Huters claims that Dai Zhen, Duan Yucai, Jiao Xun, and Qian Daxin (1728–1804) are "voices characteristic of the dominant intellectual discourse of the Qianlong era"

[61] in that during the late seventeenth century *wenren* paid little attention to theories of writing. This was not universally so: one adversary whom Jiao Xun identified was Yuan Mei (1716–98), whose "concept of belles-lettres as a more intuitive and thus clearer means of gaining access to the Dao" resulted in a "repositioning of letters at the top of the hierarchy of learning" [67]. Huters points out that because of the "antiquarian interests of the Qianlong emperor" [62], *wenren* of that period again became interested in philology and the investigation of antiquity, "paying almost exclusive attention to what Zhang calls 'academic writing' [*xuewen*]: poetry, rhyme-prose and parallel prose" [63]. Thus Huters shows that although most eighteenth-century intellectuals were uninterested in theories of writing, by the 1799 death of Emperor Gaozong, a "sea-change in mentality" allowed the Tongcheng school to retheorize the discourse as centering on prose style.

The *guwen* revival that dominated letters after 1820 managed to "focus attention of prose stylistics," but its proponents still had to avoid "submerging the philosophical and moral issues that writing was meant to serve" [78]. It is in the discussion of this wider framework after 1820 that Huters provides some evidence for my own theory: although prose theories occupy a central (if disputed) position within elite arguments over evidential research, moral philosophy, and writing, the largely textual realm that the triad represents becomes in itself a questionable site for intellectual discourse. Huters points out that in the first half of the nineteenth century, disciples who had studied with Tongcheng leaders "sought a sort of moral rearmament through increased political participation by the scholar-elite" [77–78]. In effect, disciples are taking intellectual discourse farther outside the field of "letters" than previous practice indicates. Huters quotes the words of Tongcheng advocate Guan Tong, which indicate a negative evaluation of literary intellectuals:

> When I was young, I loved to write and I consorted with the literati (*wen shi*) of the land. Of them, Mr. Fang Zhizhi [i.e., Dongshu] of Tongcheng was the best. Later I encountered worries and illness and thus, after age forty [i.e., after 1820], I realized that scholars should establish merit and that the literati were base and not worthy of being taken seriously. I told this to others and, regrettably, no one responded. Only [Fang] comprehended. [79]

Huters also quotes the comments of twentieth-century critic Guo Shaoyu, who discusses the aversion of mid-seventeenth-century writers to "empty words," in spite of their inability to divorce themselves from the literary trends of the time: "In this situation they on the one hand recognized the value of literature, but at the same time deeply resented the uselessness of empty words" [81]. Although "literature" and "useless words" seem to exist as different categories in Guo's formulation, they also merge: in the twentieth century Guo recognizes the possibility that these earlier writers saw literature *as* empty words. Even though Huters interprets the Tong-cheng school's "constant concern with writing as the main avenue of learning" as "a disposition to allow every educated person access to participation in cultural discourse," he also states that "insisting upon the moral oneness of writing made it difficult to allow for new contingencies" [91]. Thus Zeng Guofan (1811–72) had little choice but to add statecraft [*jingji*] to the triad of letters, evidential scholarship, and moral philoso-phy; even so, he had difficulty "holding the terms of scholarly discourse together" [94]. For the purposes of my argument it is significant that the addition of statecraft does not just provide a fourth fulcrum of knowl-edge, but also upsets the textual bias of the other three. Letters and evidential scholarship are clearly textual pursuits (as, to a large extent, is moral philosophy); statecraft, while still utilizing textual representation, is a category that insists on activity outside the realm of scholarship.

Huters's final position is that Tongcheng writers and others, such as those who wrote *Wenxuan*-style prose, "had a common role in raising the position of writing and bringing increased attention to it" [95]. In "mak-ing *wen* into an entity that transcended immediate practical concern, [Ruan Yuan] cleared the way for its function as a powerful, if abstract, force in intellectual inquiry," thus anticipating the modern "struggle over writing between those striving to preserve the medium as the central portion of a unified field of knowledge and those seeking to elevate letters by splitting them off from ordinary knowledge" [95]. From Huters's point of view, after 1895, "literature" in its modern sense "made explicit as never before the vital role of writing," a "category of knowledge" pre-sented within intellectual discussion as possessing "miraculous proper-ties" [96]. Huters carries out a discussion of the new "literature" in his 1988 article, "A New Way of Writing: The Possibilities for Literature in Late Qing China, 1895–1908."

In this later article Huters defines the literary production of 1895 to 1908 as "an arena of tension between utopianism and the hopes for real departure from old concerns," a position which "is at once emblematic of its importance to the overall cultural enterprise and of the tremendous frustrations involved in trying to construct that enterprise itself" [246]. Theories of literature had to try and relegate to it an authority which would allow it to meet this challenge. The five schools which emerged were the *Tongcheng school,* whose modern adherents Yan Fu and Lin Shu used archaic prose to translate Western fiction (and succeeded in elevating fiction but not *guwen*); the *Wenxuan school* of parallel writing, whose proponent Liu Shipei promoted a type of national essence [*guocui*] that removed literature from everyday affairs, reformulating it as mystically powerful; the *New Style school,* represented by Liang Qichao, who wrote a didactic, political classical style; the *novel writers,* who took literature into a more public sphere as a way to educate the masses; and the *nonconformists* such as Zhang Binglin, who was also involved in the national essence movement but rejected any special status for writing, and Wang Guowei, who emphasized the autonomy of art from social and political concerns. In these five theories, according to Huters, it can be seen that "literature was often thought of as lying close to the heart of the nest of contradictions making up Chinese thought at the time"; thus novels arrive at their paradoxical state of standing "for both the highest ideas *and* the grimmest utility" [266].

Again, although Huters's thesis is that literature becomes the central intellectual discourse of the period and is thus elevated in status, he provides some evidence for my claim that while (speaking somewhat tautologically) writing is indeed the focus of discussions on literature, within a wider field of discussion (and, to some extent, within these discussions on literature) its primacy as the most valued site of intellectual concern is under question. For example, Huters interprets Wang Guowei's severing of literature from social and political affairs not as a true separation, but as the establishment of an opposition [268]. Huters regards Wang's work as in effect hiding a demand that literature take a critical stance toward society, and he goes on to search for evidence of a utilitarian stance in Wang's claim for literary autonomy. Thus Huters does not regard Wang's abandonment of literary criticism in favor of political activism as an about-face, since "the unconscious hold on him of certain key patterns of traditional Chinese notions of writing" are evident in his writing between 1904 and 1906 [269]. The opposition between literary work/social involvement that Huters locates in Wang Guowei's writing is at the root of my argument, but his reading of Wang's unconscious structural affinity is not the only significance that could be assigned to Wang's dichotomy. Wang's decision to reject literature and take up politics can also be read as a choice that selects a more socially effective activity (political work) over what he views as somewhat useless, if transcendent work (writing).

In his discussion of Lu Xun's 1908 essay on Mara poetry, Huters quotes Lu Xun's attempt to identify literature as a powerful cultural manifestation. At the same time Huters goes over Lu Xun's claim of literary decline within China, which the young writer countered with a Kantian plea for a literature that had "use in its uselessness" [271]. Huters accurately comments that the "hopes [Lu Xun] invests in literature are unprecedented in their scope" [271]. Still, Lu Xun insisted, with Wang Guowei, that literature "worthy of the name" must take on a "negative and destructive attitude toward the society and the governing mentality of the society from which it issues" [270]. Although Huters interprets this as Lu Xun's attempt to avoid "crass utilitarianism," or to maintain some of literature's mystical powers ("to make literature at once abstract from society yet finally effective within it" [270]), I would also point out that Lu Xun is placing literature within a negative realm. Although within this schemata Lu Xun maintains for literature a socially central position, he must assign literature a negative value to allow it to continue to possess viability.

Although Huters makes a good case for the utopian formulation of literature among elite intellectuals, he also comments that "even when the calls were heeded the works actually produced in response did not come anywhere near fulfilling the optimistic demands of the critics" [272]. Is this because the works were not "skilled," the claims were overstated, literature did not truly have social power, or simply that the audience did not understand these works? Huters's research focuses on the ideas of literary intellectuals about the position and value of literary and scholarly writing within Chinese society. His acknowledgment that in fact, literary texts did not perform the miraculous cures expected, however, suggests that this utopian construction represents the desires of writers and scholars rather than their evaluation either of literature's actual status or its function. I would go one step further and suggest that there are many indications *within* intellectual discourse that the elevation of literary writing, while undoubtedly taking place in theoretical texts, is not as clearly unproblematic as these texts may indicate. Huters's revealing work does not rule out the possibility that writers and critics defended and exalted literature precisely because they felt under siege: first, through the progressively more serious attacks on textual work and its position within society that were partially responsible for abolishing the examination system and, second, because of the structural break between writing and social/political function that this abolition engendered.[11]

Huters's work clarifies an important aspect of the elevation of literature: both conservative writers, who promoted writing in one or another classical style, devised "national essence" as a literary and political ideology and opposed vernacular reform, and reform-minded writers, such as Lu Xun and Wang Guowei, constructed lofty writing as a repository of cultural and spiritual values.[12] Although some critics or writers may undermine this construction as they build it, nonetheless it exists and cannot be ignored. At the same time there are indications that writers were defending literature against various assaults as early as the late 1800s, with particular attacks aimed at the literary nature of the examination increasing into the 1920s and 1930s.[13] How can this paradox—both elevation and denigration—be explained?

Mystification and Economic or Political Power

Late Qing theorists criticized the literary slant to the examination because they felt it had not prepared them well for modern challenges, particularly those from the West. Basically, this argument rests on a questioning of the relationship between the social function of literary writing and affairs in the social world. The content of the examination was held in contempt not only because it was too literary, but also because much of it was aimed at elucidating principles of the faraway past. Thus just as the context of literary writing/social affairs was one area under discussion, the dichotomy of literary writing/ancient history was another. Some intellectuals pushed for more contemporary themes that would demand knowledge of current political affairs.

Similar arguments about the relation of literary writing to "reality," moral construction, or immediate historical circumstances also occurred at various times in the West. What follows is a discussion of one such case, which helps to locate similarities in the way literature is accorded social value and also calls our attention to the marked differences.

According to Edward Rosenheim, Western satire originally was conceptualized as "distinguished by the presence of *both* the historically authentic and the historically particular." In "The Reader in History" Jane P. Tompkins quotes Rosenheim and comments that "far from being separated from its temporal human origins by a literary persona or by translation to a level of universal significance, eighteenth-century satire is embedded in the historical setting, engendered by it, and responsive to it in detail" [212]; Tompkins indicates that Rosenheim's claim for satire "pushes the classical identification of language with political power to an extreme" [212].[14] This identification between literary writing and political power is duplicated by "poetry of the late seventeenth and early eighteenth centuries, [which] traffics in power both in the broad sense of exerting influence on personal behavior and public opinion, and in the narrower sense of dealing explicitly with political issues" [213]. In the late Qing reformers who demanded that poetry be omitted from the examination had rejected the notion that either historical immediacy or allusive language which indicated direct political comment manifested a functional political content.

Tompkins also discusses changes in the definition of Western literature and the writer in the nineteenth century that "lead directly to the view of art that has dominated criticism in the twentieth":

> At exactly the time when a consciousness of history becomes fundamental to critical thought, poetry is spoken of as transcending the influences of place and time. Just when the most grandiose claims are made for the power of poetry to transform human consciousness— poets are the "unacknowledged legislators of the world," who "bind together the vast empire of human society"—the poet starts to be described as lonely and ineffectual, a "nightingale who sits in darkness and sings to cheer its own solitude with sweet sounds." And while literature is hailed as England's most important national resource, greater than the entire Empire of India, it is also spoken of as one of the worst possible ways to make a living. [217]

In comparing Tompkins's discussion of the way in which "literature" as a category was essentialized and universalized with Ye Shaojun's 1921 plea for a more serious type of writing, we can see that a similar mythologizing process could be taking place:

> In recent issues, Shanghai newspapers have been carrying an advertisement which grieves me deeply, and I imagine there must be a lot of people who feel as I do. I almost couldn't believe my eyes at this advertisement, but there it was—unmistakably written in big, clear characters. It read: "I'd rather not take a concubine / Than to miss out on reading *The Saturday Magazine*."
> This is really an insult—a wide-ranging insult. They insult them-

selves, insult literature, and what's worse, insult others! . . . This not only leaves the future of literature uncertain and worrisome; it actually leaves the whole advancement of the Chinese nation uncertain and worrisome.

Yet we hold the following as an item of faith: only literature has the power to serve as the tie which binds together the best in the human spirit, which unites countless small and weak consciousnesses together into one great consciousness. It can expose the darkness, usher in light, and lead people to abandon their mean and shallow side in favor of more honorable and profound tendencies. How can we let its future fall subject to uncertainty and worry?[15]

Tompkins accounts for these "apparent contradictions" by the "gap that had opened up in the nineteenth century between literary activity and social and political life," where writers are "no longer the associates of powerful men," but write for "a faceless, unpredictable public rather than for a small, highly influential elite" [217]. The split that developed "between poetry and the world of affairs" led nineteenth-century critics to attempt to turn the artist's "progressive alienation from society" into something positive, reconceptualizing poetry as "the highest manifestation of culture and the greatest force for the attainment of an advanced state of cultural development *because,* unlike other forms of discourse, it has no particular uses, no loyalties, no causes to plead" [219]. Ye Shaojun is defending literature against those who use it for entertainment purposes alone; in the process of doing so he also essentializes the ideal literary writing as a unique spiritual tool.

Tompkins's argument is related to the earlier discussion of Raymond Williams in *Culture and Society: 1780–1950,* in which Williams analyzes the idea of culture. Williams's second chapter, "The Romantic Artist," traces the development of artist as romantic first in the conception of Poet or Artist as "by nature indifferent to the crude worldliness and materialism of politics and social affairs" and later in the supposed opposition between attention to natural beauty and attention to government, or between personal feeling and the nature of man in society [30]. According to Williams, during the period that corresponds roughly to the lifetime of William Blake (1757–1827), "a theory of the 'superior reality' of art, as the seat of imaginative truth, was receiving increasing emphasis" (it actually is a much older idea) [31–32]. Under these conditions "culture became the normal antithesis to the market" [35]. Chinese writers, like

Romantic writers, felt artists should "read the open secret of the universe" [39]. Yet in their romanticization of art and literature, rather than disavowing the influence of the "public," a term that centers on the writer's actual relations with society, Chinese writers increasingly moved toward recognition of the public as the ultimate and most valued subject and object of literary writing.[16]

The descriptions of Williams and Tompkins have similarities to the nineteenth-century and early twentieth-century Chinese context: writers had lost the textual authority the examination system had provided, and they had to establish the validity of "serious" writing against the claims of other approaches, such as that of the Saturday school of entertainment writing. In both cases writers were forced to struggle for a new status for writing that maintained some of its previous prestige. Yet the differences are much more striking. The relationship between the writer and power, or those in power, was radically altered through the elimination of the examination system and the changes that led up to it. Although late Qing elite writers still wrote for an educated elite, the reconceptualization of literary writing made more true the statement that they were dealing with a "faceless, unpredictable public" rather than a group which had been through a remarkably uniform, exam-oriented education. However, despite claims and attempts to the contrary (such as that of Ye Shaojun), China's humiliating political and military struggles and the implied contrast of a modern, vital Western education to Chinese learning prohibited long-term removal—through mythologizing and essentializing—of the topics and form of Chinese literature from the harsh reality of economic and political life. Theoretical concepts such as national essence which continued to thus define literature were ultimately not nearly as influential as those schools which had begun to emphasize the social relevance of literature—also a movement with early roots.[17] Whereas the early May Fourth period sees many pleas from writers anxious to improve the status of literary writing, at the same time critics are calling for a more socially engaged literature; by the late 1920s writers have gone the further step of perceiving immersion in social affairs as an alternative to literary or textual work. Raymond Williams shows the positive formulation of literature as an idealized form of knowledge and of the writer as a genius who can perceive essential reality; while this construction occurs in China from 1898 to the present, at the same time the alternative of social and political work is established as more important, more valuable, and ultimately more meaningful. Thus it is fair to say that to some extent perception of

Chinese learning as extremely and negatively textual on the part of a limited number of elite scholars and officials as early as the Song, and intensifying in the late Qing, was a development influential in working as an opposing preconceptualization that pushed literature away from what Tompkins calls the transfer of "the ultimate locus of value [away] from the context of poetry to poetry itself" [221], instead centering value on the context, or the relationship of literature to society.

As soon as literature in the West lost its elite status and audience and became a difficult way to make a living, mythologizing statements elevating it to the level of a universal cultural indicator ensued. The almost evangelical claims by late Qing scholars and writers such as Liang Qichao and then modern writers such as Ye Shaojun on behalf of "literature" reveal a similar insistence on the value of the literary—at exactly the point when the structural determiner of literary validity, the examination system, is under strong attack or already abolished. Long-standing criticisms of the content of the examination, which centered on its excessively literary nature, combined with late Qing concern about the validity of social institutions to strengthen the position of military training and practical education with direct political or scientific application and to demean the significance of literary writing *as previously defined*. Although writers tried to redeem literature by redefining it as socially involved Westernized fiction, they could not help but be influenced by the assault on Chinese learning and texts.

Education and Textual Value

On the other side of the examination system and its ideology is the education which led up to it: as long as the examinations were held, education was self-regulating [Borthwick, 6]. The abolition of the examinations brought not only a questioning of the validity and definition of the literary corpus and the writer, but also confusion about the purpose and value of education in general. In the past literacy had been the only requirement for teaching, but now teachers were required to be trained in many fields; many were classical scholars retrained against their will in the new "corpus" of knowledge, and they ended up teaching students who knew more than they did in any given subject [Borthwick, 119, 145]. This new corpus, which included foreign languages, mathematics, world history, and science, was considered to be "concrete learning" (*shixue*) and was opposed to the speculative learning which had been taught when the examination system was still operative [Borthwick, 52].[18] Because there were not many opportunities for employment in the new fields, however, students continued to seek work in civil service and teaching—the traditional fields for the educated in premodern China.

As Frederic Wakeman has illustrated, the expansion of study societies in the late Qing era prompted a redefinition of the concept of "state," which was previously conceptualized as a transmitted kingdom. The example of study societies now suggested that the nation could be formed by association of men, in which a key concept was the idea of *jun,* in one sense referring to the man able to form social organizations [Wakeman, 64]. It was in such an environment that education was seen as a crucial element in the fostering of the enlightened individual, the intellectual (*zhishifenzi*) of the modern world.

It is significant that the examination system "was called into question less by its own defects than by the inability of the Chinese polity as a whole to resist Western and later Japanese aggression" [Borthwick, 38]. At the same time it is clear that although the entire structure of the examination system itself may not have been seriously attacked in unity until late Qing times, the content had been criticized almost from its initiation, and certainly many times since Song alterations underlined the aspects of the examination that were perceived as remote from everyday life, overly formalized, and excessively literary. From both angles—the domestic evolution of criticism of the examination content and the attack on the system which was the result of foreign military victory in China—the examination and the education linked to it were seen as too literary and lacking in physical application both in the social world and in the military arena. The move toward the elimination of the *fu, shi,* and small calligraphy on the examination is nothing more than an attempt to eliminate the literary aspects of a system that was eventually considered to be an obstacle in its own right.

This trend gains concrete expression in one of the slogans of the *Qiang xuehui,* the "study society for self-strengthening" formed by Kang Youwei in 1895. The phrase "to inspire customs" (*kai fengqi*) "was partly an appeal for physical education to create a new martial *junzi* robustly modeled on the samurai instead of the effete literatus" [Wakeman, 60]. Another meaning of "to inspire customs" was "to engage in social action by breaking the coterie mentality" [Wakeman, 62]; glorification of both the physical and the social restructures these spheres of knowledge and involvement as contrasting ideologies to what was perceived as the influence of the corpus of past Chinese literary traditions and their institutionalization within the examination. The identification of foreign military power as a force originating in the classroom, or in Western education, further lessened the validity of a distinctively Chinese *wen* and stipulated the rejection of at least part of the Chinese cultural forms and the adoption of Western style education as well as writing styles [Borthwick, 42, 49]. When posited against foreign military strength, the core of what had been perceived as "Chinese culture" in the past appeared to many as empty, useless knowledge. A short time later this past corpus, including Confucian ideals, social relationships, and literary writing, was attacked almost in its entirety by May Fourth intellectuals.[19]

Affairs and Intellectual Involvement

By the end of the Qing reform-minded intellectuals had abandoned a vague concern with imperial self-development for the concrete management of local affairs. Members of a new kind of social group expressed an unprecedented concern with the nationalist issues of railway and mining rights which specifically influenced local or provincial politics [Wakeman, 1972:57]. The examination and its education, which had elevated the literary at the expense of knowledge of current events, was insufficient to meet the crisis brought on by foreign imperialist expansion: "Previously young Chinese readers paid no attention to current events, but now we were shaken. . . . After the loss of the war and the establishment of a Japanese concession in Soochow], most educated people, who had never discussed national affairs, wanted to discuss them: why are others stronger than we are, and why are we weaker?"[20]

The isolation of literary work as a negative category eventually, in the mid-1920s and later, developed into a contradiction that pitted writing against other alternatives in a battle that had no easy resolution for the writer. Out of this basic paradox grew an emphasis not only on the alternative of intellectual classification through primary involvement in the social structures of politics, economics, and military organization, but also anything symbolic of physicality or materiality which could successfully be contrasted with textual authority, such as the social and ideological domain occupied by manual labor and the worker.

Writing as Indicator: Intellectual Definition and the Nation

After 1905 those whose position in society was a result of their mastery of the interpretation of certain written texts and control of certain styles of writing were displaced from their roles; the automatic status and social orientation that came from successful participation in the examination system was no longer theirs. As civil servants in a system which claimed the authority of both moral right and of actual political power, *wenren* had occupied a neatly carved out ideological niche that granted them both status and function. With the abolition of the examination system they were forced not only to seek a new social role for themselves, but also to search for a new personal identity. For writers this included reevaluation of their selves within the framework of newly arising social and literary standards.

Even writers who had not chosen the route of the examination system as a means to position, status, and self-definition had no choice but to take a new look at themselves. The tradition of the literary recluse, the disengaged literatus who had rejected position and social role, became meaningless as the status quo underwent revision and alteration, making a socially unengaged persona unattractive and strongly challenged in the early twentieth century. European realism and later Marxism demanded that the writer take an active role in at least observing the functioning of society and recording it accurately, and perhaps also in deterministically portraying the forward march of progress. The impressionistic stance, which required the author to symbolically disengage himself from the seminal organizational structures of society, and through reference to the characteristics of the literati lifestyle establish immersion into the literary text as an appealing option, was no longer a valid alternative. By the time of the Republic the category of the Chinese "literary" was neither rejection of social orthodoxy nor reference to an alternative authority; rather, it signified the powerlessness of the Chinese traditions before foreign military power. It was, in other words, a discourse of weakness.

Late Qing Autobiography and Political Signification

The four late Qing autobiographies I discuss are modern examples of both the circumstantial and impressionistic autobiographies. They include the texts of Lin Shu (1852–1924), Yi Shunding (1858–1920), Wang Tao

(1828–1897), and Liang Qichao (1873–1929). Three of these writers are very well known; Lin Shu as the writer who collaborated with others to translate hundreds of Western works into classical Chinese even though he himself did not read a single foreign language; Wang Tao as the entrepreneur who started a newspaper and helped James Legge translate the Chinese classics into English in Hong Kong and England; and Liang Qichao as a moderate reformer noted for his excellent essay style who was one of the foremost intellectuals of early modern China. Only Yi Shunding is more obscure. A child protégé who wrote excellent poetry at fifteen, he served under Yuan Shikai. Yi was a prolific poet who wrote almost ten thousand poems.[21] Both Lin Shu and Yi Shunding wrote autobiographies that are similar to the models of Tao Yuanming and Bo Juyi, texts that basically follow the conventions of the impressionistic autobiographies. Wang Tao and Liang Qichao, reformers who involved themselves actively in new movements to alter politics, education, and the media, wrote texts similar to those of Sima Qian and Liu Yuxi, essentially conforming to the requirements of the circumstantial autobiography.

Lin Shu and the Impressionistic Stance

Although Lin Shu translated many Western works, he refused to write in the vernacular, preferring to work with someone who knew the original language and could orally translate the work into colloquial Chinese, which Lin Shu would then transform into a freely rendered classical Chinese that was unlike the original both in meaning and style. Born in 1852, Lin Shu was well-trained in the classical tradition and could manipulate the works he translated until they assumed a form familiar to the Chinese reader.[22] Although Lin's translations were very influential in altering the consciousness of young Chinese urban intellectuals, within the context of the late Qing urban intellectual scene, he would be termed relatively conservative.[23]

Other than his voluminous translations into classical Chinese, Lin Shu was known for his strong, emotional defense of the classical written language against the attempts of Hu Shi and Chen Duxiu to institute the vernacular as a major written form and for his opposition to Cai Yuanpei when Cai modified the curriculum at Beijing University, changing it into a modern educational institution. Lin also wrote stories and essays criticizing Hu Shi and others for their disregard of traditional culture and their desire to discard the gems of the classical tradition.

The autobiography of Lin Shu, *Leng hong sheng zhuan* [Biography of the cold red master], gets its name, Lin explains, from a line of poetry: "Maple leaves fall, and the Wu River is cold."[24] Although Lin tells us the name of the place where he lives, he claims to be unknowledgeable of his ancestry. He refers to his poverty and his own appearance of poverty and begins a short discourse on his relations with women; when young, he would feel respectful and uneasy whenever he saw women, but later he (literally) chased them.

Lin Shu relates his futile attempt to gain admittance to see a courtesan famous for her sexual techniques; when he tried to send some cakes in to her by means of hired help, the servants collaborated to eat the cakes themselves. He refers to *La Dame aux Camélias,* also the story of a courtesan, which he translated, to the fame of his translations in general, and to his strong emotions.

The bulk of this short essay is taken up with the courtesan incident, which, while possibly actually occurring in the life of the author, associates him with the environment of the leisurely literati and separates him from the domain of the official that designates political power. Moreover, this episode is not related to any significant conceptual or phenomenal development in the author or his surroundings; as such it is quite incidental in its relationship to the life of Lin Shu. Unlike reference to success in the examinations or to attainment of official position, reference to chasing courtesans does not allow Lin Shu an identity within a socially sanctioned context.[25] The incident itself is marked by weakness and poverty, as Lin Shu fails to see the courtesan and is mocked by the servants because of his failure. The incident functions in a way similar to that of the fanciful name in the texts of Tao Yuanming and Bo Juyi in that it allows the author to align himself with an arbitrary phenomenon and to deny a significant and causal link with designations of political power and authority.

This text contains many components of the impressionistic autobiography, including ignored ancestry, reference to poverty and writing, and the use of a fanciful name. The frame of reference locates the author in a space that has no relevance to the reigning political, economic, and social configurations of society at large. Lin Shu's autobiography is brief enough to virtually eschew temporal progression and significant spatial orientation. A comparison of the incident recorded here, for example, with the incident of transmission of power in Sima Qian's autobiography yields a striking difference. Sima Qian is situating himself in a temporal and spatial chain and seeks to rectify himself through the narration of incident, whereas Lin Shu situates himself within a discourse that implies poverty and weakness.

Yi Shunding

A slightly longer and more complex text is *Ku an zhuan* [The biography of the crying bowl] by Yi Shunding. In comparison to the autobiographies of Sima Qian, Wang Tao, and Liang Qichao, Yi Shunding's text is extremely short.[26] It begins traditionally: "Crying Bowl does not know where he comes from. As for his name, everyone knows it, so he will not tell it here" [334]. It also ends traditionally with an explanation of his fanciful name: he claims the only thing in the world worth crying about is the inability to see one's mother, so he cries every day and thus calls himself the "Crying Bowl."

Yi Shunding elaborates on one incident which occurred in his childhood. When he was five, he was taken by some thieves from Shaanxi to Sichuan and then to Hubei and along the way was captured by a Mongolian army. Yi spoke a southern dialect the Mongolian prince could not understand, so in order to communicate, Yi wrote characters out on the prince's palm. This symbolically playful incident delighted the prince, and he had Yi sent back home.

Yi comments on his literary education and accomplishments in poetry, prose, history, philosophy, and art. He briefly refers to his life as an official and his retreat into the mountains and reviews his past: "In these twenty-odd years of my life, I was first a child protege, a genius; then I went on to be a drunk, a fighter, a famous gentle man, a classics scholar, a student, a high official, and a recluse" [334].

In some respects *Ku an zhuan* is more circumstantial than the autobiographies of Bo Juyi, Tao Yuanming, or Lin Shu. Yi Shunding names some of the places he lived in or visited and specifies his age at different times as five, seventeen, and thirty [sui]. He proceeds in a more or less chronological pattern, from the incident at age five up until seventeen, when he took the examinations, to thirty, when he entered government service, and finally up to the time of his mother's death, when he wrote this autobiography. He makes reference to the examination and official service.

Nonetheless, the overall structure into which these individual parts fit is that of the impressionistic autobiography, with emphasis not on official social institutions, but on whimsical acts and events that delineate the author's self outside the political sphere. Other than a few figures from antiquity (Mencius and Confucius) which connect the author with literary and philosophic traditions, no other people are named; none of the author's teachers, friends, associates, or any other modern person is named. The incidents the author mentions correspond to designations he provides to typify some aspect of his experience; for the most part they are only mentioned and are not developed in the narrative. The designation the author provides essentializes his experience into qualities or impressions:

Incident and Designation (provided by author)

Mongolian king exchange	*shentong* child protégé
fame at fifteen	*caizi* genius
studying classics	*jingsheng* classical scholar
studying history and philosophy	*xueren* learned person
time in office	*guiguan* official
house in mountains	*yinshi* recluse
traveling east and west	*"shenlong"* "Holy Dragon"

What superficially is a chronological progression of the author's experience is undeveloped through narrative, becoming a series of designations naming certain *qualities* of the self. Whereas Lin Shu's seemingly irrelevant incident indicates poverty and weakness, the incidents or events referred to here correspond to qualities the author wishes to project as part of his identity and are similar to Bo Juyi's delineation of friends "in" some aspect of life.

Although it would be simplistic to say that a certain style of autobiography corresponds to specific political ideology, it is not surprising that Lin Shu and Yi Shunding, both relatively conservative politically, should find that an impressionistic style positions them in reference to a tradition that signifies the past more strongly than does the circumstantial autobiography.[27] The allusion to ancestry, history, actual time, and social event which is characteristic of the circumstantial text more readily corresponds to the socially engaged, nationally aware position of the modern intellectual who is unwilling to permit textual work to become the primary indicator of his social function.

Qing Circumstantial Autobiographies and Political Ideology: Wang Tao

Wang Tao and Liang Qichao lived at roughly the same time as Yi Shunding and Lin Shu, from the middle of the nineteenth century into the early twentieth century. The autobiographies of Wang Tao and Liang Qichao differ notably from those of Lin Shu and Yi Shunding in length; both wrote around three thousand characters, compared to the three hundred of Lin and Yi. In both cases the length of the text indicates a process, with the authors describing their lives from the time before their births (ancestry) up to the time of writing.

In *Between Tradition and Modernity: Wang T'ao and Reform in Late Ch'ing China*, Paul A. Cohen comments on the difficulty of classifying Wang Tao as a bureaucrat, scholar, gentry, writer, historian, or journalist.[28] He has little concern, however, over terming Wang a "reformer":

> "Reform," nevertheless, describes better than any other word Wang T'ao's central preoccupation. Wang wanted change. He wanted a more effective bureaucracy, staffed by abler men; higher status for merchants and acknowledgement of the growing importance of commerce in the economy; revision of court policies toward foreign countries and of the educated public's attitudes toward foreign learning; a greater political voice for people outside the government; and countless other modifications of the existing system. [155]

Cohen writes that during the 1860s and 1870s, when except for the newspaper, the "modern vehicles for the expression of public opinion" such as the boycotts, protest demonstrations, petitioning, elections, reform clubs, and journals of opinion which characterized the early modern period were not yet available, Wang Tao spent much of his time writing or speaking to literati, the "educated community" of China [156–57]. Of all of the scholars and writers addressed in this study, Wang Tao is the least scholarly, even though he worked with Legge on translations of the classics. Wang promoted a "complete overhaul of the examination system" to rid it of its "undue narrowness and impracticality," and the inclusion of new subjects such as "administration, current affairs, geography, astronomy, natural science, mathematics, military and penal matters, and fiscal affairs" [165]:

> Most Westerners who come to China study the Chinese language. Even if they don't learn the language they in all cases develop an intimate knowledge of Chinese conditions and a precise sense of our advantages and defects. Chinese, on the other hand, remain utterly ignorant of Western government, public opinion, geography, and customs. Most of them don't even know where [a country] is on the

world map or how far it is [from China]. There is really no cause for surprise in this. What is incomprehensible is the fact that when you ask them about such important Chinese concerns as the Yellow River conservancy and the grain transport system or military and penal matters or financial and fiscal affairs, they beg off answering on the ground that they are too busy for such things. Why is this? It is because [mastering] the eight-legged essay style has so deprived them of time and energy that even the most learned scholars are able to do no more than browse through the works of the sages and the historical records of three thousand years. Thus I have said that China's scholars are acquainted with the past but do not know the present, while the scholars of the Western nations comprehend the present but do not know the past. Yet, *it is essential that scholars who want to be of use to society place comprehension of the present first.*[29]

Wang's suggestions for the educational system were equally radical. He criticized the system's reliance on book learning as opposed to action and theory as opposed to practice and chided graduates for being "good at talking, in high-flown language, about human nature and life; they could lecture on benevolence and righteousness; they could do painstaking analyses of the most trivial minutia" [169], but could not talk about taxation and finances and were unashamed to admit it. In the 1880s Wang supported the establishment of technical schools for commoners in treaty ports, all to be publicly financed. He also approved of the first public library of Chinese books established in Hong Kong and felt such libraries would be much more beneficial than private collections which served an extremely limited number (for the most part, literati).

In *Mi yuan laomin zizhuan* [Autobiography of the old one of Mi yuan] Wang Tao provides his surname, place of residence, and lists all of his other names. He traces his ancestors from the Ming dynasty to the time of his birth. After referring briefly to some of his personality traits, he tells of going to Shanghai and lists the names of twelve of his friends there. While in Shanghai he is witness to the takeover by the Taiping forces of all surrounding areas and also sees foreigners' warships docked at the piers. When he is accused of collaboration with the Taipings, he flees to Hong Kong, where he studies, writes on the classics, and helps James Legge in his translations; later he travels to England and Europe.[30] He writes a history of the Franco-Prussian War and collaborates with others in establishing a newspaper. He travels, returns to his hometown, and goes to Japan; later he expresses great remorse over China's losses to Japan and Russia. He refers to his brother, Lizhen, his sister, Ying, and his wife Yang Mengheng, all of whom are dead at the time of writing. Wang names his second wife, Linlin, and two daughters, Wan (who died early) and Xian, who is mute, and laments the end of the Wang lineage (neither he nor his brother has any sons). In discussing his childhood Wang expresses the sadness he felt at his mother's death, his fondness for writing, and his fear that people will misrepresent him when he dies. All of his works are listed at the end of his autobiography, along with his closing justification: "To live and write one's own biography is not something done by the ancients; the Old One was afraid no one in the world will have heard of him, so he narrated himself in this way" [322].[31] When compared with the impressionistic autobiographies of Yi Shunding and Lin Shu, the most obvious difference in this text is its attention to descriptive detail of aspects of the author's daily life: names of many places, people, and works are included. The author lists his friends by name, as well as the places he visits and the titles of his works. The list as a narrative device appears frequently in circumstantial autobiographies; Sima Qian lists the chapters of the *Shiji*, and Liu Yuxi lists the places he lived that correspond to certain official titles. Wang Tao's list of friends or names of places in which certain occurrences took place is a clear reference to contemporary phenomena that fix the author in a specific social environment, and self is constructed through its relationship to these concrete external elements. Whereas Yi Shunding lists qualities, Wang Tao lists the "proper" names of people and texts.

At one point in his narrative Wang Tao expresses a wish to "go back home," live in a small house, "collect tens of thousands volumes of books," and spend his time "reading and chanting" until he is old and his teeth fall out [322]. This expressed desire implies a dissolution of his active, engaged, and specific relationship with society and acknowledges an alternative life that would involve withdrawal from and disavowal of involvement in political and social affairs. In positing an existence that is contrasted with his present life, Wang suggests the ideal of the impressionistic autobiography—the leisured literatus—and formulates this lifestyle as the symbolic option for an engaged scholar who wishes to cut off social ties.

Wang Tao's autobiography proceeds chronologically only up to a point. Toward the end of his text he begins to discuss his family—his brothers and sisters, many of whom died young, as well as his nuclear family. Wang's text makes it clear that the purpose of this digression is not to discuss his personal life, but to lament the end of a line. Neither Wang nor his brothers had sons, thus the two hundred and forty years of the known ancestry comes to an end. This, and the subsequently narrated death of his mother, he claims, are the two aspects of his life which prevented him from reaching fulfillment. The other debilitating occurrences are the verbal attacks he endured, his longing for things of old, and his fear that in the future people will misrepresent his ideas or activities. Chronology disintegrates only to invoke reasons for present despondency and for his decision to write an autobiography.

Like Sima Qian and Liu Yuxi, Wang Tao had a record to set straight. Accused of collaboration with the Taipings, he explains in his autobiography that he was only appearing to collaborate with Taiping leaders in order to gain information to be used against them. Using a longer narrative with a technique that permits reference to concrete issues allows for a "verifiable" record.

Wang Tao is an ambivalent figure who established a newspaper and worked with foreigners yet also did voluminous exegesis on classical works. Although he writes an autobiography that sets out to trace his life in the public domain, explain his misconstrued activities, and in this way present a circumstantial self-definition, his reference to a desire to escape from a life of energetic social work indicates the attraction of an opposite and contradictory life-style (if not definition).

Liang Qichao

Liang Qichao's position in late Qing and early Republican literati circles is unrivaled; he was famous as a stylist and essay writer and thus securely within the boundaries that constituted a *wenren* of the times.[32] Hao Chang claims that Liang was the most popular writer of the first decade of the twentieth century [142]. While his literary reputation and influence were enormous, changing political ideas have led some to term him a reformist, others to call him a neoconservatist, and books on Liang to invariably devote a chapter to the "reformer or revolutionary?" theme expressed so succinctly by Philip C. Huang.[33] Furthermore, like Wang Tao, Liang possessed so many roles—writer and essayist, politician, bureaucrat, public speaker, philosopher—that to some extent he defied categorization.[34]

Liang's 1898 exile to Japan because of his activities in opposing the Qing government gave him the opportunity to begin producing voluminous writings; his time in Japan was important in the development of his reformist ideas on the nation-state, the new citizen, the "historical" and "nonhistorical" races, anti-imperialistic nationalism, and the myriad of other concepts on which he wrote. But politically Liang is an "ambivalent" figure who supported reform but also was a strong sponsor of monarchy. After he visited the United States in 1903, Liang's preference for valuing the central role of domination in the political order over liberal values strengthened [Chang, 254]. He also felt the Chinese people were physically weak in comparison to Westerners and considered "physical strength an important factor in the western quality of martial prowess" and Japan's *bushido* ethics significant in the country's strength [Chang, 278].

After 1907, when his journal *Guomin congbao* stopped publication, Liang increasingly devoted himself to political activities. After the 1911 Revolution, Liang actively supported the new government [Zheng Pengyuan, 6], throwing his efforts into working for Yuan Shikai's attempts to build a constitutional monarchy and to some extent discrediting himself through his endorsement of Yuan. However, while Liang was able to fan the flames of revolution through his speeches and essays, he developed conflicts with Sun Yat-sen, worked with other moderate reformers to establish a new political party to oppose the Nationalists, and finally, in 1918, left politics and returned to intellectual work.[35] According to some historians Liang's political and intellectual work made him "one of the major players in the May Fourth Movement,"[36] while to others the "Chinese intellectual world of the 1920s was in fact passing him by," with many writers delving into social and economic issues but Liang still mired in "his emphasis on the spirit and attitudes of men" and promoting the middle way [Philip Huang, 158–59].

Self-Narrative at Thirty

Liang Qichao's *Sanshi zishu* [Self-narrative at thirty] appears to belong to an era different from the autobiographies investigated thus far. A number of pioneering elements characterize Liang's autobiography—an altered sense of temporality and a synchronicity of personal and "historical" time—which in other respects resembles the circumstantial text.[37] Liang's narration proceeds from one moment to the next, whereas previous texts go from one year, one event, or one era to the next. Furthermore, Liang's

stated reason for writing an autobiography is different than that of explication or validation: "If [my biography] is written by someone who does
not know me, how can this person's knowledge be equal to my own" [91]?
Other than in the case of self-defense, where the writer asks the reader to
accept his version of the facts, the other writers do not claim superior self-
knowledge as a reason for writing, and their texts do not promote self-
knowledge as a goal of the autobiography. In other respects Liang's
autobiography follows the tendencies established in the circumstantial
texts: he gives dates, names and place names, follows a chronological
order, and largely traces his movements in the world. Liang expostulates
not only the history of his ancestors, but also that of his home place; he
figures in these histories not merely as a specific entity in a chain of people,
but also as a precise location and time-point. Liang appears as the intersection of lines coming in from three different aspects of the past which are
manifested as the history of the human race, the history of locale, and
overriding both of these, time itself. His birth date is described in this way:
"I was born January 26 of the 2nd year of Tongzhi (1863), ten years after
the Taiping Kingdom was defeated in Jinling (Nanjing), one year after the
Qing scholar Zeng Guofan died, three years after the Franco-Prussian
War, and the year that Italy became a nation in Rome. When I was one
month old my grandmother Li died" [93–94]. His birth is known only by
the worldwide events that contextualize it. The individual, like the autobiographical subject in the text of Sima Qian, arrives in the world only
through the framework of time, place, and human history. Although it is
certainly not unusual, it is interesting that Liang mentions his study of
Shiji as one of the two textbooks he used as a child.

Liang continues to place priority on time and the overwhelming sense of
the moment. Rather than giving the year of his mother's death, he relates it
as a point in time and space: "When I was fifteen, my mother Zhao died in
childbirth with my fourth brother. I was studying in the provincial capital;
at the time there were no steamers, but I raced back home as fast as I
could. It was already too late to participate in the funeral. In all my life I
have had no regret greater than this" [93–94]. Liang describes buying a
copy of *Yinghuan zhilue*, a world geography, in a Shanghai bookstall, and
his autobiography begins by informing us that he is writing while traveling on a train in Japan. When Lin Shu relates the incident of his attempt to
send in cakes to win a courtesan's favor, or when Yi Shunding writes of his
capture by a Mongolian prince when he was five and of his writing

characters on the prince's palm, although the incidents are specific in time and place, they are not determining events in the author's life. Liang Qichao's recording of certain specific moments and places of certain acts is similar to these autobiographical incidents, but the implication of the instances or the positioning of the instances in relation to a significant context is dissimilar. The book on world geography, which he describes himself buying in a Shanghai bookstall, opens his eyes to a "new world"; Liang describes this figurative and literal discovery when he finds the existence of "the five continents and each country," which he had no knowledge of previously [94].

Liang wrote his autobiography at thirty. Writing one's autobiography at a young age is consistent with the requirements of a circumstantial approach. If the individual is a series of articulations, discrete in time, place, and person, it is advantageous to record these moments close to their happening. Therefore an author trying to write circumstantially would do best to write an autobiography at twenty, thirty, forty, and so on.[38] In such a text self-knowledge is not authorized by introspection or creative retrospection, but by a sense of moment and proximity to the occurrences the author describes. It would follow that since diaries are generally written in close contact to the time of the events they describe, they can be used in autobiographies as a type of "evidence" for the author's views, opinions, or simply his presentation of the "facts."[39] Liang formulates the self as produced through its relationship to events, incidents, and people in the socio-material world rather than as a "floating" entity that emerges from suppression of the orthodox biographical trademarks of ancestry, kinship, status, and position and association with an alternative.

Liang ends his autobiography by lamenting his inability to accomplish his aims and decrying his slavery to writing. In many respects Liang Qichao was a contradictory figure who was "liberal as well as Confucian" and "emotionally committed to the East and intellectually committed to the West."[40] Even though he defines his self through a circumstantial text, Liang mentions the importance of textual work in his life and lists the texts he wrote. As the list in his autobiography and the profusion of works he produced indicates, he was an extremely productive writer. The importance of textual work in his autobiography does not, however, indicate an impressionistic stance; through his detailed narration of historically particular events and people in the past and the present, Liang constructs a self that evolves in a distinctly circumstantial way.

Toward May Fourth

Other than a minority following groups such as *xueheng pai* and *jiayan pai*, most writers working in the teens and 1920s attempted to reorient literary writing away from a relationship with past literary traditions. Even writers such as Hu Shi, who became known for attempting to reform style and content within writing and did not emphasize the redefinition of the position of writing and of the writer in relation to society, tried to draw a clear line between the new literature and the old. The conflict of authorization that developed after the May Fourth movement frequently takes form in writers' autobiographies as an awareness of the possibilities afforded by reauthorizing the self not as a producer of texts, but as a "more active" participant within social life; in other words writers construct an antiliterary ideology.

One level of the progress of this struggle can be seen in the changing theories of the Creation Society and one of its founders, Guo Moruo. In the early twenties Guo espoused a romantic theory of literature as the expression and indulgence of the self, and the Creation Society flew the banner of "art for art's sake." By the mid-to-late twenties, however, Guo had become a Marxist, and Creation Society members viewed literature as a vital aspect of political and economic reality, now to be characterized by the slogan "art for life's sake." Within autobiography it appears that changes in literary ideology are not sufficient; writers are looking for a more radical change that orients them away from textual work and toward what they formulate to be either more physical or more politically and socially profound options.

Many of the writers of the twenties and thirties had been educated in the classics, but the abolition of the exam system disappointed only their parents' hopes, not their own. As we see in their autobiographies and other writings, most were only too happy to have escaped from the drudgery of a classical education which had consumed much of their childhood and to be able to go out into the world and seek learning in faraway places that were uninfluenced by the problems of Chinese education and its goals. Away from the infrastructure of significant texts and textual learning that they felt imprisoned anyone who had gone through the Chinese system, these writers hoped to redefine the function of writing in modern society and create a new work based on a lively, creative relationship with all aspects of society.

Nonetheless, in the autobiographies of May Fourth writers, most of which were written between 1925 and 1935, writing seems to work against the desire of the author to place himself squarely in the world of action and phenomena and gain authority through this relationship. Thus modern writers express contradiction, confusion, and disgust at literary writing and the social role of the writer. Literary work as the main authority for the self is alternately accepted and rejected as writers try to work out other options or recast themselves as workers or soldiers. The dilemma of the intellectual in modern China is encapsulated in the fate of these twentieth-century writers, who attempt, literally and figuratively, to go out into society, but are held back by their association with their work.[41]

3

Shen Congwen and Ba Jin: Literary

Authority Against the "World"

Shen Congwen zizhuan [The autobiography of Shen Congwen] and *Ba Jin zizhuan* [The autobiography of Ba Jin] both contrast authorization through reference to textual work (study and writing) with other alternatives that the author constructs as much more attractive, yet for reasons unclear in the text, unchosen. In these modern texts the "literary code" includes reference to the life-style of the writing intellectual—no longer a *wenren* in the traditional sense—and more specific reference to literary writing and the creative writer. Other textually based work, such as literary or textual scholarship, study in an educational institution, and memo and report writing in government or military organizations comes under attack in differing degrees. The process of becoming a writer is contrasted unfavorably with alternative constructions of work and the self, such as being a soldier actually engaged in fighting (Shen Congwen) or a manual laborer (Ba Jin). Yet in both cases, despite the desirable formulation of more physical career options, the authors insist on affiliation with the literary at the expense of the alternatives which they have developed.

The contradiction which results from the author's construction of two competing ideologies of self and work puts the writer, who has no choice but to locate identity in textual work, in a no-win situation. If he wants to continue work as a writer, he projects and implies the significance of the text and textual labor; if he denies this priority, consistency demands that he abandon textual work and become a worker, soldier, or otherwise physically engaged revolutionary.[1]

It is in evaluating the alternatives that writers propose to counteract the negative effects of textual work that the concepts of *impressionistic* and *circumstantial* become significant. While they do not signify priority or hierarchy, these categories indicate the relative arenas into which modern autobiographies organize experience. The two polarities in premodern autobiographies are, on one hand, a text which arranges narrative and self-definition through reference to a "literary" life-style, and, on the other hand, a text which is organized through reference to social and material phenomena. Both are textual strategies. In modern autobiographies this dichotomy embodies the way in which the text organizes the "reality" of the authors' lives; an existence which relies on affiliation with textual work is contrasted with either a social or a physical orientation. The difference is that on a superficial level, the modern autobiography elevates the physical or social approach while demeaning textual work, while at some level it adheres to an epistemology that would retain the supremacy of a textually defined life-style. Thus although it is accurate to say that the purely impressionistic autobiography has been recast as an indicator of the "un-modern" and thereby cannot be utilized by the modern writer, the "literary code" that the impressionistic autobiography promotes still exists in the modern text in the form of ultimate acquiescence to textual authority. Although it may be difficult or impossible to trace a historical development of autobiographies that leads to the modern form, it is possible to say that the organization of textual references that comprise the self-narrative is similar in both cases.

In discussing May Fourth writers and their depiction of self, Leo Ou-fan Lee writes:

> While in their lives and works the focal point was always on the self, there was a concurrent lack of inner depth in their self-expressions. Rather than searching within for a definition of selfhood, as Liu E had done in the middle section of the novel [*Lao Can youji*], the May Fourth generation of writers (with a few exceptions) often asserted their individual personalities and life-styles externally against an environment that they found both confusing and alienating. While this externalization of the self had its romantic appeal, there was a spiritual void under the veneer of radical antitraditionalism. [1985:294]

Lee notes that in writing about the self, modern Chinese intellectuals seem unable to gain a sense of inner tranquility and strength and are deprived of spiritual sustenance which is indicated, in Liu E's case, through "traditional poetry and metaphors." Lee implies that these references have been outmoded by the Westernized intellectual context that forms the environment of the modern writer [1985:293]. At the same time he mentions that modern writers have not "lost" the self; rather, "a sense of social crisis has compelled the writer to confront a broader reality" [1985:295]. I argue that the unifying "spirituality" that allows Liu E to "relate meaningfully to his environment" [1985:293] is an extension of the premodern *wenren* concept which designates certain literary and philosophical traditions as indicative of spiritual essence. Aside from the issue of whether Liu E, Yu Dafu, or Shen Congwen possessed anything that could be called "inner tranquility," the textual expression of such a quality must rely on a set of signifying referents. By the late 1920s and early 1930s the "traditional poetry and metaphors" which Liu E can successfully employ to denote spirituality no longer signify, to urban intellectuals, the same meaning. Lee comments: "Lao Can's political disillusionment does not prevent him from enjoying, without any ambivalence, the pleasures and vices that such a milieu provides: food, wine, opium, sing-song girls, and prostitutes. Yu Dafu is equally a connoisseur of such people and things, but his pleasure is invariably accompanied by remorse and shame, as evidenced in his numerous accounts" [1985:293]. Lee attributes Liu's "sense of continuity with traditional Chinese culture" and the book's resulting unity of feeling to the author's "familiarity and comfort with his cultural milieu" [1985:293]. However, by the modern period the cultural milieu of "food, wine, opium, sing-song girls and prostitutes" which signifies status and function for Liu E means traditional ideas and life-styles and opposition to reform for modern writers. There is no readily available textual method for modern writers to signify *wenren* in all of its premodern implications; the category has ceased to exist.

Given the negative construction of literary writing that exists in autobiographies of the late 1920s and early 1930s, why did anyone choose to be a writer? Why did writers continue to work rather than quit and become actively involved in one of the alternatives they proposed? Throughout this manuscript I have traced an increasing disillusionment with the emphasis on the literary that critics say the examination system promoted and claimed that the abolition of the system severed the link between the literary and political realms that gave literary writing its structural basis of authority. The abolition of the examination was one effect of a social environment which was in the process of constructing the physical and "practical" as more valuable than the textual and "impractical." At the

same time I have noted that some writers and critics championed literature as central to the modernization of China, especially in creating a
"new citizen," a concept which consumed the intellectual energies of
Liang Qichao and others. I have attempted to explain this discrepancy by
noting that whereas the *function* of literary writing within Chinese society
was diminished when the examination system was abolished, and at some
level prestige dwindled, the writers, critics, and scholars who were trained
in textual labor partook in a widespread effort to rejuvenate the stature of
literature through redefinition of its social role, embodying literature as
the repository of culture which they hoped it would continue to be.[2] While
this mythologizing of literature did not completely disappear (nor has
disappeared today), it broke down in the late 1920s and early 1930s,
when writers became disillusioned with the failure of the revolution, the
factionalism of Chinese politics and letters, the lack of progress in reform
of traditional ideas and practices, the violence against reformers and
revolutionaries, and the seeming ineffectualness of their work in changing
any of this.

This era of disillusionment is commonly recognized. By the last half of
the 1920s Lu Xun had ceased to write stories. Mao Dun penned his trilogy
Disillusionment, Pursuit, and *Vacillation* at the same time; in "Cong
Guling dao Dongjing" [From Guling to Tokyo], written in 1928, he
comments on intellectuals and the era:

> *Disillusionment* was written from the middle of September to the
> end of October 1927, *Vacillation* was written from the beginning
> November to the beginning of December, *Pursuit* from April to June
> 1928. The period from *Disillusionment* to *Pursuit,* therefore, coin-
> cided with a troublesome time in China, and the author naturally had
> many stirrings of emotion and could not help but let them show
> through. I also know that if I were more daring in words like a person
> of heroic stature, there would probably be more people praising me;
> but I have never been good at making a public display of my feelings,
> be they heroic or otherwise. When I remind myself that it is already a
> pitiful, cowardly thing to be able only to closet myself in a room to do
> some writing, to go ahead and shamelessly spout out tough words
> would be quite out of the question. I am beginning to feel that hiding
> in a room to write brave words on paper is laughable. I have no
> objection to other people doing this in hopes of deceiving the world
> and stealing some fame, trying to get people to say "he is a revolu-

tionary after all," but I myself am totally unwilling to do so. I can only, therefore, tell the truth: I *am* rather disillusioned, I *am* pessimistic, I *am* depressed, and I express these feelings in the three novelettes without the slightest disguise.[3]

Mao's antithetical relationship between writing and revolutionary activity is clear; he links his depression to his decision to "closet" himself in a room and write.

Thus although it is in this period that the negative theorization of writing and the writer becomes most prominent in the essays, stories, novels, and autobiographies of writers, it should not be viewed as an isolated period, but rather as a continuation and consolidation of previous tendencies which demote literary work and as one result of the abolition of the examination system.[4] Writers took up or continued writing because despite the now problematic definition of the writer, literary work still represented an avenue of creative expression for the intellectual trained to work with texts. Even though the structural basis for high social valuation of textual work had disintegrated, the esteem with which such work was regarded did not immediately disappear. Furthermore, there were new ideologies embedded within late 1920s and early 1930s literary campaigns—the popularization movement, the promotion of social realism, the emergence of patriotic literature, the emphasis on folk forms—that were altering the meaning of writing within society and lending the writer some hope that a new literary stature would emerge.

Shen Congwen: The Military Against the Literary

Congwen zizhuan perfectly represents the dialectic of text versus world or writing versus action. Through his self-narrative Shen Congwen redefines the relationship of writing to society, revalues writing within the context of society, and creates the writer as contradictory by virtue of the inherited codes which delimit the Chinese literary identity in the early twentieth century.

Shen Congwen wrote his autobiography when at the relatively young age of thirty. When he added an afterword to the autobiography for a 1980 reprinting, Shen commented on his speed in writing the text and on its warm reception upon publication:

This *Autobiography* is not the same as my other works. A friend of mine was preparing to open a new book store in Shanghai and jokingly asked me if I would "lead the attack." We agreed that it must be finished within one month. I am not at all used to turning in a manuscript under such urgent conditions. But in my subjective reflections of the time, I felt that since it was an autobiography, there was nothing to prevent me from throwing off all the restrictions of customs and trying a new method. So I just wrote it straight down from my individual memory. This allowed me to go over the progress of development of my individual life, and also allowed the reader to understand what kind of environment a person like me had lived in. Especially when life has fallen into complete hopelessness yet one is able to continue to work, full of bravery and confidence from beginning to end—what is the origin of this motivation? So I took only three weeks, read it over once when I had finished it, and then, breaking all precedent, sent it to Shanghai. After it was published as a volume, it was not long before it got some good reviews. Perhaps some of the readers just felt it was "unique, strange, and interesting." Only a small number of friends and relatives could understand the heaviness and misery of going in and out of hell. But as for me, I feel it is nothing but the "autobiography of a mischievous child."[5]

Shen's autobiography integrates bizarre aspects of his childhood and prechildhood into the first part of the text that covers the background of his birth or young childhood before his participation in the military. His autobiography ends at the point where he attempts to go out into the world and leave the environment that has formed his youth and young adulthood.

Military Order and Utopian Consciousness

The place of his birth exists, Shen writes in the introductory paragraph, because the military set up a garrison in order to proceed with a policy of decimation toward the Miao tribes. The violent rationale for the town's existence does not prevent Shen from describing it as a totally enclosed, self-sufficient little world endowed with a special military mystique, code, and order: it is a utopia that is characterized by a correct order in all aspects of social intercourse and absolute harmony between people and the natural world. The physical arrangement of the forts and blockhouses is in a precise layout, the peasants all live according to law, and the soldiers are pure and simple like the common people [2]. Within the town government the hierarchy among rulers is rigidly delineated, and the people have faith in this system: "The local rulers were separated into several types: at the top were the spirits of heaven, second were the officials, and in only third place were the mayor and those who performed as shamans in attendance on the spirits. Everyone deeply believed in the spirits, lived according to the law, and loved the officials" [3]. The rites and festivals of the town, voluntarily financed by the inhabitants, are carried out in accordance with rules of ancient rites, and when the natural world does not cooperate with the prescribed amount of rain, it is controlled through the dancing and chanting of costumed shamans. Each group of people engages in the business of its ancestors (those from Fujian sell tobacco, those from Canton medicine), emphasizing the continuity of ancient ways. The ruling officials are made up of a class united in marriage as well as politics. The land is fruitful, the water full of fish, and the people are ideal images that fit perfectly into the utopia Shen describes: "In the country and the town, there was no shortage of brave, sincere, perfectly ideal soldiers, and warm, soft, durable, perfectly homey women" [4].

The Material: Desire and Attainment

As the author begins to describe the young Shen Congwen sallying out into the immediate surroundings of the village, three aspects of the phenomenological world appear as powerful and attractive. One is all sensory aspects of materiality: sounds, tastes, and especially the experiences associated with water. Whenever he can, Shen steals away from school to go swimming. Symbolically and concretely using the power of writing to circumvent the pleasurable sensation of water, Shen's parents write a large, washable character on his hand in an effort to keep him out of the water. All sensory experiences appeal to Shen, but water affords him access to the world in a dangerous and forbidden but beautiful form [11, 12, 17, etc.]. He even attributes his ability to think and to recognize beauty in some part to his relationship with water. In 1939 Shen wrote an article titled "Wode chuangzuo yu shui de guanxi" [My creative writing and its relationship to water] in which he credits his ability to write to his early relationship with water: "But as for my work, which according to prevailing custom would be called 'literary work,' it may be useful to those friends who are a bit younger than myself for me to go to the roots of it, to explain it. I can say that the base of this work is not constructed on 'a certain book' or 'a stack of books,' but rather, it actually is based on 'water'" [453]. Shen places "water" in direct opposition to "books," showing that it was his desire to get away from the classroom and textual learning that pushed him and his friends out into the "world," where they learned to appreciate material phenomena that he set up in direct contrast to book learning.

Another fascinating aspect of the world is the means of material production that function within it.[6] Shen watches workers polishing needles, making umbrellas or shoes, dying cloth, and making soybean milk [15, etc.]. The third and most pervasive aspect of materiality he treasures is the strange underside of phenomena, especially the sign of their demise: death and all of its tools in the form of knives, guns, instruments of conflict and its attributes of blood, corpses, and mutilated body parts.

Shen's obsession with death and its figures continues throughout his text.[7] He writes at length about squirming fish and turtles about to die, slaughtered pigs still twitching, and by the fourth chapter the death and mutilation of humans. Shen is especially intrigued with the mutilated body parts of those executed by soldiers during the revolution. As a child, Shen goes to the execution grounds to watch corpses being eaten by wild dogs [16] and observes the slaughtering of cows as he plays in a stream: "When the opportunity presented itself I could even see that honest, pitiful stock animal when it was laid down. Because each day I could see a little, before long the way the cow was killed and the arrangement of its innards were completely clear to me" [16]. Many of the tactile and sensory impressions he longs to savor are associated with death:

> My life was brimming with questions, to which I had to seek resolution on my own. I wanted to know too much, and I knew too little, so sometimes I was a little worried. During the day I was just too wild, I went everywhere to watch, everywhere to listen, and everywhere to smell; the smell of a dead snake, the smell of rotting grass, the smells on the body of the butcher, the smell of the earthen kiln after it was rained on; if I had to speak about them, there is no way I could use language to describe them, but I could easily distinguish them. [21]

Shen fixes on the poverty of language as a tool to relate the multifarious phenomena of the material world, setting off "reality" and language as oppositional in nature. These strange phenomena haunt him when he is young and continue to do so when he is thirty: "Because of this when I returned home in the night I would dream countless strange and odd dreams. Right up to the present, twenty years later, these dreams often cause me to be unable to sleep soundly at night, and even take me back to the emptiness of that 'past' and into the illusory universe" [22].

From Freedom to Entrapment: Learning the Codes

Bizarre, sensual textual motifs are common to the first parts of many autobiographies of Shen Congwen, Guo Moruo, and Lu Xun. This inscription of the early aspect of the self as illogical, magical, and strange generally appears only in the first part of the text, when the author writes of his life as a young child, or in some cases before the birth of the author, stipulating recognition of these presocial elements only under these conditions. When authors write of their initiation into the educational institutions of society and their constriction through the norms of education and work, they relinquish frequent reference to bizarre phenomena, implying a suppression of childish interest in more primitive and genuine phenomena. In Shen's autobiography reference to strange phenomena continues as he joins the military and searches for the life of a "soldier."

Although the struggle that marks the child's transition into school education and his forced disavowal of past sensual pleasures in their replacement by textual study is often authorized by a father who insists that his child can be a scholar, the actual process of mastering the textual tools of reading and writing frequently is supervised by the mother.[8] Shen Congwen's father recognizes his intelligence, but he is first educated by his mother, who teaches him to read and also imparts to him certain qualities of personality: "Much of my education was from my mother. She taught me to read, to recognize the names of medicine, and she taught me resoluteness, the resoluteness one must not lack if one is to be a man" [8]. The moral code which comes from textual training is imparted by females, yet encoded with a male mystique. The female family members, who cannot participate in the construction of moral fibre through military activity (highly developed throughout the autobiography), can ensure that their sons (and thus they themselves) will reap the advantages of textual knowledge. Traditionally, mothers were also the beneficiaries of literary training when their sons passed the examinations and became officials.

In a later essay Shen claims that his salient motive in portraying his dislike of schools, teachers, and book learning was to expose the poverty of the "Confucius says" tradition of education which relies on memorization of the classics and commentaries:

Although the emphasis is on opposing the "Confucius says," long-enduring, ineffective educational methods of the academy teachers, most readers will probably just feel it is "interesting," and will not feel there is any purpose or significance in the writing. Because when they read my works, the era has already changed and "Confucius says" has already lost its function. ["Afterword," 77]

In his autobiography, however, there is less criticism of old-style education than of any education that is based on book learning; Shen does not deal with the differences between studying with a teacher trained in the classics as opposed to one trained in a Western-style academy.

Books Against the World: Books As World

In "Wo du yiben xiaoshu tongshi you du yiben dashu" [At the same time as reading a small book, I read a large one] the metaphor that Shen continues throughout the text begins: life is a large, interesting book that is fun to "read," whereas actual books are dull, dry, and small in both size and significance. As Shen's family tries to get him to attend school, they are in constant conflict with the young student. When Shen's father decides his son is intelligent and should attend school, formal education receives the authorization of the father and the support of the mother but is undermined by Shen's cousin Zhang, who is his collaborator in truancy, teaching Shen how to lie and thus escape not only from the tyranny of family authority, but also from the deadening training in the orthodox understanding of language, text, and culture that school represents [Shen, 12].

Like Guo Moruo, Shen Congwen begins his autobiography with a description of the place of his birth, following the conventions of the circumstantial autobiographies and locating himself in a specific spatial context. His positioning of the self within a corporeal environment is extremely precise and concrete:

When I pick up this pen and try to write a little about the twenty years I passed in this place, the people I saw, the sounds I heard, the smells I smelled, that is to say, the real, true education of life I received; when I first mention the small, remote border town where I was born and grew up, I really don't know how to take hold. I should speak with the air of one of the people of the town—it really is an odd place! It is only two hundred years ago, when the Manchus were in charge of

> Chinese land, and wanted to suppress, torture, and kill the remaining
> Miao tribes, that they sent a garrison to live here and a fort and
> inhabitants came into existence. The establishment and complete
> past of this odd place is recorded in some official documents in
> *Miaofang beijian* (Defense against the Miao), but that is just a dry,
> dull official book. [11]

Concrete, sensual phenomena are the substance of the "real, true education" that results from immersion in the specific locale of the pre-
institutional author; contrasted with this vibrant and colorful education
is the transformation of this materiality into a "dry, dull official book"
that renders the world into text and forms the basis of all formal
education.

When Shen writes these words he is already a writer, known by textual
rather than material production; he has become a writer despite a professed strong antipathy toward any "knowledge" that has come from
books rather than the "world," and despite his aversion to what he
describes as the transformation of world into text. However, his own
efforts to write about the people he sees, the smells he smells, and so on—
all of the phenomena of the world which form a contrast to the "dry, dull"
world of books—appear contradictory, as he seems to have no choice but
to follow the practice of "world into text" if he wishes to write. The
autobiography devalues writing, demoting it to a position much below a
"life" of perception and participation, yet as the textually defined identity
of the writer, it also stands as a contradictory sign of this devaluation.
Thus the writer appears to be writing against his own will, sketching a
better, nontextually defined existence, yet at the same time able to do this
only through the use of the textual tools of paper, pen, and ideology.

Shen Congwen wrote his autobiography when he was thirty, and he did
not make any additions to it later in life. Because he emphasizes the people
and phenomena he saw and otherwise sensually perceived, his close proximity to the time of these events works to his advantage, as he is able to
imply to the reader that the concrete detail with which he portrays phenomena is a consequence of nearness in time. The contradictory opposition of world/text and writer/actor and its depreciation of textual work
demands a detailed and concrete material description. The author's ability
to record phenomena close to their occurrence, or at least to insinuate
such proximity, allows for the creation of a more forceful alternative to
the textually defined existence against which he strives.

Wen *Against* Wu

As Shen indicates in the first paragraph of his autobiography (quoted above), the classical contrast between the military (*wu*) and the literary (*wen*) is the basic dichotomy of his text.[9] Shen recounts local parents' support for their children's participation in the military; the continuation of military power behind civilian rule ensures further support of an idyllic, well-ordered environment. Shen represents the military code as originating from a legendary utopia that establishes the prototypical ideal conditions of a small town that lives by ancient rites in a well-arranged manner. Military ideology provides the inspiration for this utopia, with the killing implied in military affairs muted into a ritual performed by dancing shamans with weapons wearing "blood-red" clothes.

However, Shen's father's desire that his son go to school hints at a larger context that does not grant the military the utopic, unifying qualities which it has in the village. Power and order in the world at large result rather from a mastery of the written tradition which can only come from participation in formal education. At the urging of his parents Shen goes to school but quickly finds the lure of the "world" too great and quits school to join the military. As military personnel, Shen is "studying the big book" that proves its authenticity by refusing accurate description in a text; this "big book" demands participation in the worldly events and sensual perception of phenomena. As the autobiography progresses, however, the contradiction of the intellectual seeking authority through reference to military and corporeal involvement becomes evident, and Shen emerges not as a participant, but as an observer who, after denying the textual, makes a gradual journey back to the textual as the basis of a valid identity. Furthermore, Shen incessantly makes use of textual metaphors to define nontextual endeavors, undercutting his attempts to locate an alternate authority for his life and work outside of the influence of the text.

The "World" and Sensual Experience

In "Qingxiang suojian" [What I saw at Qingxiang] Shen records a story that is almost identical to that which forms the contents of Guo Moruo's first creative story.[10] When the daughter of the chairman of the local business club dies of illness and is buried, a young man who sells bean curd digs up the corpse and sleeps with it for three days. Asked why he did it, he does not answer, but murmurs about her beauty [70–71]. Shen combines the three most vivid and striking constituents of the contrasting corporeal system he is devising—death, sex, and beauty—in a story that initiates his venture out into the "world."

In the chapter "Yige dawang" [A great king] Shen writes of a man he called the king (a title common for military leaders), a "real, true, man" who had killed two hundred men and who had seventeen wives. The respect Shen has for the king comes from the masculinity the king embodies, which Shen represents as the ultimate form of vitality in the earthy sphere he supposedly is entering. The king's extreme physicality, his power over women, and his ability to impose death almost at will on others are desirable aspects of the military environment that later become unavailable to the author when he decides to establish himself as a student. Shen makes no explicit comparisons, but as manifestations of the "big book," the king and his attributes become implicit oppositions to the "small book," or textual learning, from which Shen is escaping. The figure of the intellectual, who works primarily with texts, contrasts with the strong, physical presence of the military man.[11]

From Military to Textual

The obvious transition from an immersion into the physical and material to one whose life is authorized by writing and the text begins in "Xing Wen de mishu" [A secretary named Wen] (*wen:* writing). Wen introduces Shen to the dictionary *Ciyuan* [The origin of terms], which Shen then ironically places to the test by looking up the name of China's archetypical warrior, Zhuge Liang. One by one Shen begins to take up various texts and learn how to use them; after the dictionary he learns to read newspapers, and finally books. By the next chapter Shen finds himself jealous of students and lonely as a soldier [88–89].

Shen reflects that he is serving his country but cannot get over his growing envy of the students he sees when he is still in the military. When Shen sees the bloated body of his friend Lu Mi, who dies in a battle, he begins to question his participation in the military, wondering how and where he will die. He finally decides to leave the military and resume the life of a student, characterizing this decision as a sacrifice of power for wisdom [140–44].

The author suppresses the contradiction in authority that circumscribes his identity by partially representing his desire to "be a soldier" as thwarted by *others,* who have heard he is good at writing and refuse to let him be an ordinary soldier [103, 133]. Shen becomes known for his calligraphy and is even accorded with special honors: his superiors tell him no one but he can do the job correctly [112]. In this moment of textual displacement Shen allows the reader to believe that he has been forced into switching his priorities; he wants nothing more than to work in the army as a common soldier but is prevented from doing so. Eventually he comes to enjoy study and reads old books late into the night. By the last chapter of the autobiography, "Yige zhuanji" [A turning point], Shen goes to Beijing to *enter school* and "learn about a new world" [144]. In the last sentence, however, Shen claims he is studying "human life," the class he can never finish studying and the "school from which he can never graduate" [145].

Passivity and Textual Authority

Although Shen intellectually rejects the literary as a defining aspect of the self and develops the contrast between the sensual, material, and corporeal and the textual, the tension between these two authorizations lacks any sense of the passion and struggle apparent in, for example, Guo Moruo's text. Other than a desire to simply submit to the views of others or a fear of death, Shen provides no motivation for his final decision to become a student. However, the overall acceptance of a textual authorization that is revealed in the couching of his self-transmission within a metaphor that implies writing (big and little books, study of the world and study of books) indicates that despite his protestations to the contrary, Shen privileges the textual.

The perspective that allows the paradox between textual/material authorizations to exist without struggle is *kan renao*, or a point of view determined by passive observation. The *kan renao* standpoint exemplifies the pattern of passivity that informs Shen's text.[12] Shen's search for a materially based life develops into nothing more than a somewhat distanced observation, both in his childhood excursions and his military life. He does not fight with knives, kill, or sleep with female bandits as do others in his autobiography. Even in his childhood Shen spends most of his time watching others work, gradually gaining a sense of the way things are constructed through his observations.

Shen's "decision" to pursue a career as a writer is a logical correlation to his passive reading of the world; what he tries to present as a plunge into "life" is actually just the knowledgeable observation of the "author." Because this passive authorial position is not just displayed in his final decision to become a student (to study rather than participate in worldly affairs), but structures the entire autobiography, no transition is actually made.

Thus although active involvement in the phenomenological world is developed as the vital contrast to study, structurally such participation is only as an *aspect* of the narrator. As such, it has taken on the internal passivity of the narrative position. By situating his entire discourse on the unagitated level of *kan renao,* Shen transforms the detached, observing stance of those involved in the "small book" into a metaphor that signifies lack of active participation. In an exemplary incident Shen describes, peasants marked for execution by soldiers edge themselves away from the others and stand close to those who had come to watch, causing soldiers to forget about them and allow their escape [30]. Involvement with the text is the opposite of the material, sensual participation in life that Shen establishes as his desire, yet what he shows as the apparently innate and unavoidable negativity and passivity of a textually based stance continues to define Shen and prevent him from becoming an actor in the socio-material arena.

During the 1930s and 1940s Shen Congwen wrote many articles about literature and aesthetics, literature and society, and the technicalities of writing, some of which clarify his later views toward literature. In his 1942 "Xiaoshuo yu shehui" [Fiction and society] Shen refutes the common appreciation of fiction as just something to pass the time, claiming that the relationship between society and literature is highly complex and difficult to evaluate; any individual work can and usually does produce contradictory results, sometimes "good" and sometimes "bad." Therefore, literature and politics should not become too closely entwined, since this will result in superficial limitations placed on a complex phenomenon. In "Xin wenren yu xin wenxue" [New literati and new literature, 1935] Shen criticizes the newly created false literati of the era and states his criteria for new literature and demands on new writers:

> First, they must first recognize that modern literature cannot depart from modern society, writers are also "people," and literature absolutely cannot abandon human problems in favor of empty talk. Second, they must not only pay attention to society and the unreasonable places in social organization that need to be recreated and altered, but also must put great effort into showing their opinions and goals in their works and clarifying their likes and dislikes [168].

In short, although Shen defined literature as linked to and molded by society, he opposed a tight unity between literature and political ideology.[13] Even in this analysis Shen implies categories of "writing" and "society" which may become, against his desire, oppositional.

Ba Jin and the Alternative of Labor

In *Ba Jin zizhuan* [The autobiography of Ba Jin] Ba Jin establishes a childhood orthodoxy of familial ties, human relationships, and early study that he immediately begins to destroy.[14] His identification with a socially oppressive family gives way to understanding of and sympathy for those who labor. The family system becomes the background from which he must escape, a conceptualized "China" that collects together all of the negative forms of social interaction possible. The utopia of familial warmth to which Ba Jin refers is brief and limited to the time when he is very young, studying at home, and under the influence and control of his mother, whom he portrays as a warm, kind person who never chastised him. Although the lower classes attract Ba Jin's interest and he establishes their lives and work as an alternate to the suffocating mentality of his aristocratic family, he does not become a laborer or engage in social action to benefit others. Rather, he becomes a writer.[15]

Conflicting Ideologies: Oppression Revealed

From the beginning of his autobiography Ba Jin works to establish himself as distinct from the environment that produced him and his social ideologies as diverging from those of his parents and his social class. The process of differentiation begins with his discussion of attachment to a chicken, his "first real friend" which he loses when it is killed and eaten. This incident disturbs him and causes him to question the morality of adult humans [9–17]. His sympathy for the weak and oppressed extends to the silkworms which are used in medical prescriptions for his brother and, cured with salt and pepper, eaten by his uncle [52–53]. Ba Jin's next social affiliation is with Auntie Yang, a servant in charge of taking care of the children. He is intrigued by the stories she tells him and the songs she sings, and he describes her voice as she read characters to him and his brothers as "the only music of our youth" [22].

Ba Jin continues to describe the powerless as deserving of compassion and even empathy. He points out the difference between Auntie Yang's hands, which were rough and coarse, and those of his mother, which were soft and smooth. His life proceeds peacefully, with "no tears, no sorrow, and no hate" until this small utopia is destroyed by Auntie Yang's prolonged sickness and death [76]. Only after she dies does Ba Jin's mother tell him about Auntie Yang's history: after she gave birth to her son, Mao'er, her husband died and she was forced to become a nursemaid to support herself. When her son was two, he fell in a river and drowned, leaving her without relatives. She had been with Ba Jin's family for four years when, before she reached the age of thirty, she became ill and died. Auntie Yang is the first human catalyst to stimulate Ba Jin's increasingly revolutionary sensibility.

When Ba Jin is old enough to understand his father's work as a judge, he is appalled by what he perceives as his father's cruelty toward those on whom he passes judgment. As he watches the presentation of cases, Ba Jin is amazed that his father's reaction to the defendant's pleading is "Nonsense! Beat him," and the result is that the man is beaten until his posterior is purple and bleeding [54].

Ba Jin also notes three incidents that further decrease his confidence in the judgment of his superiors and increase his sympathy for the laboring classes. The first is Ba Jin's father's action when he heard Ba Jin say that the servants had been gambling and ordered them beaten. Ba Jin blames himself for this and cries when he realizes what he has done. Another is the beating and firing of one of his sister's nursemaids for eating a certain kind of food which would supposedly, in its very presence, influence the sister's case of measles. The third is his brother's beating of the young servant girl Xing'er. After observing these incidents, Ba Jin's conclusion is that "many things in the world are unfair" [64].[16]

This childhood environment of oppressor and oppressed is further developed when Ba Jin is beaten by his mother for refusing to bow before a picture of his grandfather and comes to hate all ritual; his mother's actions strengthen Ba Jin's ties with the oppressed [65]. When his two uncles return from study in Japan without their braids and have to wear fake ones to avoid accusation that they are part of the revolutionary party, Ba Jin is envious. The uncles represent a challenge to the reigning hierarchy of oppressors over oppressed. Ba Jin writes that when the Qing government fell and the Republic was established, his grandfather was sad, his father had no opinion, his second uncle quit his post as an official, and his third uncle gave himself the pen name "Gentleman of the Perished Land" (*Wangguo daifu*). Only the children were not unhappy [72].

The "China" which Ba Jin formulates is composed of a network of social habits that are based on lack of equality between classes and bereft of humanity between individuals. Another indicator of "China" and this undesirable past is traditional Beijing and Sichuan opera, which was a source of entertainment for Ba Jin's father, uncles, and older brother. In describing the relationship of his relatives to the actors who played the *danjiao* parts of women characters, Ba Jin implies that there may have been sexual relations that went well beyond the poetry-writing and picture-taking which he finds so despicable. Because of this implied homosexual activity, which to Ba Jin seems to epitomize the heights of upper-class corruption, he becomes unable to ever enjoy traditional opera again [82–85].

Eventually the author finds that he is spending at least half his time with servants and those whose social position is lower than his [86]. He identifies with servants and the rickshaw pullers and feels angry at their misery, finally openly declaring himself to be on their side [88]. He dislikes the hypocrisy of his superiors and has rejected all of the structures of the old society, including ritual, entertainment, and eventually, with the death of his father and the change of his family life into one full of hatred and struggle, the family system itself [88, 89, 96]. This rejection of what he has identified as the seminal institutions of China leads him first to associate with those in lower classes and then to "participate in social movements," an activity that is not described and is eclipsed in this text by creative writing after he goes abroad [88].

Writing in the Real World: Hazardous Work

In the last part of the text the author records the actual process of learning to master literature and, later, creative writing. The process that Ba Jin describes is one in which family life after his father's death was so unbearable that he took refuge in study. Yet the influence such immersion has on his general well-being is anything but healthy: "My body was bound too tightly. I could not move. I could not shake off the heavy burden on my shoulders. I used all my time to study. And books gobbled up my health" [96]. In the chapter "Xiezuo de shenghuo" [My life of writing] Ba Jin writes that when he was a student in France, he "let books eat up [his] youth" [117]. Extreme loneliness leads him to begin to write creatively, and in 1928 he sends some of his work to friends in China with the ostensible reason of having it printed for his brothers and friends to read. When he returns to Shanghai in 1929 and sees his work in *Xiaoshuo yuebao* [Fiction monthly], he is not pleased: "As for that friend who sent it to a publisher instead of to my brother and friends, I blame him for my having wasted a youth on paper, and for my having fallen into a literary life from which I cannot escape" [122]. This is the moment of suppression and displacement in Ba Jin's text: like Shen and others, he foists the decision that leads to his self-definition as a writer onto the desires and actions of others. Although Ba Jin writes all of his work from "painful recollection," literary production does not lead to relief from this agony; on the contrary, he also characterizes this life as one of loneliness and pain in which he ruins his health, his self, and his happiness [123–28]. Ba Jin finally blames the "tragedy" of his life on his inability to separate himself from books [129].[17]

Reinventing the Tradition

Both Shen Congwen and Ba Jin appeal, in different ways, to textual work as reference points in their construction of self and work, yet both denigrate its literary value for the individual or society. In a process that is echoed in the autobiographies of Lu Xun and Guo Moruo, Ba Jin frames a past that lacks vitality, the moral values of decency, human compassion, fairness, and systemic justice. This "China" is rejected, and he seeks an alternative "outside" life as a writer. Far from providing a framework for the positive definition of self and work that the author, in his outward movement away from family, seeks, his literary work emerges as even more deadly and pervasive in its ability to harm the individual who authorizes the self through it and in its inability to provide an authentic, socially valuable activity.

Both Shen Congwen and Ba Jin set up an early context of orthodox social relations that can only be maintained through ignorance. Ba Jin must ignore the unequal social structure which allows the upper classes to use and misuse workers, and Shen Congwen must remain within the utopia of his vibrant fort if he does not want to deal with the pain and suffering of military life in "reality." The military alternative is eroded as soon as Shen begins to wonder how he will die and in his envious glances at the lives of the students. Textual work as an alternative is implied and eventually accepted, but the autobiography ends when textual work begins. Throughout the text the opposition of the textual versus the active and material, or the small book and the large book, is at work. Ba Jin offers literary work as an alternative only in his actions in the last part of his autobiography, when he discusses becoming a writer and his attempts to transform experience into text. As he describes it, not only is literary work capable of "killing" him, but he doubts the social value of such work. Similar to Shen Congwen, Ba Jin elides the moment of decision that should constitute him as a writer. The literary exists as an alternative road that the author takes, yet the author presents it as extremely damaging to his developing formulation of work and self. Ba Jin leads readers to believe that he never escapes from the dire influence writing has had on his life, at the end of his autobiography equating writing with his life: "This life of writing is totally unhappy; my work is full of blood and tears. I am not an artist, and writing is just part of my life. The road of writing is the same as my life. Works of art have the same loves and hates as my life" [128]. The last words of his text question the cause of his misery, but propose no solution: "My life is tragic. I need rest, yet books are my companion. This is an unhappy state of affairs. Why is it so tragic?" [129].

Much as Shen Congwen stipulates military existence and authorization as an alternative to textual work, Ba Jin implies another choice in association with the laboring classes and, eventually, participation in social movements. Throughout the text the author develops his sympathy with and understanding of the difficulties of workers as they exist in relation to the upper classes; Ba Jin finds himself increasingly moving toward a complete identification with the stance of the workers his family employs. As he goes out of the family environment, this alternative identity moves into a mature social participation that continues to stand as a *theoretical* opposition to work as a writer. However, in his autobiography Ba Jin does not record his work in social movements, but discusses his life as a writer; within the text this literary authorization becomes the actualization of opposition to his early family life. Self-definition through social participation remains an undeveloped possibility.

Ai Wu: Social Involvement or Writing

Another example of a constructed opposition between textual and physical work is shown in *Qingnian shidai* [The era of my youth] by Ai Wu. Throughout his youth Ai Wu participates in various kinds of work, initially earning a living working in a hospital and eventually, when he internalizes Cai Yuanpei's dictum of "work is sacred," as a volunteer schoolteacher in the countryside [90]. He is sensitive about having done manual labor and fears that his friends will find out and ridicule him

[117]. When he finds himself unwelcome in political meetings in Kunming because of his worker's clothes, he writes an article on the necessary changes in society, but decides it is too dangerous to publish [119]. After this point his goals appear to change:

> In this great era, it seemed like I had fallen behind the ranks. During the day I did not wish to be with people, but only to wander in the fields, alone and aimless. Sometimes I would see the sun shining brightly on the tile roofs of the houses, the green fields of vegetables and the little streams with drooping willows beside them, and thought if I could only rent a small room, then I could live here and study and write to the end of my days. I could submit articles to newspapers in exchange for the lowest living expenses, and this would be a satisfying, peaceful life. [120]

Ai Wu has attempted to project his work as active engagement in both physical work and social affairs, yet a strong temptation is offered by a traditional rejection of this life and immersion in the detached life-style of an uninvolved intellectual.[18] Like Shen Congwen, Ai Wu utilizes the metaphor of the world as book and of life experiences as the reading of a "big book," disclosing an overriding textual mirror through which he constructs experience [117]. A life of immersion into books is initially rejected as passive and unrewarding, yet an eventual acceptance is implied both in this metaphor and in the above quoted words of the author himself.

The Literary as a Category: Effete and Ineffectual

A description of the corrupting influence of books and immersion in writing can be found in the book *Wenxin* [Literary mind], first published by Xia Mianzun and Ye Shaojun in 1933. Part of the story of the friendship between middle-school students Dawen, Lehua, and Zhiqing revolves around the contradiction between a literary identity as opposed to the life and work of a worker or soldier. An attachment to the literary is shown as harmful in many ways, yet as the title indicates, the entire book is an exposition on the literary, covering the steps to mastery of the literature and traditions of writing in China. The book was republished in a series for middle-school students in Hong Kong in 1968.

One episode that indicates this contradiction is the related past history of Zhang Dawen's family. Dawen's father, Zhang Ziyuan, was a scholar and had amassed a large collection of books in his library. As time went on the family fortunes decreased, but the number of books increased [31]. Historically, although not all government officials in China were scholars, many had an interest in literature, the classics, history, philosophy, or art, and many collected books and art. The passion for collecting reached its height during the Qianlong period of the Qing, when it was clear that an interest in art and books had the eventual effect of impoverishing a family [Ho, 142–57].

This inverse relationship between immersion in books and material prosperity takes on an added dimension, that of military capability, as the authors introduce the character of Mr. Wang, the students' teacher of literature and writing. Mr. Wang's comment on the Japanese bombing of Chinese cities is: "Foreigners mock China as a 'land of writing' (*wenzi zhi bang*). We only can use writing to protest—how ashamed we should be" [45]. The claim that China is a "land of writing" is repeated later in the book, when the authors discuss the image of the mother in ancient China and decry the lack of pictorial images of the mother that have been able to survive. On the contrary, however, many "images" exist in writing, showing the primacy accorded to writing within Chinese intellectual discourse [230].[19]

Later, Mr. Wang expresses to Lehua his concern about the tendency of students to be interested in writing and literature, but not the more "practical" classes:

> Most students in middle school have decided their fate lies in literature, and are not interested in mathematics, drawing, physics, and chemistry, etc. This is wrong. Writing is only a tool to express thought and feeling, all of which must be obtained elsewhere. You are partial to writing, but writing is empty, without substance. You all work hard at Chinese literature, but what about your other classes? This worries me. [126–27]

Lehua has no response, but Zhiqing denies the allegation. At the same time he voices a similar concern about the clear delineation between physical and mental labor that characterizes society: "We know nothing, only what we learn from magazines. Mental labor and physical labor are divided. All the clothes we wear and the food we eat is from workers and peasants, but they don't go to school. I don't want to stay in the ivory tower of mental labor. We can't just plan to be teachers, administrators, or bureaucrats, but must plan to be workers too!" [141, 142]. The main

crisis comes when, shortly after this discussion, Lehua is forced by economic necessity to leave school and become an iron worker. Echoing Shen
Congwen and others, Lehua claims he is now going to study the "book
without writing": "I won't give up study. I will go to the library. Also, I
will study the book without writing, and I will spend my efforts learning
about and experiencing in the library of society!" [143]. Although Lehua
claims to be going out to experience society, the entire endeavor is, like
that of Shen Congwen and Ai Wu, expressed within a literary metaphor.

As Lehua slowly learns the trade of iron working, he is at first plagued
by dreams of home and of his happy times in school. Little by little, these
dreams disappear, and he turns into a person positively informed by the
work experience. When Lehua returns home for the first time for the
Duanwu Festival (ironically commemorating the death of the famous poet
Qu Yuan), his new mentality and being contrast favorably with those who
have remained in school, and he is even able to use his experience in the
work environment to correct their rarified interpretations of writing and
literature.

Although Lehua's parents are worried that he may have suffered in this
transition from student to worker, they are relieved when they see him on
this first trip home. He is wearing the short blue jacket of a worker, his
hands are coarse, and his body is strong; he projects a healthy, happy
spirit. When Lehua goes to Dawen's house to visit, however, his appearance causes his friends, who are just then engaged in a discussion of
writing, to reflect back on their own situation. As he shakes Lehua's hand,
Zhiqing is embarrassed to sense the smoothness and softness of his own
hands. Another friend, Zhenyu, comments that although they don't know
how many people are starving in the world, this group still continues to
discuss "small problems of writing." Zhiqing attempts to bridge the gap
between writing and the world in his response: "You can't say that. We
discuss the proper arrangement of writing, and that is important in any
matter. Writing is a tool of action" [154]. As Lehua uses examples from
his work environment to contradict the students' interpretations of writing and language, it is clear that he is a new person, formed by his
experience in the work arena, and now capable of becoming a contrast to
the weakness and timidity of the students, and of bringing in actual,
practical, material experience to rectify their narrow-minded, inexperi-
enced, literary understanding of language and writing [157–58]. Lehua's
presence resists the tendency to turn China, as it exists in this small setting,
into a "land of writing."

The authors' efforts to bring the values of the workplace to bear on an excessively literary, alienated tradition of writing is shown in the life of the character Lehua and verbalized by Lehua's father, who tries to solve the problem of the radical delineation between literary works and the events of the world at large by suggesting that whereas old poetry took as its material a kind of romantic, "wind, flowers, snow, and moon" perspective, some new poetry is "workplace poetry." The vitality of the country now lies in the city, he claims, and poetry should be "workplace poetry" that gains its inspiration from actual city life [59–60].

Although the students still desire to put their energy into literature, the tradition has lost enough prestige that Lehua's appearance causes some consternation and reflection on their own inadequacies, and his comments and corrections are met with respect. The authors' attempt to show a minimally effective merging of workplace values with literary work is probably a reflection of what was happening to literature in a society influenced by realism and Marxist literary theory. The presupposition of this union is that literature as it was and still is remains a textually hermetic form divorced from another "reality." Mastery of past literary traditions and the ability to discuss styles and literary history is not as important as knowledge that comes from a material, physical existence that is typified in manual labor and in military capability.[20]

According to research by Arif Dirlik, the theorization of labor as an alternative to intellectual work has its modern roots in the early days of leftist discourse, a time when radicals were making attempts to contact laborers. In the spring of 1920 early Communists such as Deng Zhongxia initiated efforts to hold discussions with townspeople and villagers, acts which met with little interest.[21] Even more importantly, during this early period the term "labor" entered into the "language of radicalism" in the phrase "Labor is sacred," which was displayed in Cai Yuanpei's calligraphy in *Xin qingnian* [New youth] in 1920 (and noted by Ai Wu). However, although Cai's interpretation of "labor" included the work of intellectuals and capitalists, in the May 1920 issue of *Xin qingnian* (a special issue on labor), Chen Duxiu rewrites "labor" to mean work with the hands: "Who are the most useful, the most important people in the world? People who are confused say it is the Emperor, or those who become officials or read books. I say they are wrong. I say only those who labor are the most useful and the most important."[22] Shi Contong also concluded a letter to *Awakening* (supplement to the *Nation Daily*) with the words "I am deeply ashamed that I am still not a worker," contributing to the "adulation of labor" that Dirlik documents. Significantly, Dirlik points out that the first contribution of radical intellectuals to the May 1920 issue of *Xin qingnian* was their calligraphy [186] and notes that before "the factory could emerge as the 'battlefield' for social revolution, radical intellectuals had to lose their faith in the communal and labor-learning experiments of the May Fourth period" [188]. In other words intellectuals had to be forced away from association primarily with other intellectuals in communes and labor-learning groups and thrown into a relationship with labor and laborers in society at large.

The contradiction over self and work which motivates the students of *Wenxin* is precisely what is internalized in the autobiographies of Shen Congwen, Ba Jin, and others and makes up the central dilemma of their textual self-definitions. Although Shen Congwen seeks to escape the role of the textually defined and plunge into the world as a worker or a soldier and Ba Jin identifies with the working classes and becomes a social activist, both appear to have little choice but to take on implications of passivity, degradation, and humiliation when they switch their orientation and work with texts. The most intriguing paradox is that the writer's work is almost always forced on a seemingly unwilling subject, who unsuccessfully fends it off and eventually succumbs to the desires of others, fate, or the requirements of the nation and agrees to conform to this unwanted existence. These writers present the prestige of textual work as high enough to draw in and catch even those who actively resist it, making them unwilling participants in a system of textual signification. Shen Congwen and Ba Jin must be pulled into roles as students and writers, and they persist in inscribing this work as detached from the more valuable jobs of social worker, soldier, or manual laborer. "Reality" is embedded in these latter occupations, and only here can the self become a positive construct.

4

Hu Shi and Lu Xun: Writing, Identity, and Race

A comparison of Lu Xun (1881–1936) and Hu Shi (1891–1962) can lead one to the conclusion that they were almost opposite in their approach to Chinese culture. Lu Xun became the hero of modern literature and society in post-1949 China, whereas Hu Shi was criticized repeatedly, a small portion of his works becoming available only recently. In Taiwan, Hu Shi became a well-known cultural and political figure, whereas until recently, Lu Xun's works existed only on the black market. Although Lu Xun never joined the Communist party, he was supportive of many of its goals and severely critical of the Nationalists, especially in the last years of his life. Hu Shi eventually became the president of the Academia Sinica in Taiwan, but not before serving as Chinese ambassador to the United States from 1938 to 1942. Despite obvious political and cultural differences, the autobiographies of both Hu Shi and Lu Xun express concern with the meaning of textual work, either scholarship or literary writing, for the modern Chinese intellectual. Although both could be called first-class intellectuals, to some extent both construct textual work negatively and offer alternatives that appear more attractive.

The alternatives to literature or textual scholarship that Lu Xun and Hu Shi present are revolution and physical work for Lu Xun and revolution and scientific work for Hu Shi. Neither explicitly and absolutely rejects textual work, yet they are similar in their construction of textual work— either literary or scholarly—as a realm separate from the alternatives and to some extent negatively formulated. For Lu Xun literature is useless to revolution and in opposition to physical work. For Hu Shi, textual research is separate from revolution and inferior to scientific research because it is done on paper alone. Whereas both Lu Xun and Hu Shi devote themselves to work with texts, they deny the absolute viability of this mission, subordinating it to other areas that claim the primacy of material production, evaluation of material phenomena, and physical work. Both writers claim that excessive emphasis on textual work can be damaging to a nation and a race and in fact has harmed China. Lu Xun and Hu Shi look outside national boundaries as they formulate their textual ideologies, linking race, nation, and textual work in a triad that recognizes the specificity of Chinese social and intellectual life.

Lu Xun and the Zhengren junzi

For Lu Xun, 1925 and 1926 were a turning point in his career and mark the time when he was forced out of Beijing; during these two years he kept up a running battle with the "upright gentlemen" led by Zhang Shizhao (1881–1973) and others who formed the conservative faction of letters in Beijing.[1] According to reports by Ouyang Fanhai, the May 30th Incident changed Lu Xun's consciousness and direction, especially when students at Women's Higher Normal School where he taught were killed demonstrating in support of the Shanghai workers and students and against the pro-Japanese government.[2] Lu Xun had previously become a vocal enemy of Zhang Shizhao, minister of education under Duan Qirui, when he joined in with students to effect the ouster of the school's conservative chancellor. Before leaving Beijing for Xiamen in 1926, Lu Xun intensified his struggle with the conservative group, making fun of them because they insisted on promoting "scholarship" and "research" and branding social affairs as "trivial matters":

> Before the March 18 Incident, what kind of airs did the "upright gentlemen" put on? First, Chen Xiying announced that starting January 1, 1926, he would have nothing more to do with trivial matters. Second, Chen Xiying announced that he was going to do research, and said that even for a small topic, he must look at over one hundred books: "If one wants to study in detail the abridged *Four Books,* one must use several hundred or several thousand books as reference." And if one wants to understand the true meaning of the *Four Books,* one must study the commentaries and theories of scholars of the Song, Ming, Qing, and even Han. The third I have already discussed.

Chen Xiying announced that the combined libraries of all the colleges and universities in Beijing, private and public, did not equal the number of books of some individuals. . . . The sixth was that Feng Chuan and Tao Menghe were going to write a book, and first published a few sections in *Xiandai pinglun* [Modern criticism]. The book would not be completely finished until the year 2025, so contemporary people or those born ten years from now had no hopes of seeing it. Just from that one could see how great and fearful it was.[3]

Within the social context of developing revolutionary ideologies that were being fueled by events such as the May 30th Incident and the murders at the women's college, traditional scholars were establishing themselves as antirevolutionary. This process contributed to a reworking of the meaning of scholarship and textual work, which increasingly became seen as ultimately conservative or, within a "revolutionary" context, debilitating. In Lu Xun's writing textual research is becoming part of an antirevolutionary ideology that sees scholars standing against "action" and outside the realm of social affairs. This dichotomy is repeated in Lu Xun's articles on literature and revolution.

Revolution Against Literature

Lu Xun expresses his ideas on the relationship between a given society and literature in "Wenyi yu zhengzhi de qitu" [The diverging roads of literature and politics], a talk given in 1927—just after he wrote *Zhaohua xishi*—at Shanghai Jinan University:

> There is a school of literature that advocates separation from human life and discussion of the moon, flowers, birds and the like (in China it is not so simple, as there is also the morality of the national essence school, which does not even permit discussion of the likes of flowers and the moon; I won't discuss it here), otherwise they want only to talk about "dreams," or the society of the future, nothing too immediate. . . . There are some literary people in Beijing who despise the writers who write about society; they think that if even the life of a rickshaw puller can be described in novels, isn't this just destroying the law that novels should write about a poem giving birth to love between the beauty and the scholar?
>
> Post-nineteenth century literature is not the same as pre-eighteenth century literature. Eighteenth century English novels were for the pur-

pose of providing entertainment for ladies and girls, and were full of pleasantries and wit. In the second half of the nineteenth century, novels developed a close relationship with problems of human life. When we read them we feel totally uncomfortable, but we contain our anger and finish reading them. This is because the literature of the past seems to talk about another society, and we can only appreciate it; the literature of today is about our own society, but the literature of the past is like watching a fire from across the river: there is no personal danger. The literature of today will burn you up right along with everything else, and there is no way you can avoid feeling it deeply. When you do feel it, you have to go out and get involved in society![4]

Lu Xun emphasizes the close relationship between writers, readers, and literature with the contemporary society in which the text functions and traces the development of literature as fostering social involvement and moving away from purely literary or aesthetic discussion.[5] However, although Lu Xun constitutes literature as an element of society, how influential is it in radically altering society?

In his essays on literature and its social role, and particularly from 1925 until his death, Lu Xun theorizes literature and revolution as somewhat antithetical.[6] In four essays written in 1927, Lu Xun clarifies the role of literature as possibly a catalyst but ultimately not influential in promoting revolution or assisting once it is underway.[7] "Geming shidai de wenxue" [Literature in a time of revolution], which was first presented as a talk at the Huangpu (Whampoa) Military Academy, is Lu Xun's longest essay on the subject and succinctly formulates the dichotomy of "calling out" (literature) as opposed to "acting" (revolution). In the beginning of the talk Lu Xun describes those who discuss literature as "the most useless, most powerless people":

> Those with true strength don't open their mouths, but just kill people. Those who are oppressed say a few words, write a few characters, and are killed. Or if they are lucky they are not killed, but since every day they call out, expressing their misery and inequality, the powerful continue to oppress them, mistreat them, and kill them. There is little the oppressed can do to oppose it. What is the value of literature to humanity? [312]

During the rest of the talk Lu Xun continues to depict literature as weak and of limited social value and, more importantly, as indicative of national weakness in that people who devote themselves to "calling out" are unable to take decisive action:

(1) Before a great revolution, all literature sees the unfairness and misery of various social conditions. It calls out its misery and inequality; there are many literatures like this in the world. But these literatures, which call out misery and inequality, have no influence on the revolution, because calling out misery and inequality has no strength, as one's oppressors will pay no attention. The mouse squeaks and squeaks, but despite the quality of the literature it squeaks out, the cat won't be polite when it starts to eat the mouse. *So when there is only literature that calls out misery and inequality, there is no hope for that race: it has stagnated at the level of calling out misery and inequality.* . . . So what it amounts to is that literature that is calling out misery and inequality is just shouting "unfair!", and the oppressors merely feel relieved. . . . Since it is useless to call out, races that have great strength to fight back, and hold a latent power will awaken. A sad sound will become an angry roar; when literature that is an angry roar emerges, the time of fighting back is almost here. They will already be very angry, so literature that is close to the explosive times of revolution will always have the voice of anger. It wants to fight back, it wants revenge. There was some of this kind of literature when the revolution of Soviet Russia was about to begin. But there are also exceptions like Poland; even though it had a literature of revenge early on, its actual revenge relied on the European war.

(2) When revolution arrives, literature disappears, it has no voice, because everyone has been affected by the tides of the revolution, and *has gone from calling to action.* Everyone is busy with the revolution, and *has no leisure to discuss literature.* Then there is another level of people whose livelihood is in danger and have barely enough time to find bread to eat; how could they feel like discussing literature? The conservatives have been attacked in the tides of revolution and are furious; they can no longer sing about their so-called literature. . . . When you are busy, literary works cannot exist. Those carrying a pole must set it down before they can write essays; those pulling a rickshaw must set it aside before they can write essays. In a great revolution all are busy and poor; this group is fighting with that group, and are intent on changing society. There is no time or energy

to write essays; so during a great revolution, literature may as well temporarily be silent.

(3) When the revolution has succeeded and society is calm, people's lives are relaxed and literature will again be produced [italics mine]. [314–15]

To Lu Xun literature emerges from leisure and exists within the dichotomy of words against action. Furthermore, literature is not part of material production: set against pulling a rickshaw or carrying goods on a pole, literary writing appears superfluous and unnecessary. Lu Xun goes on to deny claims that Chinese literature is for the commoner; he points out that almost all literary writing in China is written for the elite: "After they are full of food, they take a rest on a recliner, holding a book up to read" [317]. Entreating the audience of "revolutionary soldiers" to avoid undue respect for literature, Lu Xun reaffirms his belief that literature, an elite object out of the realm of material production, has little influence on revolution [318].

In "Geming wenxue" [Revolutionary literature] Lu Xun repudiates the idea that "revolutionary literature" can be created either by calling it revolutionary or by including in the writing a preponderance of words such as "hit" or "kill" [407–8]. In "Wenxue yu han" [Literature and sweat] Lu Xun criticizes those who posit literature as an indicator of eternal human nature. Recognizing that "literature," like "human nature," is not an absolute form but rather a discursive category that changes with history and culture, Lu Xun chides Chinese critics of literature for their romanticization of both writing and human nature. In "Wenyi yu geming" [Literature and the arts and revolution] Lu Xun again attacks the idea that "literature is the precursor of revolution" [419]. Throughout these essays Lu Xun expresses a negative apprehension of literature that places it in opposition to action, revolution, work, and material production, a stance clearly indicated in his autobiography, *Zhaohua xishi* [Morning blossoms picked at dusk].

Lu Xun wrote part of *Zhaohua xishi* in Xiamen, but part had been written in Beijing before he left to go to Fujian. Ouyang Fanhai analyzes Lu Xun's comment that he "did not want to think of the future" and so thought of the past and on the social relevance of the piece:

Half of *Zhaohua xishi* was written in Beijing. This is to say that not only when he was lonely and locked away in the Xiamen library did he think of the past, but when he was involved in the fiercest struggle with Duan Qirui and Zhang Zuolin, he was also thinking of the past. So if we understand his comment, "I don't want to think of the future," as Lu Xun escaping from society, it is far more ridiculous than understanding it as Lu Xun's bitter hatred for the contemporary dilemma. So we can see that recollections of the past springing up in Lu Xun's heart, and his study of ancient tales [at Xiamen] are oppositions only within the context of the contemporary dilemma, and were not produced out of a fundamental opposition.[8]

Nonetheless, Ouyang admits that 1926 was a year of "crisis" for Lu Xun, who for many intellectuals had come to represent "new" ideas until this time; by 1928, after this period of transition was over, Lu Xun became embroiled in a series of conflicts not only with the neoconservatives, but also with "revolutionary" groups such as the Creation Society, which had changed its orientation from an early "art for art's sake" to a promotion of revolutionary literature. Thus Lu Xun's status as promoter of the new was questioned as he himself was in the process of questioning the meaning of literary work within Chinese society.

Forced Out of "China"

Lu Xun's *Zhaohua xishi* [Morning blossoms picked at dusk] was written when the author was forty-five years old; he died at the age of fifty-six.[9] This brief autobiography does not cover Lu Xun's life comprehensively, but it does proceed chronologically and move through the first part of his life in a regular manner. To a much greater extent than Shen Congwen or Ba Jin, Lu Xun develops a triad of three interacting segments of self that combine in a profoundly negative apprehension of existence and work. As in previous autobiographies, textually oriented activities such as study are implicated; the other two aspects of this negative authority are perception of the self as *nationally* specific and as *racially* determined. Unlike Shen Congwen, Lu Xun does not structure his autobiography as an obvious contrast between the textual and the material; rather, he constructs a more extensively degrading persona of which textual studies become only one aspect of the debilitating experiences and defining paradigms the Chinese intellectual must pass through.

Like Guo Moruo, Lu Xun follows a path away from an initial nucleus of family and its immediate surroundings to the slightly greater environment of formal schooling, to schooling away from home, and finally out of China. Both Lu and Guo structure their alliances and departures in terms of insiders and outsiders: they successively leave "inside" communities in a progressive move toward the final departure from the "China" of past experience which is elaborated in the first part of their texts.[10] After arriving at the ultimate outside destination of Japan, however, Lu Xun is unable to establish himself as an insider, forcing him to directly confront the issues of nationality, race, and cultural experience which prompted his departure. Within this reconsideration, which is implied throughout the autobiography (including the first parts), Lu Xun evaluates the texts and textual approaches which have formed him.

Lu Xun formulates his early childhood as magical and fascinating, a period to be contrasted with a later time when he becomes numbed by the requirements of conforming to Chinese social institutions. The first essay in the autobiography, "Gou mao shu" [Dogs cats mice], narrates an episode from his childhood. Its main figure is his grandmother, who tells him fables and stories full of magic and fantasy. For the child narration has the power of transformation, changing the world into a marvelous place. In the same chapter the author attacks his enemies in the literary world, with whom he kept up a running battle of the pen for many years. Placed side by side with his childhood transformations, this bitter attack forms a destructive contrast to the magic that the tales engender and foreshadows the ruination of this childhood world and its replacement with an unpleasant social order.

In the next essay, "A'chang yu Shanhai jing" [A'chang and *The Classic of Mountains and Seas*], the narrator as a character has disappeared, and there are no comments or intrusions from adult sensibilities. Lu Xun is still a child, and the object of his desire is a book filled with drawings of strange creatures: "But that was my most beloved treasure; looking at it, they were all there: the human-faced beast, the nine-headed snake, the one-footed ox, the sack-like monster Di Qing; Xing Tian, who 'used teats for eyes, and his navel for a mouth,' and 'danced with spear and shield'" [359]. The book is procured for Lu Xun by a servant he calls A'chang, whose real name or history he does not know. As an essentially anonymous figure for whom Lu Xun provides little socially significant data, A'chang is an appropriate character to transmit mythical values. A'chang reputedly has some mysterious qualities of her own—she tells Lu Xun, for example, that she has the ability to stop cannons from shooting. As the text progresses this magic world is destroyed through the joint invasions of adult sensibilities and formal education, and references to these fantastic items are replaced by descriptions of social interaction. Lu Xun depicts the illustrated book the servant A'chang procures as crude but wonderful in the physicality of the illustrations; what makes the book appealing to the child is its nontextual nature or the lack of words. The pictures provide the text with a type of magic that the child can appreciate only before he begins to "grow up," or participate in the socializing and normalizing structures of education.

In the next essay fascination moves into terror as the magical text gains a closer association to the web of signification formed through texts and their application in the adult world. In "Ershisixiao tu" [The picture book of twenty-four acts of filial piety] Lu Xun sees illustrations of children flinging themselves into rushing rivers or being buried alive in their attempts to be filial; he perceives that the pictures could be relevant to his own situation and begins to fear his aging grandmother, who may require a similar show of filial piety from her grandson. The adult, Lu Xun writes, having read numerous books, could propound countless arguments to oppose such practices, but it would be useless to the buried child. In this written tradition of piety, the creation and continuation of which is textually enforced by scholars, text-magic, or illustrations that provide a physical image accessible to a child, has been replaced by a picture-text that supports and continues a powerful social ideology.

Up to this point the author has delineated two traditions of the text, one a popular tradition characterized by physical and military images and marvelous phenomena, the other illustrating a frightening and yet orthodox social practice which is forced upon children. In the next piece, "Wuchang hui" [The fair of the five fierce gods], the tradition of enforced textual learning impinges on and destroys childhood altogether. As Lu Xun is about to leave for the Fair of the Five Fierce Gods, an event which he has never attended and which is attractive only through hearsay, his father calls him back to memorize an unintelligible passage from a classical text. This text, the *Jian lue* [Outline of history], is supposed to be valuable to study because "you could learn the approximate course of events from ancient times to the present." The enforced memorization of this text squelches the spontaneity and joy of the festival—where, ironically, stories from history would also be acted out physically on stage. When Lu Xun does get to go to the festival, it is too late to redeem his pleasure: "Even so, I wasn't as happy as they were. When the boat sailed, the scenery by the river, the cakes and cookies in boxes, even the bustle and excitement of the Fair of the Five Fierce Gods when we reached Dongguan—none of them seemed very interesting to me anymore" [373].

The authorities of text and father combine to kill the spirit and joy that derive from an active involvement in the physical activities the community provides. The text is posited in opposition to this world and has the ability to erase the participatory excitement that the festival can engender.

At this midway point in the autobiography Lu Xun begins to move out of his childhood fantasy world that has been muted by early studies into a social arena dominated by the text alone. The representative of this transition is the piece named with the appellation of the god Wuchang, or "Life-is-transient," the most friendly and human of all the gods. Wedged in between two essays that depict the authoritarian figures of father (tradition) and teacher (text), Wuchang appears as a human form in the inhuman world. Within the autobiography this juxtaposition gives the figure its value; in one respect Wuchang is the point where the autobiography moves out of the human (childhood) into the inhuman (social institutions), yet the ironic opposite is also superficially true: the autobiography moves out of the inhuman (fantasy) into the human (the "real" world).

Lu Xun makes his full transition out of childhood in the next essay, "Cong baicaoyuan dao sanwei shuwu" [From the garden of a hundred plants to three-flavor study], where the formal educational system functions. The symbol of his previous text-free existence is the multifarious garden, full of marvelous creatures and plants, where he has played at his home. This garden must be abandoned for the schoolroom with its small, unstimulating garden behind, which is only a shell, or symbol, of the powerful garden of childhood the author has left behind.

In a critical study of this chapter of *Zhaohua xishi*, Wu Tianlin emphasizes the mysterious physicality of the garden against the study:[11]

> First, using precise, lively language, Lu Xun exhibits the various kinds of natural scene and object in the Hundred-plant Garden, such as the "caiwa," "shijinglan," "zaofu tree," "sangkan," "crying cicada," "calling son," etc. In this both passive and active description of scene and object, language such as "jade-green" "glistening," "tall and big," "wine-red," "plump and fat," "always moaning," and "lithe" are used to liven them up. [3]

Lu Xun describes the "scene and object" of the garden in all four seasons, completely exhibiting "the life and pleasure of the hundred-plant garden" [6]. This setting is contrasted with that of the three-flavor study to the east, where the "rituals of beginning study" [7] take over and "the life of studying can only be difficult and boring" [9]. Wu comments that many critics have regarded the garden and the study, with all implications, as showing "two themes; one illustrates the author's leanings towards a beautiful, free, happy life, and the other shows the author's rejection and criticism of the feudal education of the private academy." Wu, however, regards the two opposites as possessing an "internal relationship" and only one main theme of the deadening, corrupt, and reactionary education of private academies [10–11].

Lu Xun is criticizing educational practices, but in a way that puts them in contrast with nontextual alternatives and implies a valuable nontextual realm of knowledge and experience that is rejected from studies in the academy. Lu Xun attempts to bring in an element of the previous world when he asks his teacher about the existence of a legendary insect, said to be the incarnation of a man who was unjustly slain; when doused with wine, the bug was supposed to disappear. His teacher's terse and displeased "I don't know" sets the parameters of what will constitute the authority of the text: no intrusions from the "outside" will be allowed.[12] The negativity of textual training and perspective, as well as the inability of past phenomena to interact with present reality, is apparent in the next sketch, "Fuqin de bing" [Father's illness], where the medical quacks who kill Lu Xun's father appropriate the written word in the placards they hang in front of their houses, which proclaim their ability to bring the dead back to life.

In "Suoji" [Fragmentary recollections] Lu Xun leaves China to go abroad to Japan to study. His disillusionment with tradition and schooling culminates in the scene with a neighbor, Mrs. Yan, who mocks him because of his lack of understanding of some vulgar illustrations in a text. Illustrations, once innocent representations of mythical understandings, now have come to represent a social reality that is beyond the understanding of the child; even in its most childlike form of an illustrated work, the text no longer possesses its magical qualities. Lu Xun leaves home to go to a naval academy, where ridiculous exercises in language contribute to his disillusionment. Extremely simple lessons in English ("It is a cat, Is it a rat?") next to abstract and obtuse Chinese writing assignments ("On How Clouds Follow the Dragon and Wind the Tiger") make up the jarringly incongruent environment he characterizes as murky, confused, corrupt, and inexpressible. He decides to go "out" once again, this time to Japan.

Lu Xun has moved from a magical and physically expressive childhood to learning at home, to schooling in his hometown, to schooling away from home, and finally to study abroad. When each position betrays him in turn, he leaves both the China and the negative "China" he has formed through selective use of his experiences. Through his continuing flight, Lu Xun attacks the authorities of family, history, education, and written tradition that have defined his identity up to this point.

Japan: An Alternate to "China"

The Japanese individual who dominates the sketch "Tengye xiansheng" [Mr. Fujino] is Lu Xun's teacher at the Sendai Medical Academy in Japan. Unlike Lu Xun's teachers in China, Mr. Fujino appears as a kind man who goes out of his way to see to the needs of the young foreign student. Mr. Fujino teaches Lu Xun anatomy and corrects both his notes and the drawings he copies from the blackboard. When Lu Xun copies a drawing of blood vessels incorrectly, Fujino insists that he move the vessels into the positions they actually hold in the body. Lu Xun portrays the Chinese teachers as existing in a textual world so hermetic that as they chant their texts, they often totally forget the students' existence; Fujino, on the other hand, enforces a rigid correspondence between the text and nontextual "reality."[13]

Also contrasted with Mr. Fujino are the "students from the Qing Empire," always gathering in groups under the symbolic cherry trees, trying to learn ballroom dancing. These students wear their queues, the sign of Manchurian domination in China, curled on their heads; their national origin implies cultural traditions to be dispensed with.[14] As soon as Lu Xun begins this sketch, he rejects the possibility of availing himself of this "other" place, language, and culture to negate what he is narratively constructing as the essential Chinese being; in the first line of the text, which has given birth to various interpretations among Japanese translators and critics, he writes "Tokyo was not so extraordinary after all" [409].[15] This sentence, coming at the beginning of the narrative, implies a predetermined image of a foreign land that is radically different from China, an "other" that is conceptualized as the binary opposite of the "China" which has formed the basis of the author's negative experience to this time. When Lu Xun arrives in Tokyo and sees Chinese students learning ballroom dancing, he realizes that Japan cannot be this ideal "other": it cannot meet his expectations in providing the environment in which he can disregard the disquieting issues of nation and race, but actually pushes him toward a recognition of nation and race as ontological categories unavoidable in the interpretation of experience. Although the Chinese students who have disguised their queues and are attempting to alter their cultural manifestations through the acquisition of new manners and styles are one example of a temporarily successful identity change, Lu Xun ridicules this alternative as absurd and meaningless. He has rejected "China" and the past, but a viable option is unavailable to him in this alienated context.

Return, Race, and Nation

"Mr. Fujino" contains a description of the well-known and controversial scene of Lu Xun's transformation from a student of medicine to a would-be writer. At medical school in Sendai, Lu Xun sees some lantern slides of the Japanese army beheading Chinese citizens in China and notices a group of Chinese spectators, watching passively and curiously on the sidelines. This passive voyeurism so appalls him that he decides to switch his endeavors from medicine, which can only cure the body, to literature, which he believes can cure the soul.[16] The scene's implication of inherent passivity, racial humiliation, and human debasement is the background against which Lu Xun turns to literary work. The consciousness of the writer is formed under conditions which stipulate recognition of the validity of race and nation as determining and absolute categories.[17] Guo Moruo uneasily and repeatedly returns to this point through a series of struggles; Lu Xun's definition of national stance is a precondition to his narrative that is presented, as we shall see, in the preface of his autobiography.

This scene has also been the object of interest among Japanese critics, some of whom view Lu Xun's privileging of the execution as an essentializing of the fundamental Chinese character. In a discussion of Dazai Osamu's story "Sekibetsu" [Sad parting], Ozaki Hideo explains Dazai's portrayal of Lu Xun as someone who simultaneously becomes the Chinese who was shot *and* the people watching.[18] Lu Xun takes on the body of the victim as well as the passivity of the audience, combining the two stances into an ultimate Chinese "nature" which becomes his motivation for writing. Hirakawa completes the circle of referentiality by claiming that while Soseki writes as though he were shooting scenes with a camera, Lu Xun points the camera at himself [142]; Hirakawa finds that the "hidden topic" of this piece is that Lu Xun discovers he is Chinese and can't avoid being so, but does not like it [141].

Lu Xun begins his "Short Preface" (written after the body of the text in 1927) with a discussion of symbolic return:

When a person has come to the point where only memories remain, his life is tedious, of course, but sometimes, unexpectedly, not even memories remain. In China, there are circumscribing rules for writing, and the affairs of the world still rush on in a spiraling course. When I left Sun Yatsen University a few days ago, I recalled leaving Xiamen University four months ago. Listening to the drone of the planes overhead, I strangely remembered the planes that circled everyday above Beijing one year ago. I even wrote a short essay then, called "A Perception." Now things are such that I don't even have this "perception" anymore.

"Circumscribing rules" prevent the written word from straying too far from an established norm, and worldly matters seem unable to progress. Memories are lost in this eternal return and have lost a corporeal referent:

There was a time when I kept recalling over and over the vegetables and fruits I ate as a child in my home; caltrops, horsebeans, water bamboo shoots, muskmelons. These things were so fresh and delicious; they were the enchanters that made me long for my home. Later, when I tasted them again after a long absence, they were nothing so extraordinary; only in my memories did they retain their old flavor. Maybe they will beguile my entire life, making me constantly turn to the past. [340]

Lu Xun compares himself, the writer sitting at his desk writing, to a cut-off branch that is sitting in water on his desk. Although both are immobile and isolated, the branch manages to produce lovely green leaves, whereas the writer exists in a time that is "like years of death" in the midst of life. He refers to the setting sun and the west window, both traditional images of death [339]. The return to which Lu Xun refers in his preface corresponds to the return to both "China" and China at the end of his autobiography, when he rejects his outward movement and returns to a confrontation with nation, race, and the challenge of creating a valuable text that will not be limited by the "traditional" framework of past education or the alien mark of the demeaning "text" under creation by Chinese students in Japan.

As previously noted, Lu Xun destroys the possibility of a positive alternative experience in Japan at the beginning of his sketch "Mr. Fujino"; the illusion of cherry blossoms shimmering like light, pink clouds is destroyed when he realizes that under the flowers are groups of "students from the Qing empire." In the final sketch in his text, "Fan Ainong," Lu Xun leaves this false paradise to return to China. According to his own text, Lu Xun's initial contact with the student Fan Ainong occurred in Tokyo, when Lu Xun demanded that a telegram be sent to protest the assassination of Xu Xilin, one of Fan's teachers and a well-known revolutionary. In Fan's opposition Lu Xun sees signs of what he has now established as the "Chinese" qualities he despises: cowardliness, passivity, and humiliation. He identifies Fan as a representative of all of these qualities and as an obstacle to change.

When they meet again in China, Lu Xun is an administrator and Fan is a derelict who cannot hold down a job and is despised by his acquaintances. Lu Xun and Fan frequently go drinking together; and through this friendship Lu Xun learns that Chinese students in Japan regarded him as arrogant and unapproachable. Lu Xun describes his switch from medicine to literature as made under the pressure of national humiliation and in an environment of racial discrimination, prescribing a recognition of race and nation as integral to the writer's consciousness. Fan Ainong possesses the combination of qualities Lu Xun despises, and yet Lu ends up friends with Fan. Fan Ainong is an ambivalent character with which to conclude his text, yet he is an appropriate symbol for the resolution which Lu Xun effects.

Writing his autobiography in 1926, Lu Xun posits national and racial consciousness as a precursor of a valid literary role for the writer; in 1927 he claims that a nation which wishes to get on with the revolution should not waste its efforts in literary work. The essays discussed at the beginning of this chapter, all of which were written in 1927, document Lu Xun's tendency to brand literature as antirevolutionary, anti-action, and useless. Although his famous switch of focus from medicine to literature would appear to belie that negative authorization for literature, the antitextual bias also appears in his autobiography in the delineation of textual study as separate from and less interesting than the phenomenal world. In either case Lu Xun maintains the categories of text and society/material phenomena; although he attempts to redeem literature by giving it a basis in social knowledge, he grants it little transformative power.

Hu Shi: Piles of Rotten Paper

Hu Shi's *Sishi zishu* [Self-narration at forty], which describes his life only up until he leaves to study in the United States, constructs a critical account of the formation of the Chinese scholar, historian, and literary theorist.[19] Not only in Hu Shi's autobiography, but also in his lectures and articles on scholarship and the work of the historian, he locates excessive textuality, or an excessive concern with textual work aimed toward textual goals, as an unfortunate but persistent aspect of the work of the traditional Chinese scholar. However, even though Hu identifies extreme textuality as a problem peculiar to Chinese scholarship, the solutions he proposes do not allow scholarship a nontextual orientation.

According to a preface written in 1954, Hu Shi wrote *Sishi zishu* in seven sections from 1930 to 1933. As Hu Shi explains, he is unable to complete his autobiography because of his inability to return to a united China:

> But my fiftieth birthday (December 17, 1941) was exactly ten days after the Japanese air force attacked Pearl Harbor without warning; I was the Chinese ambassador to Washington, and had no free time to write an autobiography. My sixtieth birthday (December 17, 1951) was the third year after the fall of the mainland, and the second year of the Korean War; of course I was not in the mood to write the autobiography of an individual. [II, 1]

The "individual" writer and scholar is determined in the national and political issues to which Hu refers, and these issues prevent him from completing his text.

As he states himself, Hu also regarded the writing of an autobiography as a distinctly historical enterprise: "I told my friends: 'I will write on my youth at forty, on my study abroad to my maturity at fifty, and on my middle age at sixty' " [II, 1]. In an earlier preface dated 1933, Hu emphasizes his view of the autobiography as a historical document:

> In these past years, I have felt strongly that China is extremely lacking in biography, so I have been all over advising my superiors and friends to write their autobiographies. What is unfortunate is that they all agree, but are unwilling to start. . . .
>
> Once I ran into Mr. Liang Shi'i, and earnestly urged him to write a self-narration, because I knew he had played an important role in Chinese political and fiscal history, and I hoped he would leave some historical material for future historians. I know writing his autobiography would be a way for him to wash away his crimes, but that would not matter, as practised historians have ways of telling. It is

more important that he himself write about his own motivation, about clues behind the scenes and his observations from the special position which he is in. [I, 1–3][20]

In this description autobiography is a unique document that can maintain its value as history while providing a specific individual view of this history. It can combine the objective and the subjective in an approach that is at once historical and individual.

Hu Shi's role as historian and scholar is determined in this stance and is based on a link between the historical writing he does and the objective world. Yet this definition of the historian is challenged by another textual approach that threatens to destroy this fragile relationship. On one hand Hu gets "corrections" to his autobiography from friends—implying that the text mirrors a concrete objectivity—and on the other he must deal with the urge to fiction:

> I want to explain the arrangement of this book. I wanted to select some interesting topics from these forty years, and write something in the form of fiction for each topic, like the first [essay] on my parent's marriage. This plan was approved by the now deceased Xu Zhimo, and I felt happy about it, as this method would be a new road for autobiographical literature, and it would allow me (if necessary) to use false names and places to describe emotional aspects of life that are too intimate. But in the end my historical training went deeper than my literary training; when I had finished one essay and arrived at the years of my childhood, I unconsciously abandoned my fictional structure and went back to the old road of strict historical recitation. [I, 2–3]

Therefore, the fictionalized story of Hu Shi's parents' marriage, which he knows only from hearsay, must be set off from the rest of the text and marked as a "prologue" within the autobiography. To place it with the part of the autobiography defined as "history" would be to allow fiction, obviously a step farther into the subjectivity of the individual, to contaminate the objectivity of history.

Hu's prefaces reveal facets of his approach to history, literature, and the composition of the intellectual; other lectures and articles by Hu deal with the same issues. From this brief discussion it would appear that Hu Shi regards both history and literature as textual artifacts, yet literature is more "textual" in that it is to a greater extent removed from objective reality than is history, which can maintain a more direct representative connection with this reality. Autobiography, the individual textual interpretation of the objectively historical, falls between history and fiction, much as the intellectual individual is located between the two textual poles of history and literature; both autobiography and the intellectual, however, most likely will tend toward one or the other. Thus Hu's historical training "unconsciously" pushes him into a historical rather than a fictional autobiography.

Like Shen Congwen and Lu Xun, Hu Shi includes hearsay and mythical elements that do not correspond to his standards of historical accuracy, placing them in the "prologue" to indicate their semifictional nature. This piece, "Xumu: Wo muqin de dinghun" [Prologue: my mother's engagement], tells the story of his mother's marriage to Mr. San, a powerful man twenty or thirty years her senior. Hu Shi begins the prologue with a description of a spirit festival, enhancing the mythical elements of the environment which existed before his birth and emphasizing bizarre phenomena such as the incense carriers who stick the hooks of the incense burner into their flesh but do not bleed. References to such phenomena cease after the author moves out of the prologue. Although according to the author much of the information in the prologue is extrapolated from bits and pieces he heard as a child, the text is authorized by a brief quote from Mr. San's diary.

In the text of the autobiography itself the issue of the relationship between the text and its nontextual referent, which Hu Shi grapples with in the prefaces, becomes a problem of the scholar-historian. Hu's intelligence is noted by his father when the boy is only three, and the father decides that he should study; characteristically, his first teacher is his mother. As Hu's family is able to give more than the regular tuition to send him to school, the teacher pays special attention to the young student and he progresses rapidly [32]. When Hu Shi describes his childhood years, he portrays bookish tendencies at a very young age that are contrasted with the active outdoor-loving life-styles of the other students. Because his health is not good, Hu spends his time studying instead of playing; he provides a list of the books he read as a child and claims that he liked books. Hu's total immersion in textual studies is indicated in his amazement at one of his cousin's lack of interest in school: "I often felt it was strange: why was Sizhao always trying to play hookey? Why did someone willingly undergo beatings, deprivation of food, and scoldings by all rather than go to school?" [24].

When Hu goes to school in Shanghai, he becomes interested in Liang Qichao's writing and lectures and also in the revolutionary work that is going on in the first decade of the twentieth century. However, Hu's involvement in the *Tongmeng hui* or other revolutionary groups or activities is limited because, he writes, his classmates perceive him as a potential scholar:

> Among the teachers and students at the public school, there were many members of the Revolutionary Party, so it was easy to get hold of *Min bao*, published in Tokyo. During vacations, students would sew the paper into their pillows and take it inland to pass around. And there were some extremely active students who would force those with braids to cut them. But I was in public school over three years, and no one forced me to cut my braid, nor did anyone urge me to join the *Tongmeng hui*. Only after twenty years did Mr. Xin Mao tell me that at the time the members of the *Tongmeng hui* had discussed it, and all recognized that in the future I could work in scholarship. They wanted to protect me, so they did not urge me to join the *Tongmeng hui*. [65]

According to this description, not only does Hu himself see his salient characteristics as those formed by his relationship to books, but those around him also recognize his scholarly qualities, and through their recognition he is "protected" from involvement in social movements. The motivation for his life of scholarship is partially placed on others and presented as their desire for him. Hu implies a contradiction between the role and identity of a scholar, who is constructed through textual studies, and a revolutionary, who is defined by activity in society.

In the last section of the autobiography, "Bishang Liangshan" [Forced up Liang Mountain], Hu Shi describes the arguments he had while he was developing his theories of vernacular fiction as a student at Cornell University. Although "Liang Mountain" is a clear call to revolution in its reference to the Northern Song gang of rebels and the novel based on their activities, the context of the revolution is delineated by a subtitle: "Wenxue geming de kaishi" [The beginning of a literary revolution]. In response to criticism of his promotion of the vernacular to replace the "dead" classical language, Hu comments: "I knew there had been vernacular literature before and that it could not be considered new fiction, and I also knew that the new literature needed new ideas and a new spirit. But I confirm: no matter what, a dead language cannot give birth to a living literature" [124]. Although Hu does not deny the validity of an approach that concentrates on the content of writing, he prefers to place his energy into changing the "tool" or form of literature and into solving what he identifies as the major problem of Chinese literature: "At this time I already had recognized the nature of the problem with Chinese literature. I clearly recognized that the problem was in 'there is art (*wen*) but no substance (*zhi*).' How could the defect of art over substance be remedied?" [109]. Echoing late Qing criticism of Chinese letters as without substance, Hu calls for the promotion of substance over art. Underlying Hu's use of concepts like "tool," "form," and *wen* as opposed to *zhi* is an emphasis on writing as a tool that is more pervasive in his critical essays than his search for substance. Even more importantly, his solution to this perceived textuality is the use of the vernacular.[21] When Hu is later attacked by Marxist critics, they lock onto and overstate his tendency to emphasize language over content, depicting him as an excessive formalist.[22]

Despite his criticisms of vernacular fiction, Hu gave it a high evaluation in its ability to discuss concrete problems of daily life.[23] He also encouraged contemporary writers to be realistic and write about the struggles of everyday life, placing literature, like history, in a more direct relationship with a nontextual referent and contradicting the portrait of literature as somewhat removed from reality that he presents in the prefaces to his autobiography [Grieder, 87]. Hu expresses a belated desire to be a scientist, a field he perceives as nontextual and refreshingly material. Thus literature and history are lumped together as fields of study whose textually defined nature will outweigh any differences and will cause the researcher to become a scapegoat for all the ills of China at the time [Chou, 199].

It is well known that Hu Shi held extremely critical, if often contradictory, views toward most of the textual artifacts of the Chinese past. In his 1921 lectures on the reorganization of the "national past" (*guogu*), however, Hu is not so much dissatisfied with China's past as he is disgruntled with the definition of the scholar and the methodology he uses that has come out of that past. According to Hu's discussion, the Chinese historian/scholar is informed by a disorderly, unsystematic, random gobbling of textual artifacts [*Guoxue*, 33–37].

Hu Shi proposes approaching the past through an historical method that systematizes and even reinvigorates it for contemporary scholars. Even so, the method Hu proposes is a specifically and strongly textual endeavor; in these lectures the practice of history does not consist of an attempt to redefine or reinterpret past phenomena through texts, but rather to redefine, reinterpret, or reorganize texts that are regarded as historical artifacts in themselves. The four means of organizing the "national past" are historical/textual in nature. The first is to use annotations, punctuation, separation into chapters or sections, commentaries, and translations into the vernacular to make the books of ancient China accessible to all. The second is indexing, which can eliminate the necessity for large-scale memorization of texts, a "waste of time" possible only for the aristocracy. The third is the method of "calculating the bill," which is to write compendiums to the major texts that would provide a contemporary evaluation and starting point for students. The last is to compose histories of the major disciplines, such as the history of society, the history of religion, the history of law, economic history, and literary history, using a "systematic historical approach" to deal with each subject. These histories would prevent the disastrous intellectual situation Hu describes: "We often see scholars with several rooms full of books, who have read a countless number; but if we ask if the scholar has any systematic concepts, the answer is no. History is a natural system that can be used to look at the traces of changes in society, and changes, progression and regression in scholarship" [*Guoxue,* 36]. After listing and explaining these four methods Hu Shi discusses his own attempt to apply his principles to the *Shijing.* The examples consist of tracing various meanings for several obscurely used characters and defining their meaning in a commentary. This application of the historical method clearly has as its goal the explication and organization of texts.

In later work Hu presents the whole of Chinese studies as hopelessly textual. In "Zhixue de fangfa yu cailiao" [Methods and materials for study] (1928) Hu compiles a chart comparing Chinese and foreign scholarship from 1606 to 1687. On the Western side, beginning with the invention of the microscope in Holland, are Sir Isaac Newton's (1642–1727) work on differential and integral calculus and his *Principles of Natural Philosophy,* William Harvey's (1578–1657) discovery of the circulation of the blood, John Napier's (1550–1617) invention of the logarithmic chart, Robert Boyle's (1626–91) *New Experiments Physico-Mechanical* in 1660 and his 1661 work *Sceptical Chymist,* which began to lay the foundation of chemical theory, and others. The Chinese side is represented by Gu Yanwu's work on phonology and his *Rizhi lu* (1670), Yan Ruoju's (1636–1704) *Shangshu guwen shuzheng* [Inquiry into the authenticity of the Classic of History in ancient characters], and Song

Yingxing's (b. 1600) work *Tiangong kaiwu* on the applied sciences and the use or disuse of the *bagu* writing style. Hu's chart constructs Chinese scholarship as extremely textual (work on texts about texts) and Western scholarship as delving into physical properties and manifestations:

> On the Chinese side, other than Song Yingxing's work *Tiangong kaiwu,* all of it is just scholarship on paper. It is great progress to go from *bagu* to the evidential research (*kaozheng*) of ancient phonology, but in the end it is still work on and about paper.
>
> In these few decades, western scholarship has already gone the road of the natural sciences. [*Guoxue,* 166–67]

Hu claims that the investigative method of Chinese and Western scholars is the same, but the materials investigated by Gu Yanwu and Yan Ruoju are simply texts, whereas Westerners study actual objects. He decries the limitations of texts:

> Written materials are limited; even if you drill in here and there, you still cannot get past the boundaries of this pile of paper. . . .
>
> The size of the universe has increased many ten-thousand fold in these past 300 years, and the average lifespan of the individual has lengthened by twenty years.
>
> But our world of scholarship is using up our energy on a pile of rotten paper! [*Guoxue,* 167–68]

Furthermore, textual research can only produce the "evidential method," which Hu characterizes as a "passive use of materials," whereas the materials of natural science can produce the "experimental method." Such a method leads to a delving for a much deeper understanding than merely what the eye can behold, for it prompts the researcher to develop new means of investigation, such as the microscope, to get beyond his or her limitations. According to Hu, work on textual materials is constrained because it only allows investigation of various texts and prohibits this outward development. Therefore, experimentation is based on "bold speculation, and careful search for evidence," and the researcher is forced to think creatively and work out theories that can be proven or disproven [*Guoxue,* 168]. Textual studies, or paper on paper, limit the methodology and hence the creativity of the researcher and result in "dead methodology." Hu tried to apply the methodology of evidential research to his own work.

Ironically, in this 1928 analysis Hu Shi is emphasizing the materiality of

the text over its ideological content. His metaphors of the text as a pile of
paper and of textual work as paper on paper are extremely material and
point to physical boundaries rather than limitations in ideology or application. Hu views scientific work almost as unconfined by any material
boundaries. In discussing scientific work he brings out ideological aspects
such as speculation, creativity, and understanding. Hu's metaphor of
textual research in China as circumscribed by the actual physical existence
of paper and ink, which not only prevents the researcher from moving
outward but also determines his or her method, underscores the extremely
physical alternative to Chinese scholarship that he feels exists in Western
work.[24]

Chinese Scholarship and Literature: Overdetermined Textuality

If Hu's analysis of the extreme textuality of Chinese scholarship is correct,
the reasons for such a phenomena are far more complex than a mere
choice of materials and must be related to traditional concepts of the
relationship between political power and the mastery of texts, as well as
philosophical, ethical, and literary paradigms. Yet Hu's focus in the comparative chart and in his discussion is clear: the problem lies *not with
intellectual work* per se, but rather with the textual focus of the research
traditionally done in China. Therefore, the role and identity of the scholar
is central, and the stance he or she must take is that of investigating not
texts, but the world at large.

It is precisely through this textual nature of history and of the work of
the Chinese historian and scholar that Hu constructs self and work in his
autobiography as well as these other lectures and presentations. Although
Hu wished he had been a scientist, as many have pointed out, Hu Shi
and others—Lu Xun and Guo Moruo, for example—began their studies
abroad in scientific fields and only later switched to textually defined
studies: history and textual research for Hu Shi, history and literature for
Guo Moruo, and literature and translation for Lu Xun. All of these
intellectuals were cultural critics who wrote voluminously on Chinese
society. As Hu Shi has shown in his analysis of the organization of the
"national past," the problem of evaluating Chinese history is as much
defined by the work and methodology of the historian as scholar as by the
problematics of that history itself. This intersection of a supposedly objective history and the subjectivity of the individual scholar is the exact point
in his autobiographical preface, written much later, where Hu Shi claims

that his unconscious mind intervenes in the autobiography, pushing him as far as possible toward what he then portrays as the less textual pole of history and away from the literary. However, as Hu discusses historical work, we see that his vision of history is as textual as the fiction from which he turns, and he places history, literature, and philosophy together as textually defined studies that are in opposition to the sciences.

The "Hu Shi" of the PRC: An Antitextual Ideology

Much of the criticism directed at Hu Shi in the mid-1950s focuses on his opposition to Marxism and his advocation of reform over revolution. However, a number of critics single out Hu's definition of scholarship and its excessively textual orientation.[25] In other words contemporary critics accepted Hu's vision of an overly textual Chinese scholarship and then attacked him for doing what he criticized. In "Pipan Hu Shi zhexue sixiang de fandong shizhi" [Criticize the reactionary nature of Hu Shi's philosophical thought], Sun Dingguo interprets Hu's call to "organize the national past" as advice to the Chinese people to spend their time boring into old piles of paper; for Sun the negative side of this effort is that people will remove themselves from the revolutionary struggle and China will remain in its "semi-colonial, semi-feudal" state. The contradiction between revolution and textual study, or between the revolutionary and the scholar, is the same as the contrast Hu implies in his autobiography. Sun claims that Hu's thought shows little progress between 1921, when Hu raised the issue of "organizing the national past," and 1928, when he wrote "Methodology and Materials in Research" and proposed that the textual "evidential method" was inferior to the "experimental method" of the natural scientist. Sun rejects Hu's differentiation of methodology or materials and postulates the choice as one of socially relevant work or academic exercises. Both possibilities exist whether the material is textual or natural phenomena [161–67]. In his focus on socially relevant research, another critic, Jin Yingxi, agrees with Sun's critique. Jin organizes his discussion of Hu Shi's approach to literary research around the issue of concern with ideology, or content, as opposed to form: "The reason he wrote 'Dream of the Red Chamber' and other essays is to attract the readers attention to secondary issues of the form of language or the personal history of the author, and to cover up the ideological content and social background of these great works" [259]. According to Jin, application of Hu Shi's theories on research will result in an unwarranted demarcation between textually oriented study and nontextual reality, including the political aspect of reality. To Jin, Hu's opposition of historical materialism to textual research is clear in his research on the *Shuijing zhu* [Commentary on the *Book of Waterways*], a book he treats as a "rare object" [259–66].[26]

In *Hu Shi fandong sixiang pipan* [A critique of Hu Shi's reactionary thought] Li Da points out that although Hu made statements opposing the textual research of Chinese scholars, actually his own work is nothing but textual research, redefined to include texts from an area slightly larger than that constituted by the classics. Thus if Hu's work is an example of his newly defined "scientific" textual research, this method is no different from the textual research of previous Chinese scholars:

> Hu Shi . . . emphasizes that his method of textual research is a scientific method, and moreover says "actually it is very easy to explain the scientific method," it is just "to respect reality, and to respect evidence." But his textual research method is completely guided by his idealism, and is certainly not any sort of scientific method. We must not be deluded by the terms such as "reality," "evidence," and "physical evidence" that he uses. When Hu Shi refers to the so-called "reality" of "human affairs" that he studies it is only his subjective experience, or a reality chosen according to subjective interpretations. . . . Now, the arena in which his method of textual research functions is the "pile of old paper," the texts of the ancients, things which are white paper upon which black characters are printed. Here, what he calls "reality" and "evidence" are all words and sentences in books, so when he is making a hypothesis and seeking evidence, he must utilize words and sentences from books as "evidence." [67–70]

What Li Da favors is a redefinition of research as not only textual research (*kaozheng*) as done by Chinese scholars of the Qing, but as research (*yanjiu*) which may include textual research that focuses, as in the past, on questions of authenticity or authorship, but which has the ultimate aim of enlightening the reader about the social background, ideology, or aesthetics of the work.

These three critiques show that contemporary critics as well as modern writers grappled with the problem of aligning textual work up in relation to nontextual work or phenomena. Like Hu Shi, the contemporary mainland critics attack traditional letters as overly textual. Solutions are proposed or implied by both parties: working in society as a revolutionary rather than a scholar, becoming a scientist, or redefining textual labor to link it more strongly to the phenomenal world. The goal of the newly defined materialist scholar is always oriented toward explaining, interpreting, or changing the world and cannot be limited to issues defined by the material existence of texts alone.

Despite his perception of and protest against the textual bias of Chinese scholarship, in his own lectures on methodology, materials, and the organization of the "national past," Hu Shi still delineates a role for the historian that does not escape from the boundaries of textual research. In his autobiography as well Hu emphasizes his childhood affinity with books and his father's and classmates' perception of his suitability for scholarship rather than any other type of work; although he decries the lack of content of traditional Chinese literature, which "has art, but no substance," and states that literature needs new ideas, he concentrates his work on the essentially textual solution of adopting the vernacular. The opposition of the historian and scholar against the figure defined by action in society, such as the revolutionary, or by interpretation of the physical world, such as the natural scientist, is implied in Hu's later comments in which he ironically refers to his lifelong work on the *Shuijing zhu,* which he continued while working in the Gest Library at Princeton as a retreat to an "ivory tower" [Chou, 193]. Although Hu Shi, like other May Fourth intellectuals, constructed the intellectual arena as oppositional, he himself continued his work as a textual scholar and historian, and this identity made him an easy target for Chinese critics in the 1950s. Going one step further than Hu Shi, these critics propose a redefinition of textual studies that forges a strong bond not only with corporeal phenomena, but also with ideology and history. Thus they effectively eliminated the possibility of textual studies existing as hermetic academic exercises, recreation, or affirmations of the intellectual stance. In opposition to Hu Shi's materialistic description and analysis of the text as paper and ink that refers back only to previous texts, Marxist scholars redefine the text as an ideological indicator that must be bound to a material reality and deny its validity to the scholar and society at large as a material artifact in its own right.

5

Guo Moruo: "China" versus China

Modern writers wrote circumstantial autobiographies, tracing ancestry, identifying the names of people and places and specific times, positioning their narrative within a progressive time frame, referring to historical and contemporary figures, discussing their own roles as public figures, and in general situating themselves within political society as a referential context. This worldly orientation has not excluded the increased subjectivity which some scholars identify as beginning in Qing times and culminating in May Fourth romantic writing.[1] The autobiography which traces "actual" occurrences, albeit with other than historical principles as organizing ideologies, provided to the May Fourth writer definition as a modern figure who had succeeded in creating an ideology of modernity that placed the literary intellectual squarely in the middle of social affairs and phenomenal happenings.[2] Narratives which trace history in time and physical/social existence in space situate the writer within common social reality rather than in reference to textual practices now branded as "past." However, writers still often try to make it appear that they have no choice but to give in to pressures on them to become writers or scholars and struggle with the very dichotomy they construct. Despite its new definition, literary work does not seem to have authority sufficient to protect it from unfavorable comparisons with revolutionary work, manual labor, and military affairs. The new circumstantiality writers invest in their writing helps reorient literary work as more socially effective, but doubts remain that it is still a detached, isolated, hermetic type of work that produces and maintains elite social groups. In other words literary work is simply still too textual.

Social Relevance: A Solution to Textuality

Because his autobiography includes segments written in the 1920s, 1930s, and 1940s, Guo Moruo, more than any other writer treated here, investigates the option of reconstituting literature as directly relevant to social and material production. This issue was also dealt with at length by other critics writing during the same time. In *Wenxue wenda ji* [Questions and answers on literature], an apology for literature written in 1935, critic Zheng Nong attempts to define literary writing as both part of and valuable in understanding contemporary society. He structures his argument around three questions: what literature do we need, how should we read literary works, and how do we go about writing? In answering the first question Zheng states unequivocally that "literature already is not something solely for the entertainment of literati and cultured gentlemen" [1–2], but "is something that uses symbols (words) to express the complexity of a specific social life" [2]. Zheng then eliminates from consideration all literature which is not relevant to contemporary society in China, including *Guwen guanzhi* and *Honglou meng;* these two classical works are compared unfavorably to Lu Xun's "Ah Q zhengzhuan" [The true story of Ah Q] and Mao Dun's *Ziye* [Midnight].

When he answers the question of "how should we read literature," Zheng places literature in even closer proximity to the social sciences by inscribing it as a kind of social science itself:

> In looking at literature, most people feel it is by nature different than social science. Actually, this is not entirely correct. This error arises because people regard literature as a type of entertainment. In essence, literature and social science alike express the true reality of society. But social science is a theoretical dissection, whereas literature is a description of life: the difference between literature and social science lies only in the methods of expression. Social science is a direct appeal to the logic of the reader; literature utilizes the feelings of the reader to get to logic. To read social science, one needs a calm, cold mind; to read literature, one needs rich emotions. This must be understood before we can discuss how to read literature. [5]

Thus Zheng claims that *because* pure emotion is the essence of literature, it can be written by anyone and should not be mystified as under the sole control of literary intellectuals [9].

As the title indicates, Zheng's book is arranged as a series of questions from friends and acquaintances about different aspects of literary study or the production of literature, and his answers. His basic stance is that literature is valuable, but only if constituted in specific ways. Thus in an essay to a friend who used to be a "bookworm" but now has come to the conclusion that "reading books is useless" [20], for example, Zheng outlines his fundamental approach to literary study. First, one must avoid locking oneself in a room, closing one's eyes to society, and reading without end, a practice which will turn one into a "useless object" [22].[3] Next, Zheng opposes reading at random without a specific stance and without searching for social relevance. Third, he is against memorizing or learning facts without gaining the ability to apply them to specific social problems. Behind Zheng's exhortations is his belief that "theory is the guide to actual life, and actual life is the content of theory; we cannot say that actual life can unilaterally contain study, but neither can we separate study from actual life" [23–24]. Thus the study of classical Chinese should be, first and foremost, a way to allow students to demystify *guwen* as an absolute repository of knowledge [29–31].

Much of Zheng's effort goes toward devaluing and then redefining what he calls a "literary lifestyle" similar to what is outlined within impressionistic autobiographies:

> As I have previously discussed, our lives should be the starting point for the study of literature. So if we want to increase interest towards literary books, we must turn our lives closer to the literary lifestyle. What is the literary lifestyle? Scholars of before took literature as an individual plaything or as something to be studied in the study. So their most ideal literary lifestyle is "close the door and study," "my ears hearing nothing outside the window." But our understanding towards literature is different now, and our literary lifestyle certainly is not "close the door and study." Our literature is not knowledge of books, but is the representation of broad social life. If social life changes, literary currents change. Therefore, we can say that our literary lifestyle is change itself. [33–34]

The reason students complain that vernacular writing is easy and ancient texts more interesting and challenging is that teachers do not understand the fundamental relationship between literature and society and thus do not know how to teach a literary work that is not textually difficult [34–35].

Even though he values literature highly, Zheng, like the writers discussed in this manuscript, constructs two categories of literary work and social activity. He describes premodern intellectual life as working within these categories, which are set off against each other and basically opposite. His reinscription of literature is as a "new" category that has absorbed the latter; now socially engaged and relevant, literature must abandon its previous existence, which insisted on maintaining a hermetically complete textual world that would only suffer from ties with "the outside." Literature is now nonelite and contemporary, and specialists as well as commoners should be encouraged to write and read it.[4]

In his own establishment of himself as a writer, Guo Moruo rejected the *wenren* definition which placed the intellectual outside the parameters of social intercourse; his refutation implies a struggle against a commonly held notion that writers are indeed different from those who work in more socially relevant occupations. In 1926, two years after Guo announced his new Marxist ideology, he wrote "Wenyijia de juewu" [The awakening of a litterateur], in which he not only expounded on his support for realist, socialist literature, but also argued against those who hoped he would refrain from engaging in social movements and preserve his talent for literary work:

> Among this small group of opponents [to my ideas on social thought], there are some who stand totally in opposition to me in their thinking. For example, there is a group who is head over heels in love with the heroic ideas of nationalism, and a group of young anarchists, both of which have attacked me verbally and in print. They say, "You are a writer. You should write some poetry, write a few novels; why spend your time talking about 'isms!'" I think this kind of talk is laughable: as if a certain ideology should have a special person assigned to handle it, and their patriotism or anarchism should be discussed only by themselves, with "writers" placed to the side. It's really laughable. . . . To say that someone devoted to literature should not publish essays on social thought—not only is this not specified by law in any country, but also it is simply an absolute error to say that those who are working in literature should not be tainted by social thought. In society, this erroneous idea is very powerful, and easily can enter the minds of young people interested in literature and confuse their will.[5]

When he reformulates himself as a revolutionary writer, Guo rejects what he presents as the prevailing conception of an elite, detached intellectual writing about emotions or ideas. Writers must write "realistically" about social reality.

In his famous "Geming yu wenxue" [Revolution and literature], also written in 1926, Guo elaborates on the writer and his or her position in relation to social phenomena. First, he refutes what he believes to be the essentially "Chinese" idea of a writer:

> So-called writers, especially our Chinese so-called writers, are "other" people existing in an "other" place. Their lives are filled with wind, flowers, snow, and moon, and they have no concern with the affairs of the world. When the affairs of the world are peaceful, they may be able to sing a song about peace, but when change is afoot, their lives are threatened. They are rather cool towards revolution, and either take a superior attitude or expend all their efforts in cursing it. With old-style intellectuals or new-style intellectuals, we can frequently find actual examples; from their points of view, literature and revolution cannot stand together.[6]

Guo also points out that revolutionaries despise literature: "We often hear those actually engaged in revolutionary work say: Literature! What is the value of something like literature to our revolutionary mission? It is just the plaything of young ladies and girls; it is the forbidden fruit that decadent youth steal for nourishment when they listen, enthralled, to classroom talk. Those working in literature are not worth a dog's farthing" [Guo, "Geming yu wenxue," 364]. In an attempt to recoup the social value of literature, Guo claims that revolution and literature should have the same goals and that there is basically no contradiction between them: literature is the vanguard of revolution. In his articles and essays this is the stance that Guo maintained throughout the rest of his life. In his autobiography, however, Guo expresses a seemingly contradictory concern about the value of literary work. Eventually, he comes to the conclusion that literary work and revolution can be placed together, but not for the same reasons as he gives in this 1926 essay.

Guo Moruo: Ultimate Litterateur

To say that Guo Moruo devalued literature may appear ridiculous; critics firmly identify Guo as one of the first romantic modern writers and then one of the first Marxist revolutionary writers in China. His early poetry was a landmark in May Fourth literary experiments and was highly influential among young intellectuals. Furthermore, Guo was not only well known as a writer, but as a scholar as well; it would be difficult to find another person whose career and social persona was as linked to textual work as was that of Guo Moruo.

In his book *The Romantic Generation of May Fourth Writers,* Leo Ou-fan Lee traces Guo's early interest in literature and his suppression of "literary inclinations" to pursue the "practical" study of medicine.[7] Guo traveled to Japan in 1914 to take up studies there. In discussing Guo's sentimentalism as "more apparent than real, more for public display than as private emotion," Lee brings up Guo's development of a public entity through reference to Western literary works and quotes Guo's own words about his debt to certain works of Western literature (and some Chinese writers, such as Qu Yuan) in bringing him the "romantic spirit" [1973:183]. Guo's sons had three rabbits that were named Byron, Shelley, and Keats, and when he went for a trip with his friend, the playwright Tian Han, they represented their time together through reference to literary figures [Lee, 1973:184–85]. Lee documents Guo's inscription of the hero as poet and comments on Guo's romantic appropriation of political problems in his early poetry.

By 1924 Guo had announced his conversion to Marxism, yet kept literature in an important position as the vanguard of the revolution.[8] In 1926 Guo joined the Northern Expedition forces, eventually becoming vice-chair of the political department. As Lee points out, Guo associated his name both with Nationalists and then Communists, eventually making it onto a Nationalist list of dangerous intellectuals and exiling himself to Japan from 1928 to 1937, where he worked prodigiously in scholarship, literature, translation, and essays. When he returned to China, he headed the literary propaganda section of the political department of the Military Affairs Commission until 1940 and again began to write. Lee comments that Guo moved "with apparent ease" between realms of literature, scholarship, and political activity [Lee, 1973:198–99]. In this chapter I question not only the "ease" with which Guo altered his work and identity, but also the relationship between categories of textual work— literature and scholarship—and those of physical labor—physical revolutionary activity and labor—that Guo constructs. Although Guo engages in work in both textual and nontextual realms, it is not without the struggle of creating these categories as oppositional that he is able to represent himself as a writer, a scholar, and a soldier.

Nation, Race, Writer

Virtually all of the autobiographies of the Republican era begin with recollections of the author's childhood days. In Lu Xun's *Zhaohua xishi* and Guo Moruo's four-volume autobiography, the constructed "China" of earlier times—which the author inscribes as corrupt, illogical, and pervaded with ridiculous traditions—becomes an integral constituent in the self the author creates and confronts. Nation, race, and the meaning of textual work as it relates to nation and race are some main concerns in the autobiographies of Lu Xun and Guo Moruo.

Guo Moruo, Lu Xun, and Ba Jin depict their early years as first peaceful and then either chaotic and traumatic or simply unappealing. The breaking point frequently is the author's initial education outside of the household; sometimes, a death or breakdown in family order causes the change. The author gradually loses faith in what he has inscribed as the totality of the past and makes the decision to leave China and divorce himself from the conceptualized "China." As race and nation are incorporated within the category of "Chinese writer," however, the break cannot be complete and is a source of conflict as the writer searches for alternative authorities outside these parameters.

Myth and the Orthodoxy

In *Moruo zizhuan* [The autobiography of Guo Moruo] mythical or bizarre occurrences form a contrast to social orthodoxy, which is evoked through reference to various aspects of normative elite social existence: the examination system, status and position, and the family. As in other autobiographies, early emphasis on myth-creating incidents, texts, or occurrences evaporates as orthodox social behavior assumes a greater role.

Guo Moruo begins the first volume of his autobiography, *Shaonian shidai* [The era of my youth], with several statements disclaiming his genius and denying that his text is in any way similar to the famous authors of confessional autobiography in the West, Rousseau or Augustine. Obviously aware of the Western autobiographical-confessional tradition, Guo simultaneously denies its validity and places his own text in contrast to this tradition. At the same time he does not situate his autobiography in relation to any texts within the Chinese tradition, which did not recognize a distinct genre of autobiography. Affiliation with a premodern tradition would not permit Guo to use his text to indicate the newly emerging "modernity," in the creation of which most progressive May Fourth writers participated.[9]

The first volume of Guo's four-volume autobiography includes three texts written at different times; "Wode tongnian" [My childhood], written in 1928, "Fanzheng qianhou" [Before and after the revolution], written in 1929, and "Chuqu Kuimen" [First time out of Kuimen], written in 1936. When assembling his autobiography in 1947, Guo commented that he places them together because they seem to be of the same era and to possess the same motivations. The organization of the essays is basically historical but not entirely chronological.

The first pages of "Wode tongnian" abound with references to mythic or superstitious elements of life. For example, Guo discusses the trees of his birthplace and mentions a type of banyan (*rong*) tree called a "yellow-horn" (*huangjiao*) which sends out shoots to attach to other trees when it gets large. According to local superstition, when the tree gets too large it turns into a spirit or demon (*jing*) which has the ability to attach itself to people and haunt them. Those who were ill could nail a piece of red and green material to the tree for good luck. This botanical animation is followed by the short story about what Guo terms a "tragedy of the era"—the tale of the single successful examination candidate in their town, an old man who was killed by the young concubine he was privileged to take after he finally passed the examination on the tenth try. The text follows with descriptions of many strange and marvelous things: bandits listed by nickname, ghosts, dreams and crazy people [I, 7, 12, 13, 26, 53, 56, 78, 126]. The last reference to a ghost is qualified: alone on a night road, Guo is afraid of ghosts even though he does not believe in them [I, 128]. During this section, Guo Moruo unwillingly attends school, participating in the normalizing education that will become more important as he gets older; in the next section, "Before and After the Revolution," Guo comes of age and the references to ghosts cease.

Hu Shi, Lu Xun, and Guo Moruo all follow the pattern of framing the mythological elements into the section of their texts which belongs to early childhood or, in the case of Hu Shi, before his birth. They construct myth—events or traditions with no apparent explanation or modern means of understanding—as occurring only in or before childhood. When education and other social institutions begin to regulate the individual's life, phenomena are placed within an "understandable" framework and "logic" appears; incidents which do not lend themselves to inclusion within the framework's borders are simply excluded. However, as is shown in Guo's story of candidate Chen's rise and rapid fall and the progress of the entire autobiographical story, the "original" social orthodoxy which consists of the examination system, the education that leads up to it, and the subsequent success of the candidate and his rise to high levels of officialdom is no longer viable as a normative tradition. Therefore, as Guo "ages" and moves into social relationships and institutions, he constructs "childhood" not only as a contrast, but also as undermining the validity of orthodox tradition.

Destruction of Orthodoxy and the Childhood World

Guo Moruo begins his autobiography with a description of his hometown—a narrative pattern consistent with the basic orientation of a circumstantial autobiography—which locates the subject in a specific time and place. Although Guo identifies locale, historical background, and local characteristics, the names used ultimately are nonreferential to corporeal phenomena. For example, the area is called "fragrant country of flowering crabapples" (*haitang xiangguo*), but the fragrant crab apple flowers which determine the name have long since ceased to exist. The actual name of the town, Sand Bay (*Shawan*), refers to a sandbar to the north of the city that "is said to be" the ruins of the old city; the new site was acquired when the Du River flooded the old city [4]. There is a temple to King Han, but Guo does not know if it is Han Shizhong of the Song dynasty or Han Xin.[10] There is a stone tablet to someone named Lin in honor of his filial piety, but no one named Lin exists in the town.

The nominal reference is unclear or does not exist, making the name suspect and calling the reader's attention to the unreliability of the author's circumstantial framing of his environment. All four examples which Guo provides are false nominations in that either the referent does not coincide or is probably inauthentic: the name of the area refers to nonexistent crab apple trees, the name of the town comes from hearsay which cannot be substantiated, the reference of the temple is uncertain, and a person named Lin to correspond to the name on the stone tablet cannot be located. The autobiography locates the self circumstantially but undermines the impact of situating the individual within a specifically and commonly named locale by bringing in examples where name no longer accurately refers or perhaps never did refer.[11]

The next two sections of Guo's work describe bandit activity in the area, a part of society that in most contexts is an unattractive underside to orthodox social interaction. The bandits are listed by last name and nickname: Big Guy Xu, Third Monk Yang, Third Monk Xu, Third Dog Wang, Third Rascal Yang [I, 6]. Also mentioned in these short sections are the unnamed groups of scholars, police, ghosts, landlords, middle-income families, the original inhabitants of this area, and the outsiders from other provinces that form 80 percent of the population of Sichuan. In six pages Guo sketches these groups and describes some of their conflicts, articulating each clearly in relation to the others. Only the bandits and original inhabitants are given names. Guo connects the underground society of bandits with a literary work that is also not part of an orthodox textual tradition: "We [children] felt Yang was a good friend, like someone in *Sanguo yanyi* [The romance of the three kingdoms] or *Shuihu zhuan* [The water margin]" [I, 11].

These three parts of the text form the section numbered "one" in the first chapter of the first volume of Guo's autobiography. The first, the description of his hometown, is characterized by reference to physical structures, monuments, trees and flowers, and the visible examination candidate. At the same time there is an incongruity between the name and the actuality, and the value of nomination is suspect. The second section describes the social organization of the author's childhood society, focusing on the elements of bandits and ghosts. It is characterized by specific names or references and the quality of being underground or unorthodox. Although these underground forces are at conflict with the representatives of orthodoxy (police, scholars) in this section, the author identifies this world as interesting and as resembling society fabricated in popular premodern fiction.

The third section shows the connection between the orthodox and unorthodox aspects of society. One relationship results from common origins: "Most of the bandits were sons of middle income families—they were blamed for not being responsible, but there was nothing in society for which they could be responsible" [I, 11]. This short passage reveals an opposition of alternative realities and the questionable ability of orthodox society to provide social and individual stability. The second tie is antagonistic, as the bandits have a sense of justice and prefer to attack rich landlords. The third is the juxtaposition of underground society with regular society that is implied in the lack of contact between them, as the bandits will not harm those from their own home. Underground society exists parallel to, but not interfering with, orthodox society of the same locale.

These three sections form a paradoxical background to the birth of the subject. Like Liang Qichao, Guo situates his birth in a context of world events: "I was born in 1892 in that bandits' nest, three years before the Sino-Japanese War, seven years before the Wuxu [1898] Reform, nine years before the Eight-Power Allied Forces entered Beijing, and when the old, great, empire of China was coming to an end" [I, 12]. Up to this point Guo has constructed the immediate environment of his birth; now he begins to trace his ancestry, which also has a less than upright side. The "interesting episodes" of his family background are not, he writes, "glorious history," but are colorful incidents about which the family elders bragged. For example, one of his great-grandfathers took the risk of buying sick pigs to ship down the river to sell and got rich when the pigs recovered.

These backgrounds—local underground history and the author's personal ancestry—form two pasts, one or both of which could authorize the present and allow Guo to define himself as continuing certain traditions or practices. Shen Congwen provides himself with the role of transmitter through his initial construction of the military utopia, the fort town of his prechildhood which makes military participation a viable social endeavor. In his construction of these pasts Guo acknowledges that they describe social realities and orientations for certain people or in certain eras, but they are rejected by the author as personal possibilities at the time he writes this text.[12]

One past, to which Guo belongs by upbringing, is the orthodoxy (*zheng*): upstanding and manifested, it is the tradition of the successful examination candidate and government official. This past is symbolized by the candidate Chen, whose story is told at the end of the first section immediately following the contradictory description of the author's locale. This past is also what the author calls the "old, great, empire of China" that is coming to an end as Guo Moruo is born. As is shown by the story of Chen's vain success and subsequent humiliation and death at the hands of his concubine, this orthodox tradition is no longer an accurate indicator of function and status. The other past, the underground tradition of bandits (*fan*) and its corollary in popular literature, as well as the escapades of Guo's immediate family, is an attractive contrast, but because of the author's upbringing and his parents' desires to see him well-educated, it is unavailable except from the perspective of the child.[13]

Guo bases his rejection of orthodox and unorthodox traditions on the chaotic social transformations that occurred as the old empire of China was coming to an end and implies that there are no acceptable foundations for a new construction of self for anyone—bandit or scholar—whose birth or life coincides with the downfall of the great tradition.

As Guo Moruo describes his initial attempts at study, he refers to a *xiucai* in a past generation of the family and to his own initial attempts to learn to write and to study poetry with his mother. From *Section Four* on, "My Childhood" is essentially a narration of normalizing education.[14] Like many writers at this time, Guo does not enjoy his early education, claiming that he is sick of school after three days. "Chinese" education, whether in an old-style recitation school or in a "modern" academy, comes under criticism by many writers working in the 1920s and 1930s. Writing poetry is an activity that contains its own punishment in the teacher's demand that students sit in their chairs until they could write it well. Learning is accompanied by frequent beatings and humiliations, which thoroughly drive out the desire to learn that had spontaneously occurred when Guo was four. The huge tradition of literature and the text, with its memorization of classics that a child could not possibly understand, forms a prison which is broken only by contact with the "outside" world [I, 35]. The Western written tradition amazes Guo because of its physicality: there are pictures in the books, and there is space under the words and sentences, which do not go on forever as the unpunctuated Chinese text appears to do to the beginner, but have an ending marked by a dot [I, 36].[15]

Education and the Bankruptcy of the Orthodox

Guo Moruo continues to comment on the classical tradition of letters as an outdated and even totally worthless tradition that not only is no longer valuable to the young student with "modern" sensibilities, but is based on false principles. Classical education appears only as a cause for ridicule. Guo discusses the case of Liao Jiping (1852–1932), a classics scholar of the late Qing, and his evidence that some of the classics are forgeries.[16] Guo's teacher supports Liao and believes in his theories and accuses Zhang Zhidong and Wang Renqiu, two scholars who were students of Liao, of plagiarizing Liao's material. One piece of evidence for this accusation is the meaning of a divination done from the characters of their names [I, 64]. Guo lists the unattractive nicknames students give elementary schoolteachers they dislike. One of Guo's high school teachers is described as devoting half of his time to his studies, half to teaching, and half to himself, so he is called "Mr. Three Halves" (*Sanban xiansheng*) [I, 95].[17]

In the late Qing dynasty teachers were often intellectuals who had failed the examinations or passed only the lower level exam and were unable to become officials.[18] Teachers usually did not have enough property to live off, and their only hope for advancement was in future success in the examinations. They were dependent on their employers and lived a life without guaranteed status [Borthwick, 19]. Because of an oversupply of teachers at the end of the Qing, some were forced into the degrading position of having to come to the students rather than having the students come to them to be taught [Borthwick, 20]. A common derogatory term for teachers, "Mr. Winterhearth of Three-Family Village," which described the teacher as someone who taught children from farming families during the slack season, shows the low status and ridicule to which the teacher could be subjected [Borthwick, 25]. The inclusion of the teacher in the family shrine was part of the conceptual structure and ideology that defined the teacher as related to the role of Confucius and thereby honorable and was not necessarily related to the actual position of the teacher in society [Borthwick, 20].

In fiction and autobiography of the 1920s and early 1930s, which is often written by authors who underwent some classical education before or around the abolition of the examination system, the teacher in general is portrayed as disliked by young students, partially because of the drudgery of memorization of classical texts forced on the students and partially because teachers were underpaid scholars with no power in the greater political world. However, as teachers were in control of training students for participation in the examination, they were in a symbolically significant position; although most teachers had little political power or social status, theoretically any one of their students could rise to great heights. The teacher is at the crux of educational reform and as the pivot point deciding what should be transmitted, old or "modern," is in a crucial position. Both Lu Xun and Guo Moruo, two of the earliest born of this group of authors, establish the teacher as a critical juncture through which education, and by extension the orthodox tradition of classical letters, is shown to be invalid.

"Wode tongnian" contains almost the only explicit reference to the author's sexuality in the entire four volumes. Guo Moruo describes his sexual awakening, which occurs when he is about nine or ten. Watching the wife of his older brother standing in a bamboo grove, he feels that he wants to touch her hands [I, 46]. Guo reports that by the age of ten sexual feelings prevent him from concentrating in school, and at eleven he masturbates regularly. There are further references to masturbation and homosexual temptations and activities in the rest of this section. In the other volumes there is reference to love but almost nothing on sex.

Guo attributes his early sexual awakening to the awareness of sexual difference he gained from an unconventional reading of the *Shijing* [Classic of poetry] and the *Sanzi jing* [Three-character classic], as well as some old stories such as *Xihu jiahua* [Romantic tales from the West Lake] [Guo, I, 49–50]. By imposing an unorthodox, personal reading on classical texts such as the *Shijing*, Guo alters their reception and turns them into documents outside the framework of classical education.

At the same time Guo enjoys reading a work which overthrows the orthodoxy of texts in another way: the *Wei shangshu kao* [Investigations into the fake *Book of History*] by Yan Baishi, which uses textual research to prove the *Guwen shangshu* [Book of history in the classical language] by Mei Yi to be false, thus overturning the authority of one of the pillars of Chinese history. Young people, he writes, love to expose the secrets of others; in this case the "secrets" are the basis of the learning transmitted by and through teachers and scholars. Through reference to the deconstruction of the *Book of History* in the new text debate, Guo carries out his own autobiographical deconstruction. This is the third link in his negative presentation of the possibility of realizing a viable past in the present, which he has precluded through his description of the humiliation and death of the examination candidate, the undermining of old texts through unorthodox interpretation, and the entirely negative nomination and portrayal of teachers, the transmitters of orthodox learning.

In her contemporary autobiography *Woman Warrior,* which is written in English and takes the life of a Chinese-American girl as its topic, Maxine Hong Kingston uses images of ghosts and bizarre interpretations of reality to give expression to an oppressive and often illogical pressure that comes from being partially defined by the Chinese female tradition while attempting to establish an identity in the modern, and in her case foreign, world. In the first part of her autobiographical novel, she includes ghosts, strange foodstuffs, and odd conversations as the basis of her daily life. Eventually she escapes this nightmare by establishing her identity in a foreign language as a professor of English and later as a writer; even a once-removed tradition can only be exorcised from its hold on and in the self when it is displaced by an "alien" system of writing and knowledge.

Guo Moruo's text contrasts images of ghosts, moonlight, sex, dreams, robbers, opium, and sundry humiliations with references to the classics (forged), teachers (ridiculous), classes (useless), history (fake), and names (absurd) in a narrative that alternates these positive (negative) and negative (positive) elements. The narrator in *Woman Warrior*, growing up in a working-class Chinese family in America, finds that the old codes do not fit: nothing out of the past that her parents relate to her can mesh with her experiences growing up as a Chinese-American girl—especially one who excels in scholarship. For Guo the old system of meaning is no longer significant in the new society that China is becoming, and the elements of this code become ridiculous as he is learning them. The orthodox understanding that is passed on to both Guo Moruo and Kingston is transmitted through narrative; in Guo's case the texts that form the basis of orthodox learning are the tool of transmission. For Kingston the oral narrative of her mother and the others in her immediate environment should provide her with a proper understanding of the "past" which is significant to the formation of her self. Both authors, however, insist on imposing their own interpretations on these "texts," undercutting orthodox understanding and through this process, moving toward formation of a new, radical self that devalues and revalues the past.

The Rejection of "China"

"Fanzheng qianhou" marks the first change both in the identity-subject of the autobiography and in the narrative structure. Thematically, Guo strengthens political elements and widens the scope politics includes. Narration of the relationship of the self to the outside world increases, displacing the limited context of the early childhood years. Guo depicts a young man growing up, beginning to act upon his environment rather than being defined by it. Within this context three aspects of this newly realized arena are exposed as false: schools and teachers (continued and intensified from the last section), idealistic student movements, and the revolution. Following the orthodox road of becoming an official, which was eliminated as a possibility in "Wode tongnian," is not reconsidered, although Guo expresses shock when his brother, who originally was concerned only with "saving the country," joins the corrupt forces of the government, becomes an official, and eventually starts to smoke opium [I, 222, 296].

In the last section teachers were ridiculed, but now they are criticized for their superficial and slavish imitation of foreigners in language and method, their purchase of fake foreign university degrees, and their implied positing of foreigners as a validating higher authority of knowledge and position. In Guo's text the native tradition of teaching and learning is impotent, but the attempts to replace it with a superficial gloss of foreign learning are absurd.

At the end of the Qing Dynasty and in the early years of the Republic, students who had spent two or three years abroad came back to China as a "master" or "doctor" and became professors at the best universities, replacing what Guo portrays as a degenerate system of learning with a ridiculous alternative. Using Chinese characters with sounds similar to foreign words, such as *bu-luo-ken* (English: broken) or *a-na-da* (Japanese: anata, "you"), the "false foreigners" would approximate the sounds of foreign languages, pretending to be able to speak these languages and relying on the ignorance of their audience to complete this deceit.

The crucial function of language and its powerful, if misleading, effect is evident in Guo Moruo's description of Cen Chunxuan, once governor-general of Sichuan. The people of Sichuan were "more afraid of officials than of Hades," but Cen was loved because of his beautiful language [I, 236]. When returning to Sichuan after a long absence, he sends a short telegram:

> I have been separated from my Sichuan brothers, old and young, for nine years; I don't know if my Sichuan brothers have missed me or not, but not one day has gone by that I have not thought of my brothers. You have run into unfortunate circumstances, and this has caused us to meet once again. The feeling of so many years of separation cannot overpower the sobs I feel when I shake your hands again. When I crane my neck and look to the west, I do not know where the tears fall from. My Sichuan brothers, think for a moment what a state my heart is in now. [I, 236]

Another official, Duanfang, sends a "ten-thousand word" telegram full of words like "I, the great minister," in which he brags about killing and incurs the hatred of the people of Sichuan.[19] However, Cen never makes it to Sichuan, but Duanfang arrives and never leaves. Language is powerful but does not seem to correspond to "reality." Cen uses language to include himself in the pseudo-familial group of "Sichuan people" and thus ingratiate himself as a natural ruler; Duanfang situates himself without, as a subject looking at an object. Duanfang, however, is able to assume the position of ruler.

The episode which ends "Fanzheng qianhou" destroys the moral authority of the military and the possibility of language functioning as a medium to communicate truths. Guo Moruo describes how Jun Changheng, a warlord in Sichuan and a graduate of the Military Preparatory Academy (*Wubei xuetang*), chose his mistresses at whim from the population [I, 259–60]. If the woman were married, he approached her husband, who had little choice but to accede with a phrase that became associated with this warlord and synonymous with sexual intercourse: "I am willing to fulfill my duty" (*yuan jin yiwu*) [I, 259]. Jun also gave a lecture at the Youth Association entitled "Heroes and Sexual Desire" in which he utilized a triangular argument to prove his virility: all heroes love sex, I love sex, thus I am a hero. In the phrase "I am willing to fulfill my duty," the meaning and function of language is overturned: what the speaker means is that he is giving permission to Jun Changheng to have sexual intercourse with his wife and mocking rather than fulfilling his duty.

Further deception or betrayal is symbolized in Guo's essay on his marriage, "Heimao" [Black cat], which he places directly after "Fanzheng qianhou." In this sketch the author writes about the time right before he is to leave Sichuan, an event he describes in the following "Chuqu Kuimen" [Leaving Kuimen]. The metaphor used for his arranged marriage is that of a black cat concealed in a bag: a man thinks he is buying a white cat, but when he returns home, he finds the cat in the sack is black. When he finally sees his bride on their wedding day, Guo is dismayed to see that she has "a nose upturned like that of a gorilla" and bound feet. His future wife is not the modern woman he expected, but an uneducated girl who belongs to the old "China" the author is about to leave. Mixed in with this description of his betrayal in marriage customs are references to the betrayal of the revolution. Guo discusses the disastrous circumstances after the revolution, when power quickly fell into the hands of vying warlords, a situation that called into question the motives of revolutionaries and their supporters. Rituals of marriage and revolution thus both appear strange and senseless and are unable to serve as self-validating ideologies.[20]

Guo's flight from Sichuan as represented in his autobiography is an escape from a world that is amoral, deceitful, and passive. This world is degenerate on the inside as well as degenerating from the outside: at the end of "Heimao," Guo writes that everyone should remember that Sichuan's "revolution" (*fanzheng*) began with the building of the railways—with inroads and outroads built into the self-contained western province. Sichuan is shown as more than just a province; it is a state of mind that exemplifies all aspects of the Chinese tradition from which Guo wishes to escape. By the time he leaves Sichuan he too is corrupted—he drinks, plays mahjong, and in general is known as a rascal (*danshen*) [I, 297].[21]

Guo Moruo leaves Sichuan in 1913, when he is twenty-one years old. The essay "Chuqu Kuimen" was written in 1936, seven years after the other parts of this volume. By this time Guo has become a "revolutionary" writer. His picturesque description of the conflict between the green and the red waters, where the red conquers and completely submerges the green, is usually interpreted as a metaphor for the eventual victory of the Communist revolution. His expressed fear that he cannot make it through the gorge indicates the metaphysical trip out of the mental state labeled "Sichuan" as well as the transition to a revolutionary writer (and person). Nothing prepares Guo for the sight of foreign war boats docked on the river and for the Chinese passivity and failure to oust them [I, 312]. He recalls his desolation at the small mountains and bleak scenery of the cradle of China's ancient civilization and utilizes images of moving corpses and marching tombs to reveal his disillusionment with the "China" he has constructed [I, 314]. However, Guo's excursion from Sichuan into outer China turns out to be a failure and a disappointment in every respect: school is boring, he is humiliated by his lack of knowledge of English, and he does not have enough money. His supreme embarrassment occurs when he is asked to write an essay on the topic of "Total and Unit," and he does not even recognize the mysteriously transliterated words *tuodu* and *moro* that signify total and unit [I, 318].[22]

By the time he leaves Tianjin for Beijing and eventually Japan, Guo has written to a friend: "Tianjin's total cannot hold all the units of other places" [I, 321]. In his articulation of the world into discrete units, Guo positions himself either inside or outside any given unit. The largest unit in the text, which forms the totality from which the author is escaping, is "China," an historical, national, cultural, and racial entity that functions purely as a conceptual unit. Other units such as "Sichuan," "student," or "soldier" and some abstractions such as "poverty" or "humiliation" are all contained in this past. The eventual departure from both China and "China" stipulates an interaction with another physical and conceptual entity indicated in the foreign ships Guo sees and actually initiated in the last sketch in this volume.[23]

By the time Guo began writing his autobiography, he already had knowledge of nations and customs outside "China" and China. Guo's narrative delineates the self as separate from and rejecting most of "China." This rejection occurs several times throughout Guo's autobiography; in the first volumes his deliberate construction of inauthentic education, immoral military, and repressive social mores form the foundation for his flight away from "China."

Passing very quickly through the rest of his time in "outer" China, Guo Moruo finds himself in a difficult position: "Shijie zuinan dezhe" (The most difficult thing to get in the world) (subtitled "Leyuan waide pingguo" [Apples outside of paradise]) is the title of the short section at the end of this volume which marks his departure from China. When he is traveling to Japan, Guo recalls his experiences on the train to Korea. A Japanese man, seeing Chinese people among the passengers, asks his friends to watch over his wife when he leaves. Guo gets his revenge when the woman supposedly flirts with him and offers him an apple. Obviously familiar with the story of Adam and Eve's expulsion from paradise, Guo Moruo applies it as an ironic metaphor for his own exit out of China and "China." The metaphor is apt: although he realizes his own humiliation in his rejection of "China," Guo writes that he is "too hungry" to resist—in other words his total repudiation of things Chinese has left him with little sustenance. Nonetheless, he is conscious enough of his position to garb "foreign" in the clothes of "woman attracted to him," effectively changing his defeat into an Ah Q-style victory over the weakest manifestation of the foreign entity.

Internalization of the Nation

At the end of the first volume of his autobiography, Guo leaves both China and "China." The second volume of his autobiography, *Xuesheng shidai* [Student days], contains three essays specified as autobiography, four essays called "autobiographical prose," and five essays "outside the collection." The three essays of autobiography are "Wode xuesheng shidai" [My student days], written in 1942, "Chuangzao shinian" [Ten years of the Creation Society], written in 1932, and "Chuangzao shinian xu" [Continuation of "Ten years of the Creation Society"], written in 1937. "Xuesheng shidai" is a short essay to bring readers up to date on the author's life from the end of the revolution to his participation in the Creation Society. The bulk of this volume is in the next two sections, which trace the author's involvement in the Creation Society, a group established by Guo Moruo and other writers who had studied together in Japan. The four essays of autobiographical prose are "Imazu jiyou" [Records of a trip to Imazu] (1922), "Shanzhong zaji" [Miscellaneous records in the mountains] (1925), "Lupan de qiangwei" [Roses by the roadside] (1925), and "Shuipingxian xia" [Below the waterline] (1927). "Shuipingxian xia" is an unfinished record of the author's trip to Yixing in Zhejiang to look into the effects of the warlords' battles. The five "works outside the collection" are short essays on various topics that were written between 1923 and 1936. These essays were included in the present volume in 1947.

On February 4, 1928, Guo wrote a postface to this collection (not including "works outside the collection"), stating that the volume is mixed and contains stories, sketches, travel notes, and essays. The collection is defined by history and, he claims, divided up by history: May 30, 1925, the day when British police in the Shanghai international settlement opened fire on students demonstrating on behalf of striking workers, divides his life into prerevolutionary and revolutionary stages. Thus many of the small incidents he writes about are only parts of his "private life," he tells us, and not truly significant [II, 403]. According to the author, the importance of this volume, therefore, is that it shows the road a member of the intelligentsia should be taking and also the changes one individual went through when he took this road [II, 404].

From the end of the last volume and increasingly in this text, participation in and description of politics occupy a significant position and come to represent an alternative to the role of the writer. At the same time, however, Guo portrays himself as pursuing his career as a writer, an occupation which seems to lock him within an already determined significance that he finds confining. His autobiography shows literary writing as negatively determined work with little social significance.[24] "Chuangzao shinian" and its continuation trace the author's involvement in the Creation Society and the many literary and personal feuds between its members and those of other literary groups, especially the Literary Research Society.

The essay begins in a defensive stance as Guo Moruo attempts to set the record straight in regards to the Shanghai literary scene. Lu Xun had published an essay called "Shanghai wenyi zhi yipie" [A glance at the literary scene in Shanghai], in which he criticizes the Creation Society and especially Guo Moruo, implying that they were "vandals" who failed at making money so decided to participate in the revolution [II, 25]. The attack on Guo's sincerity as a revolutionary writer is a serious blow to a writer who is attempting to define his work and self within the context of social activity, and Guo uses the next three or four hundred pages for self-defense and explanation.[25]

Guo Moruo expresses sensitivity about his national origin and defends himself against criticism from both foreigners and Chinese. His decision to stay in Japan for such a long time results in self-castigation as well as defense when in May 1918, after China signed an unfair treaty with Japan, many Chinese students left their studies in Japan in protest, returned to China, and branded those who decided to stay behind as traitors.[26] Guo defends his decision to stay on three accounts: one is that he has a wife in Japan whom he does not wish to leave (although his reluctance disappears in later years), and another is that he is economically unable to leave. Furthermore, he insists that returning to China would have little effect on the situation there. Guo claims that his patriotism is as profound as that of those who chose to return.[27]

In this volume which traces Guo's development into his literary and scholarly career, the contextual referents include the literary society (writing), patriotism (nationalism), a traitor, a corpse (death), rape (degradation), writing, and rejection. The rest of this volume further illustrates the author's ambivalence toward his profession. He vividly narrates his many attempts to conquer his leanings toward literature, which he describes as an unpatriotic and useless activity. As he is in the process of becoming a writer, Guo simultaneously denies the value of literature; like many who eventually became writers and others who took up other careers, Guo feels it is appropriate that students at the time were interested in science, which could modernize the country and build up its industry and technology [II, 56].[28]

Almost all of the criticisms of his work which Guo raises are directed at him as a literary figure.[29] That writing should be his career, or that he is forced to rely on his reputation as a writer in intellectual intercourse, is a source of constant shame. Taking money for writing causes Guo a great deal of grief [II, 93, 113, 197]. Although he rejects money as an equivalence for writing, he is incensed when he does not get paid for writing [II, 186].

At one point at the beginning of "Continuation," Guo creates a vision of the writer as a carrier of the disease of "hysteria," which may infect the entire race. In their ability to spew up the toxins, writers can benefit both themselves and the race [II, 171]. Writing is specifically determined in race and works as the process of spewing forth a sickness within a race, which will then result in a cure. Guo Moruo describes the Chinese as dejected, listless, mutually jealous, and cruel [II, 171] and compares a scene on the train, where Westerners sit grimly reading, Japanese discuss theoretical issues, and Chinese drink, eat, and play poker with prostitutes, to the humiliating international situation [II, 80]. At one point he even writes that he never wants to set foot on Chinese soil again—a sentence deleted from the four volumes published in 1978 in Beijing.[30]

Other than writing, which supposedly can cure many ills of the nation or race, another "medicine"—revolution—is also mentioned, yet left undeveloped at this point [II, 171]. Guo points out that he wrote his translation of *Dr. Faustus* on Japanese paper and cannot accept the fact that he has to publish his classical studies in Japan because the Chinese press will not publish them. The humiliation heaped on citizens of a poor, powerless country, especially those studying in the relatively wealthy and imperialist Japan, is well documented in the literature of the May Fourth Era. In Yu Dafu's story "Chenlun" [Sinking], for example, the protagonist is plagued by the fear that the Japanese schoolgirls he sees on the street are laughing at him. Guo's story "Canchun" [Withering spring], describes a Chinese student in Japan who attempts to commit suicide by leaping into the ocean that would take him back to China, yelling "Long live!" as he jumps. Ironically, within the autobiography Guo's sense of powerlessness and humiliation is increased by his inability to effect a difference between himself and his literary writing despite conscious attempts to do exactly that. Perception of writing and race as profoundly negative combine in Guo's portrayal of himself as powerless and degraded.

In "Chuangzao shinian xu" another form of redemption from the ill effects of literature is proposed in its redefinition as socially significant. After his reference to writers as the carriers of a racially determined disease of hysteria, and to the cure as a spewing forth of toxins in the form of writing, Guo Moruo proceeds to describe his attempts to establish his work as purveyor of socially relevant literature. When asked to speak at the Silkworm Lecture Institute in Hangzhou, he decides to talk on the topic of "The Social Mission of Literature"; he finds the hall well packed, but unfortunately, before he finishes, one-third of the audience has left [II, 177]. Despite this setback, Guo pursues his interest, translating texts from the social sciences at the same time as he writes short stories. However, his interest in art and involvement in literary societies continues, even though he alters his aesthetic ideology, recognizing the limited cultural basis of standards in beauty and art as opposed to the conception of art as an eternal essence. Guo sees that his activities in literary circles are inextricably bound up with petty quarrels and factionalism—political infighting is determining his artistic existence [II, 127, 254, 264]. Nonetheless, this knowledge does not enable Guo to extricate himself from factional struggles or to avoid discussions on the meaning of art, and he continues to feel anger when criticized by personages of the literary world.

Guo's renunciation of his study of biology coincides with a turning point in literary ideology, a shift away from a more subjective, personal approach to literature toward "socially relevant" literature and the social sciences [II, 84–85]. By reinscribing literary work as a type of scientific sociology and learning about the "science of literature," Guo places writing under the powerful validating sign of science [II, 203]. With literature defined as "science" rather than "art," Guo has redefined writing as an objective tool, complete with its own laws and rules, that can be used to observe reality. Although Guo relinquishes his study to become a biologist, he retains his scientific bent through this realignment of the literary and the material. Together, the definition of literature first as socially relevant and then as a scientific discipline proposes a potentially effective solution to Guo's negative inscription of literature as useless. By altering the context of referentiality Guo turns literature into part of the social and material world, realigning it with positive indicators of objectivity (science) and social action (revolution).

The failure of this radical redefinition, however, is expressed in the last pages of "Continuation" [II, 226–74], which is marked off from the rest of the text. The concerns in this part of the essay are almost exclusively literary, and Guo succinctly expresses his lack of faith in language and in the institution of literature in China.[31] And finally, language and writing are connected with disorder in general in a quote from Wu Zhihui, who said: "If literature does not die, great disorder will not cease" [II, 255]. Guo extends this quote into the ironic "a living literature gives rise to great disorder" [II, 255].

Like Lu Xun, Guo Moruo connects the problematics of race and nation to what he constructs as the powerless stance of the writer. Guo undergoes a contradictory struggle to establish a viable identity as a writer in an environment where the concurrence of historical and contemporary significations of writing do not allow a positive identification.[32] Like Shen Congwen and Lu Xun, Guo Moruo creates a paradox: he attempts to establish himself as a writer while denying that literary work is desirable or valuable on any level.

Guo Moruo repeatedly refers to the concept of curing, a metaphor common in discussions of "what is wrong with China." There are several "cures" for China's problems in this text: science, love [II, 131], capitalism, communism, and revolution. Guo and other writers who switch from the study of medicine to literary work to cure the spiritual ills of the nation attempt to add literature to the list of cures [II, 171]. Out of this effort comes the relevance of "revolutionary literature" as a means of realigning literature as a positive social force. Yet even as a cure, literature retains unpleasant aspects, appearing in Guo's autobiography as a vile substance, with the writer acting as a carrier of disease. The cure for the individual and the race, the spewing up of toxins in the form of writing, is an image in direct opposition to the traditional concept of the writer as purveyor of morality and of writing as a transmitter of morality (*wen yi zai dao*).

The remainder of Guo Moruo's *Xuesheng shidai* consists of a miscellaneous assortment of essays written at various times that range from half a page to fifty pages. Some of them relate to aspects of Guo's personal life, such as his philosophical description of his wife's pleasure in raising chickens in "Putishu xia" [Under the Bo tree] or his reflections in "Lupan de qiangwei" [Roses by the wayside], and others, such as "Imazu jiyou" [Record of a journey to Imazu], describe his experiences and impressions on trips. The longest, "Dao Yixing qu" [Going to Yixing], describes his trip to Yixing to investigate the damage done by warlord armies fighting in the area. It is unfinished, but the part that he did finish records his disillusionment with the Chinese as a race, and his identification of race and "national character" as categories through which social phenomena must be apprehended.

Although the area of Yixing is ravaged by war, and many of its inhabitants killed, Guo Moruo feels it is the fault of the people themselves: "I felt they themselves had looked for death. They had raised pigs, and the pigs had gone crazy and had bitten them to death; who could shed tears for them?" [II, 331–32]. Through numerous seemingly bizarre references to language and writing, Guo connects problems in literature and language to what he perceives as racial and national inadequacies. One example is Guo's discussion of an essay he wrote at the time entitled "Ruce" [To the toilet], or "coarsely speaking," "Meiyou saniao de jihui" [No chance to piss] [II, 352], sloughing off objections that words like "shit" or "piss" should not be used in literature. According to Guo, this taboo is an inconsistency among the Chinese, who would defecate on a public street but did not dare write about it. Guo's objection brings out the lack of correspondence between actual situations in society and their reference in literature, implying that literary standards are false and misleading if interpreted as reflecting life. Guo also points out that the people of Yixing like only to eat, drink, and gamble, but they do not like books [II, 362]. The library at Yixing is adorned with a sign written by the late president of Beijing University, Cai Yuanpei, but remains closed. Guo comments that Cai should have written "book coffin" (pronounced *tushu guan*) instead of "book hall" (also pronounced *tushu guan*, "library"). Despite his professed disdain for literature, Guo equates book learning with culture, and blames the people of Yixing for developing only their carnal desires and ignoring the advantages of study, which presumably would produce more cultured, less violent soldiers.

In 1928 Guo claimed that this volume was a motley group of essays organized by historical principles. Whereas this may be true, the text is also a thesis on the powerless position of the Chinese as a race and of literature as a social discourse within Chinese culture. Writing is toxin, riddles, and dead libraries, and race is soldiers, prostitutes, and the apathetic commoner. The writer's contradiction in self and work that results from the negatively inscribed categories of the literary and the national/racial is explored in the next volume of Guo's autobiography, as he increasingly recognizes that what he has constructed as the essential attributes of literary writing prevent him from developing a positive modern ideology of self and work.

Literary Authority

Volume three of Guo Moruo's autobiography, *Geming chunqiu* [Spring and autumn of the revolution], contains essays written from 1927 to 1948. The first, "Beifa tuci" [On the road of the Northern Expedition], was written in 1936, ten years after the expedition began. "Qing kan jinri zhi Jiang Jieshi" [Please take a look at the Chiang Kai-shek of today] and "Tuoli Jiang Jieshi yihou" [After taking leave of Chiang Kai-shek] were written in 1927, right after Guo Moruo left the expedition. "Haitao ji" [Collection of ocean billows] contains seven sections, written at various times from 1928 to 1948. "Gui qu lai" [Returning coming going] contains fourteen sections written from 1933 to 1937.[33] The last piece, "Ganyuan zuo paohui" [Volunteering to be cannon dust], is a "record in the form of a play" that was written in 1937.

In his introduction to "Beifa tuci," Guo Moruo complains that he falls short of writing true history because other than his weak memory, he has no materials [III, 2]. He claims personal participation in historical events as his motivation and justification for writing this text: "I feel I am qualified to write this story because I participated [in the Northern Expedition] from Canton [back] to Canton" [III, 2]. According to Guo, his presence for the duration of the expedition qualifies him to report it accurately.[34] After 1924 Guo became increasingly interested in revolutionary and proletarian literature and the social relevance of literary work. An early discussion of this change in direction is in "Xuesheng shidai," when the author speaks with Shen Hou [II, 131–33]. Shen Hou, who opposes individualism and the holiness of love, says to Guo: "Love desires to possess the other. It is selfish. This is in opposition to socialism and communism. . . . If you want to become a Communist, why do you advocate the holiness of love?" Guo relates his inability to answer the question and in this volume begins to view what he had previously viewed as problems unique to the Chinese race as social issues dependent on conditions that can be identified and corrected. That negative or positive perceptions of any race become functions of political, economic, and social conditions and are related, in the case of China, to oppression from other countries is acknowledged but not developed in "Xuesheng shidai."[35] In "Going to Yixing" Guo blames national problems on the inherent shortcomings of the people themselves, locating weakness not in the individual, but in the race. In *Geming chunqiu* the author gains a new perspective on issues of racial perception and literary production. However, the contradiction of a negatively inscribed writer against the inviting alternatives of a worker or active revolutionary does not disappear, but is intensified as Guo is unable to resolve the problem.

Guo Moruo's acceptance of revolutionary literature and of the writer's responsibility toward the revolution reorients questions of self and work. In "Xuesheng shidai" Guo embraces revolutionary literature as one possible "cure," both for the illnesses of China and for the limitations of literary work in China. The question that emerges in *Geming chunqiu*, however, is whether a revolutionary or progressively deterministic role is possible for literature in China. In this part of Guo's text, which deals directly with the definition of the writer and the status of writing, Guo repeatedly rejects literature and writing, opting for a role of active involvement through revolutionary work—a struggle that suggests skepticism about the ability of the writer to redefine writing and the writer so as to assume a positive social role.[36]

In his military work Guo finds that the intellectual can, to some extent, discard his textual role and participate actively in the military struggle or the revolution. But the fate of the writer after the revolution is the complication introduced in the last volume of his autobiography, where Guo Moruo attempts to construct a postrevolutionary "writer."

Position, Rank, and the Intellectual

In the third volume of his four-volume autobiography the author consistently refers to the obstacle of rank and title—"being an officer"—in his efforts to work for the revolution. Guo notes that when he runs into a friend at the train station in Pu Che, the friend calls him "Mr. K" [III, 25].[37] Shortly after this incident a political officer of the Fourth Army who used to be a student at Canton University calls him "Commander K." [III, 28]. Guo records the comment of a landlord at whose farm they stayed when he discovers that Guo is a university professor: "No wonder he is so refined!" [III, 62].

Guo refers to China as a country "built on the skeletons of 'warlordism' and 'bureaucratism'" [III, 70]. In his economy of intellectual worker/physical laborer, working as a soldier seems to be an honorable if unpleasant profession. Working as an officer, however, entangles Guo in a mesh of allusions to the elite position of and benefits that accrue to intellectuals. Furthermore, working as an officer appears to cast doubt on Guo's objectives, disparaging his true revolutionary impulses and conveying hints of improper incentives.[38] Guo criticizes the "comrades" participating in the revolution, alleging that only 30 percent are sincere while 70 percent just want to be officers [III, 117].[39] Guo insists he does not want to be an officer [III, 101], while his friends criticize him for being an officer rather than a writer. His reply is that he does not feel like writing and has decided to give up literature entirely [III, 186]. For one year he does not write anything at all.

In this first section of the third volume of his autobiography, Guo has given up literature and is establishing himself through military involvement. Nonetheless, two aspects of this new role disturb him. One is the prospect of inauthentic motivation; the other is the possibility of having expended his efforts in the wrong direction in his work for Chiang Kai-shek. Other than protesting, or taking the apparently unthinkable step of giving up his officer's title and joining the ranks as a common soldier, there is little Guo can do to defend himself against the first accusation. He can point to his future actions for the Communists to defend himself against the second. Several lines from his diary at the time are directly quoted; because of the proximity of the writing to its referent (Guo's ideas and emotions at the time), the diary can substantiate Guo's sincerity:

> The tragedy of revolution probably will have to occur. I always have the feeling of trying to do something great, but of having no strength. This time, the result may be that the fate of being a writer forever has been forced on me, but I want to oppose this to the end. The work of the revolution can be discarded, but the spirit of the revolution cannot. For me, the road is already clear; the only way is to resign. From beginning to end I have been a tool, but fortunately, a tool used on the right road. Of course, I was not sad or angry, and it seems I was too immature. Other comrades were even more immature, and watched for me to change, but I was too immature myself. Various fortunate and unfortunate coincidences have formed the present situation. It seems I already have been thrown out from the angry tides of revolution onto a barren island alone. [III, 163–64]

The decision to be a writer is constructed as an inevitable result of fate: as in the autobiographies of Hu Shi and Shen Congwen, an outside agent is forcing Guo to be a writer (or scholar), while the author has opposed it as vigorously as possible. At other points in the text Guo implies that others have forced his association with textual work despite his attempts to dislodge himself. For example, Deng Yanda insists that only Guo can do the work of censoring newspapers and handling other writing-related tasks in Hankou, so Guo has no choice but to go there and assume these responsibilities. Deng also tells him that the political section (which handles all propaganda in pamphlets, newspapers, plays, etc.) will collapse without him [III, 98]. Chiang Kai-shek wants to turn over all work that has anything to do with writing to Guo [III, 146], and Guo notes that Chiang specifically asks him about his work on a classical text he completed when he was in Japan. Guo persistently contextualizes his textual or literary work within a passive framework in which *others* play the role of teacher, forcing him to write. Thus he elaborates a defeat that comes not from his own inadequacies or his desire to perpetuate himself as a writer; fate and others force his surrender toward a seemingly irresistible channel of literary or proto-literary work.

Toward the end of "Tuoli," Guo describes himself as one who is "as if having been thrown out of the torrents of revolution onto a barren island alone" [III, 164]. He comments: "A person working in a group can forget every thing. The group's will is his own, like a huge furnace melting all individuals together in one piece. But when a spark shoots out on its own, it can only feel isolated and eventually will be extinguished. Isolation is the consciousness of the individual lifting its head. I became this spark" [III, 164]. In Guo's ideology revolutionary work represents submission to the will of the group and reliance on mass authority as opposed to individual consciousness and subjectivity. Intellectual work "throws" Guo out of partnership with the revolutionary group into isolation; eventually he sneaks into the international settlement in Shanghai to buy books from the imperialists [III, 190].

Alternatives

Shen Congwen sets military work in direct opposition to study in an educational institution and a life based on knowledge and understanding of material phenomena against the knowledge and understanding that comes from texts. In the end he returns to textual study as an observer rather than participant, with the new job of converting phenomena into text. Lu Xun wants to leave China and its textual and educational traditions and study medicine, which he initially theorizes as a cure for China's ills. Eventually he returns to China as a writer, implying recognition of Chinese social reality as the basis from which he will write. Guo too ascertains certain oppositional categories (such as military or revolutionary work) that he constructs against writing; in the final volume of his autobiography he develops ideologies that reclassify literary work as worthy social labor.

The first active alternative is developed in "Haitao" [Ocean billows]; with the exception of "Lihu zhiqian" [Before leaving Shanghai], all of the pieces in this section were written in 1947 or 1948. They cover the period of the author's life after he left the Northern Expedition in 1927. "Lihu zhiqian" is a diary that has daily entries from January 15 to February 23, 1927, a time when Guo was recovering from a bout with typhus. It includes a short introduction written in 1933. The last section of the book, "Gui qu lai," contains thirteen titled essays and a play. This collection was written from 1933 to 1937 and covers Guo's return to Japan and subsequent return to China in the thirties. "Haitao" is a narrative based on place; each title contains the name of a place and is the story of Guo Moruo's sojourn in that place. Much of it is a day-by-day account of the problems he encountered on his journey.

Immediately following the August 1 Revolution (1927), when Guo left Lushan, he agreed to take some messages from Zhang Fagui to the city of Nanchang.[40] Since at the time of this trip he did not do any writing, this account of his journey was written in Hong Kong in 1948. He portrays himself as the carrier of a message, a body working for the revolution rather than a mind observing and commenting. Guo revels in this separation from the restricting role of the intellectual. On a hand-pushed railway cart on the way to Tu Family Village (*Tujia zhuang*), Guo delights in his trip through the countryside in the company of the workers propelling the cart:

> This was true happiness! When we passed this line everything would be our own kingdom! The sun shone especially brightly, the southern winds blew with a special fragrance, the fields were an especially enchanting green. The two rows of rails shone with a silvery white light, as if they had readied themselves just for us; smoothly, without the slightest resistance, they took us towards the happy grounds of revolution.
>
> And our worker friends pushed with special vigor; we only saw the two sides of the forest unceasingly fly away behind us. The great land before our eyes was alive, everything was laughing, everything was running, everything was singing mightily in the long winds. Everyone was part of us, and on the cart there was nothing we did not talk about without the least bit of reservation. [III, 206]

The author recalls an exhilaration resulting from a sensuous appreciation of the sheer physicality of his circumstances. Because of his fine relationship with his "worker friends," who are doing the hard work of running the cart, he is able to animate his environment; all material phenomena are in empathy with his flight toward the "happy grounds of revolution." There are no references to the ambivalence of working as an officer or an intellectual, and he optimistically recalls the many times he has *escaped* death [III, 210, 213, 220]. The idealized, romantic affirmation of self and surroundings is created by the glory of working physically for the revolution. The intellectual writer has been replaced by a physical form engaged in critical social work.

Guo Moruo's new, positively engaged self and profession, however, is also short-lived. He maintains a good friendship with the workers, but he does not run the cart himself, and he retains the knowledge that he is not a soldier, but a scholar whom Chiang Kai-shek does not find worth killing [III, 220]. The happy beginning of "Haitao" quickly transforms into the passive, degraded figure of a writer and intellectual. Euphoria lasts through three sections, "Tujia zhuang," "Nanchang yiye" [One night at Nanchang], and "Liusha" [Flowing sands]. By the end of "Liusha," Guo Moruo comments on the peasants' recognition of his different, academic background. Although because of this recognition they are kinder to him than they would have been to a soldier, the possibility of developing a rapport without "the least bit of reservation" no longer exists.

The end of Guo's ideal interlude is foreshadowed when he is beaten by soldiers at Tu Family Station and loses his glasses. Later he falls into a large ditch because he cannot see and cannot function without the accoutrements of the intellectual. Finally he remarks that the one thing he has not lost is his red pen, what he calls "the best symbol of the intellectual" [III, 240]. He buys some simple clothes for two dollars and is transformed back into the insecure intellectual.

In "Spirit Springs" the briefly happy revolutionary worker is completely gone. As an intellectual, Guo worries about his value to the peasants and the revolution: "This old man was chairman of the peasant association, after all, and he was responsible and orderly in his work. But in my heart, I, on the other hand, felt a sense of terror. He had exhausted himself worrying about our safety, but after all, what were we worth? Were we worth their rescue?" [III, 248]. Guo relies on literary comparisons, remarking that the village setting could be from the vernacular novel *Shuihu zhuan* and complains that he has no books to read [III, 250–52]. As he mulls over his problems, it occurs to him that the answer to his query of place, work, and value is in his red-tipped pen, the only thing which he has not lost: "And the answer? Already it seemed vaguely to exist. In the tile kiln ruins of Yan Suan Liao, I had already lost everything that I had on me. The only thing remaining was a red Parker pen. Wasn't this a concrete answer in my unconsciousness?" [III, 253]. In his return to the helpless position of the writer, the only act of value Guo can accomplish for the old man and his relatives is to write out some calligraphy for them, and this art/writing, he laments, is worthless [III, 254].

Toward a New Writing

From this point on in this volume Guo abandons his struggle to find an authorizing realm for self and work outside letters. "Before Leaving Shanghai," written in 1928, is virtually a list of the books he is reading and the pieces he is writing.

Guo begins to read translations of foreign literature and social and economic theory, including Lenin's "The Party's Attitude Towards Religion" and parts of *Das Capital*. His efforts revolve around the reclassification of literature as a form of action that implies social significance. Guo decides literature can be forgiven for being unrevolutionary but not for being antirevolutionary. He develops an anti-essentialist theory that reaffirms his rejection of the so-called "eternal nature" of literature and attempts to take literature out of the category of the "arts" and recraft it as a form of political knowledge and ideology.

This project proves difficult, and Guo comes up with his most ingenious and damaging images for the writer and the writer's work in the process. Diarrhea, coal dust, and the sick writer, a person with a deathly white face and poor posture who belongs to a race that eats itself appear in this section [III, 262–65]. Four times, Guo compares writers as a group to a "race that eats its own flesh" [III, 253, 257, 262, 264], similar to the octupi he reads about in a children's magazine. Guo states that writers' practice of eating their own flesh accounts for the acidity of their urine and calls writers the "urine of cats" [III, 263–65]. In his January 29 diary entry Guo tries to convince himself that he is valuable to the revolution and does not need to be a worker to write proletarian literature. Also, he reasons, Marx and Engels had fled abroad as well, so his flight to Japan should not be permanently damaging to his individual integrity.

The essays "Kuazhe donghai" [Stepping across the eastern sea] and "Wo shi Zhongguoren" [I am Chinese] concern Guo's life in Japan after he fled China in the late twenties. When the Creation Society was shut down in 1929, Guo worked in classical research but found he could not publish his works in China; however, persecution by the Japanese police prompted his eventual return to China.

The last chapter of *Geming chunqiu* takes the paradoxical title of "Returning, Going, Coming."[41] The problem is one of perspective: what is the point from which one can identify a movement as returning? The story of the chicken provides a metaphor for the problem. Some of Guo's neighbors in Japan borrow a chicken, and when the hen is returned (to her

"native land" [III, 359]), the other chickens peck her. She loses her freedom and spends her days hiding in a soysauce barrel. Finally she disappears and then reappears, but by this time the family is no longer sure it is
the same chicken. The implied problem is Guo's future return to China: is
this act a type of returning, will he be "Chinese" like he was before, and
will the others in his homeland accept him?

"Langhua shiri" [Ten days of wave crests] is a diary of a vacation Guo
took with his family at a Japanese beach. Repeatedly, Guo refers to the
Chinese race and his own status as a member of this race. In a cafe he visits
he feels the waitress purposely turns up the radio so he can hear the words
"Manchuria . . . China . . . abnormal . . . imperial" [III, 371]. In the fourth
essay, "Yong" [Carbuncle], the author is relieved that his white corpuscles
can fight off a serious infection, and the ability to struggle is represented as
a racial and national quality: "Although I was Chinese, my corpuscles still
had the power to resist foreign enemies!" [III, 397].

In *Zhang Ziping zizhuan* [The autobiography of Zhang Ziping], published in 1933, Zhang Ziping tells of his happiness at his eventual success
in the examination to choose students to go abroad. Even though he had
to borrow money to go, Zhang felt like he must put up with anything in
order to leave and become a "freed bird" [98]. Like Guo Moruo in the
third volume of his text, Zhang Ziping is delighted to leave China, especially what these writers all show to be a burdensome and irrelevant
education. However, Zhang leaves China with a sense of responsibility
that implies a positive identification with the nation: "As I was leaving, I
turned and said: 'Motherland! I am leaving! I won't come back without
fame! I don't know when I will see you again!' " [102]. Upon his arrival in
Japan, Zhang is required to wait seven days until he can have a physical
examination. The doctors who eventually give him the physical have
unclean teeth and are dirty in appearance, causing him to remark that
"Japan's exterior is no better than ours!" When he asks a friend and
discovers that Japan boasts a developed army and navy, however, he
decides that Japan is indeed better than China [107]. Still, like Lu Xun,
who was dismayed by the sight of students sporting queues learning
ballroom dancing under cherry trees, Zhang initially feels that Japan is
not as different from China as his previous perception had caused him to
believe. However, although Zhang claims he felt he was from "Great
China" and regarded all things Japanese as "small," as the narrative
progresses he comes to see Japanese students as cleaner, Japanese girls as
more feminine, and Japanese society as more interesting and complex

than that of China [116, 125, 126]. As a Chinese student, Zhang was excluded from social integration; making little progress in his Japanese language ability, he wastes his precious study time by sitting in Chinese restaurants or walking in red light districts.

Zhang's intensifying attraction to Japanese society corresponds to a developing national and racial consciousness. Prejudice against Chinese students on the part of Japanese teachers and the general populace combines with Zhang's previous ideas of China's backwardness to make Zhang insecure of himself and his studies. Zhang's friend Cai wishes to resolve his own similar dilemma by returning to China and participating in the revolution, but for Zhang this is not a serious possibility [129].

Guo Moruo, Lu Xun, and Zhang Ziping conceptualize a "China" from which they escape, arriving in Japan becoming the victims of a beleaguered consciousness of racial and national inferiority. In Ba Jin's autobiography "China" is presented as an objective totality which becomes an intolerable burden and forces the author to move "out" to Shanghai and then to France. Life in France, however, is swallowed up by Ba Jin's almost obsessive attachment to books, first in study and then in the writing of fiction. In all cases the hoped-for relief underlying their flight from China is unrealized.

"Gui qu lai" is an essay on race, writing, and revolution. Guo makes the decision he has tried to make many times before: like the title of the play that ends this volume, he leaves his red Parker pen in Japan, "volunteers to be cannon dust," and goes back to the front lines in China [III, 429]. In the final volume of his autobiography, Guo resolves problems of self, work, value, literary writing, physical labor, and revolutionary participation on which his autobiography is an extended discourse.

Resolution

The subtitle of Guo Moruo's final volume of his autobiography, *Hongpo qu* [The song of rushing waves], is "Kangri zhanzheng huiyilu" [Memoirs from the Anti-Japanese War]. While in Hong Kong Guo Moruo wrote this volume for publication in the serial *Chating,* the supplement to the Huashang newspaper edited by Xia Yan. It consists of sixteen chapters, each of which is divided into six parts suitable for publication as a serial. As Guo adds in his 1950 postface, in November 1948 he left for the liberated areas, thus ending his autobiography after writing one month in advance to cover up his departure. By 1950 he writes that he feels separated from what he has written as if it were part of a "different world" [IV, 240]. Guo revised the memoirs again in 1958 for publication by Renmin chubanshe in Beijing. Although Guo lived until 1978, he did not make any more additions to his autobiography.[42]

The author again asks readers to read these memoirs as historical material, and they are the closest to pure memoir of all of the four volumes of the autobiography. The first 240 pages, also subtitled "Hongpo qu" [Song of rushing waves], cover the year 1938, when Guo had left Shanghai. As the Nationalist political apparatus moved inland, he made his way to Chongqing in his native province of Sichuan. "Hongpo qu" does not include his time in Chongqing. The name of the serial comes from a song written by Guo's friend Zhang Shu, who had worked with Guo in the political bureau of the Nationalist party. During one of the frequent bombings of Guilin, Zhang had argued with his wife; instead of taking shelter, he stayed outside with his daughter. Both were killed and Zhang's wife went insane, spending the rest of her days singing this song.

Guo's time in Chongqing is covered in "Shaoyao ji qita" [Peonies and other things], which was written in 1942, 1944, and 1945. Guo calls this selection "autobiographical prose." It does not cover his life systematically, but is a series of short essays on topics as diverse as peonies, motherly love, worms, and shadows. "Sulian jixing" [Records of a trip to the Soviet Union] is Guo's diary from his trip to the Soviet Union in the summer of 1945, when he was invited as a delegate to a memorial meeting for the 220th anniversary of the Soviet Academy of Sciences. "Nanjing yinxiang" [Impressions of Nanjing], written in 1936, records the time he spent in Nanjing and ends his autobiography.

At the end of 1927 Guo already is writing articles on his life as a writer and listing the influences in his work [III, 281]. By the time he writes these memoirs Guo Moruo is an accomplished and well-known writer and scholar. When he is invited to Russia, it is as an expert in Chinese literature and history. In "Hongpo qu" he focuses on returning and repeating; in "Shaoyao ji qita," with remembering, and in "Sulian jixing" and "Nanjing yinxiang," with physical, spiritual, and textual monuments.

Guo himself actualizes many returns in this volume, using the motifs of repetition and return to unify essays written at various times. As I have noted, the name of "Hongpo qu" comes from a song sung over and over by a woman crazed with grief [IV, 233–34]. The author's physical progress, from Japan to Shanghai and from Shanghai back to Chongqing, is a return to his native land and province. He abandons his wife and children in Japan, marries a young Chinese woman, and has four more children. Guo describes time as a perpetual return: "During the times when history is at a stand still for long times, it is as if some flowing water has left the main current; all it can do is swirl around and around" [IV, 6]. Guo identifies his own and his comrades' duty as breaking through this eternal return and preventing history from replaying itself again.

When he is grabbed by soldiers in Wuhan, Guo must use his old title and return to his old rank of assistant commander before the soldiers will let him go [IV, 15]. The Nationalist party is reestablishing its defunct political bureau and wants Guo to return to his old post of chairman. All of Guo's friends urge him to come back to work in the political bureau and going back to 26 Taihe Street "seems just like returning to my own home" [IV, 40]. When Guo returns to Changsha, he comments: "This is the place where Qu Yuan had wandered, the place where Jia Yi had sobbed, and the place where I had worked for a short time during the Northern Expedition: I had been separated for twenty years, and now I had returned again" [IV, 27]. Although he links himself to the romantic, misunderstood, patriotic writers/political figures of the past, Guo also identifies the locale as the place he worked during the Northern Expedition, a time when he experienced his most serious concerns about the function of a writer.

In *Geming chunqiu* the essays of "Returning, Going, Coming" indicate a confused perspective regarding the return. In this volume the predicament is resolved: "returning" means returning to one's native country and language. Although the problems of writing and the writer are still being argued and there are debates between the "art for art's sake" and the "art for life's sake" schools of art theory, Guo allows the issue to be decided for him at Yan'an, the "holy spot of liberated China" [IV, 238], in Mao Zedong's epoch-setting "Talks on Art and Literature." For Guo the seminal aspect of Mao's lecture is that he clarifies the function of art: "art takes the workers, peasants, and soldiers as its object" [IV, 167]. Mao's theoretical pronouncements provide a foundation for socially effective literary work, an issue that has plagued Guo throughout his autobiography. Writing is valid because it assists in promoting the interests of workers, peasants, and soldiers, removing the responsibility of definition from the author and the possibility of significance from the individual. The author's duty is to ascertain that through experience and practice, and despite his or her intellectual education, he/she understands the needs of these classes and possesses skills and techniques appropriate to a literary form which takes the "people" as its subject and object.

In "Sulian jixing" and "Nanjing yinxiang" the author discusses the human tendency toward the construction of monuments, both physical and ideological. Guo goes to Russia "with the spirit of the Tang monk going to get the scriptures" [IV, 317], monumentalizing the USSR as a repository of truth. This spiritual monumentalization of Russia as an ideal nation continues in the comments the author makes about every aspect of Russian life and people. The Russian people understand the human need for entertainment [IV, 390], Russian scholars freely show their materials to others [IV, 475], and the relations between parents and offspring are honest and warm [IV, 376]. Inequalities, such as the lack of women in government, are brushed away: "The way I looked at it, this was only a matter of time. The Soviet Union had been established as a nation just 27 or 28 years ago; if 27 or 28 more years went by, the situation would probably be different" [IV, 450]. Guo's itinerary is basically a visit to all of the monuments the Soviet Union has to offer: museums, factories, Tolstoy's house, research institutes, temples, the Writers' Union, the Pushkin Palace, and even its Chinese scholars—living monuments who speak in classical Chinese. A few lines from Guo's quoted entry into a guest book at Tolstoy's house reveal his tendency toward erecting monuments:

> I am like a bearer of gifts coming to an ivory tower; breathing in the quiet, solemn air that the great philosopher left behind, I recognized Tolstoy's lofty character even more concretely. Although his study, living room, and books all have been left behind in solitude, it is as if they all are telling me: "The master has just gone out, he is taking a walk in the woods just now!" . . . But at the same time, I even more concretely recognize the greatness of Lenin and Stalin. Their wise leadership has preserved the treasures of humanity for posterity. Everything is for the people. They have not only caused this superior cultural legacy to educate the people of their own country, but also to educate humanity. [IV, 484]

Everything is legacy—something left behind by death, but monuments are still alive in their ability to educate the people.[43]

China, by contrast, fares very poorly, and Guo's travels make him more conscious of China's poverty. When Guo arrives in Iran, he feels total desolation. The barren and destitute scenes of Iran cause him to wonder why one of the four great civilizations of the world has degenerated so [IV, 339]. But when he asks an Iranian servant, the answer is: what about China? Guo writes a poem to express his feelings, of which I quote the last stanza:

> My abilities are few, my responsibilities heavy,
> A naked man, an empty fist, who can drum up my courage?
> I am like a fish out of water, a bird in a cage.
> I mourn the culture of Parthia, already gone without a trace.
> But this recalls an echo: is not China the same?
> You who know shame must ask this question; where can you hide?
> [IV, 346–47]

Guo is obsessed with questions of nation, culture, and race and cannot stop thinking of his home [IV, 338]. Several times Guo compares China with Russia, each time pointing out China's deficiency. Relations between father and son are terrible in China, for each is like an "iron walnut," but in Russia a father will even ask his son if he agrees to the father's remarriage. The rites in an Islam temple in Russia are the same as those in China, but in China their artistic meaning has been lost [IV, 407]. Walking in a park, Guo cannot get over a feeling of melancholy for his country [IV, 412]. He asks himself why China could not be like the defenders of Stalingrad, who kept the invaders out [IV, 433]. Asked whether China has books for children, he can only reply that writers in China write only for their own glory, thus children's literature could not possibly exist [IV, 438].

When Guo visits Nanjing, he is concerned with physical monuments rather than spiritual edifices. He describes the buildings at length. He visits the place where Emperor Wu of the Liang died of hunger and the Great Hall of the People, the newest construction in Nanjing, where he has a meeting with government officials. He also visits the Historical Research Institute in the Central Research Institute [IV, 510–11].

Guo Moruo finds Nanjing oppressive and constantly feels the humiliation of the Chinese people in the basic order of things [IV, 567]. In China, Chinese buildings seem to "bow" to Western structures, and ironically, MacArthur, an American, is asking the Chinese to help keep peace in China [IV, 545]. The upside down arrangement of physical and spiritual relationships is illustrated by the tilt of the freedom bell, which looks up toward the skies, not down at the people [IV, 532].

In "Nanjing yinxiang," which marks the end of the autobiography, Guo loses his pen for good (Section 15: "A Lost Pen"). This is the pen, he points out, with which he wrote the play "Qu Yuan." Throughout the autobiography, and increasingly toward the end, are references to the poet and statesman of the state of Chu who drowned himself in melancholy, convinced he was a misunderstood patriot. In the future, Guo claims, the boundaries of his writing will be contained by Mao's Yan'an theories, making literary work relevant to the reality of the laboring classes and the writer's role dependent on the extent to which he or she can remold him or herself away from intellectual origins and toward identification with workers, peasants, and soldiers.

Although he loses his pen, Guo does not stop writing poems, and reference to poems as well as short essays appear in profusion in these last sections. However, some examples of the kind of writing Guo works on reveal a new context of referentiality. Before Guo leaves for Russia, he writes out forty-two pages of characters (calligraphy) that he has promised others [IV, 319]. He writes out and quotes in full his greetings to a meeting of the Soviet Academy of Sciences [IV, 362], and prepares other scholarly talks [IV, 390]. He writes poems in commemoration of his visit to a factory [IV, 415] and of his learning to eat rice with his hands [IV, 419]; he writes an essay, "Impressions of Soviet Russia" [IV, 434], a poem commemorating his visit to the Mayokovsky Museum [IV, 442], and makes a draft of his article "The Two Roads of Chinese Literature" [IV, 444] and leaves it in the Soviet Union as a memento. He says that he wrote a poem commemorating the loss of his pen [IV, 571].

This writing is mostly commemorative, descriptive or scholarly. After 1949 Guo Moruo assumed many roles, one as the star of the poetry of praise (*gesong wenxue*) who produced commemorative poems praising the leaders of China or some progressive aspect of life in China. The issues that consume Guo and other writers—writing, race, nation, and authority—are dealt with decisively in Yan'an, when the long-term effort to create a "new literary intelligentsia, open to revolutionary ideas but rooted in the culture of rural China" culminated in the party rectification that redefined the role of writing through "relatively clear and detailed guidelines . . . not only for the creation and propagation of literature and art, but also for the role of intellectuals—including the literary intelligentsia—in the revolution" [Judd, 389, 396]. Theoretically, the problem of the intellectual self was resolved as the issues of race, nationality, and literary work were determined. The "transformation of literature and art based neither on a changed political allegiance by writers and artists nor on a changed literary and artistic practice . . . but rather on a more fundamental change in their social position" that Mao proposed was not accomplished immediately [Judd, 399], but through a series of political and ideological movements that have continued up until the present. In almost all of the campaigns involving intellectuals of post-1949 China, literary figures have occupied important positions on both the offensive and defensive sides. In many movements "intellectual" and "literary" seemed to be nearly identical, and campaigns not only dealt with the issue of the intellectual's social position, but also with the intellectual's responsibility toward society in literary and other textual work.

For the May Fourth writers solutions to their negative inscription of literary work range from abandonment of any kind of textual work and immersion into the physical existence of a soldier or worker to the redefinition of literature as a form of knowledge and action both socially significant and materially accurate. The quest for a realist art form in the 1920s is one remedy, as critical realism at least in theory turned literature into a "reflection" of or comment on social conditions. Chinese socialist realism and Marxist literary theory intensified the bond between social reality and literary writing by allowing that literature could not only reflect society, but could also play a more deterministic role in influencing social directions and events. Although Mao's theories realize and conceptualize the problem of negative literary authority and provide "revolutionary" solutions, the solutions are undermined by insistence on a commemorative orientation for the new literature. Commemorization allows the writer only the role of identifying and applauding the achievements of policies established by the new political elite and denies them the opportunity for realignment with the socio-material world. Because Guo Moruo wrote the last part of his autobiography after the Yan'an Forum, he is the only writer investigated in this manuscript who was able to neatly solve the paradox of working as a writer while conceptualizing literary work adversely. The solution was redefining the writer as a commemorative agent of the new regime.[44] In this essentially conservative role Guo is one of the few May Fourth writers who was able to continue as a writer and critic in the People's Republic of China.

Conclusion

Writers and Modern China

In this conclusion I want to summarize my argument, analyze implications, and in the process address some compelling objections that readers and colleagues have directed at various parts of my manuscript.

In the early twentieth century writers experience a crisis in authority: they want to write, but both in their theoretical articles and autobiographies, express doubt about the ability of literature to influence social life. It should not be controversial to say that in the essays and autobiographies of Guo Moruo, Shen Congwen, Lu Xun, Hu Shi, and Ba Jin, confusion about and disbelief in the efficacy of literary works or textual scholarship to maintain a valid social function within Chinese society causes the authors to criticize and even overtly abandon textual work. As alternatives, the authors propose the more physical options of revolutionary work, military work, and manual labor, all of which appear more interesting simply because they are physical and more socially valid than textual work. Because the writers cannot seem to get away from writing, however, some of them eventually try to redefine it as closer to or part of material production; Guo Moruo, in particular, works and reworks the possibility of allowing literary writing a role first as an impetus to revolution and then as a producer of commemorative ideology.

However, despite their superficial demotion of textual work, writers not only continue to write, but also at some level privilege textual work over the alternatives they present. Hu Shi is a good example; even though he compares textual work unfavorably to Western science, he structures his own work on textual principles. Guo Moruo, Shen Congwen, and Hu

Shi all more or less show the motivation for their work as coming from others, and in the first two cases against their own desires. *Others* see writers as literary intellectuals and force them to engage in textual work; the implication is that without this pressure they would be free to be revolutionary soldiers. Even Lu Xun presents himself as forced out of medicine and into writing by his growing national and racial awareness. Ba Jin writes against his will and despite the effect of literary work on his health and happiness, and only because some friends made the "mistake" of thinking he would like to have his work published.

The structure that writers establish posits two alternative codes of existence. The first is a code of action: positive and socially effective, this code includes various kinds of productive, physical work. Science demands investigation of material phenomena and thus falls within the realm of this code. Revolutionary work, especially physical work as a soldier, and manual labor are both formulated as valuable and potentially progressive. The second is a code of the text: negative and of limited or no social value, this code includes literary writing and textual scholarship. Within military work the more intellectual endeavors of memo and report writing come closer to this code than do physical jobs such as running, riding horses, and using weapons. These codes, like the impressionistic and circumstantial autobiographies in the premodern tradition, are ideologically opposite poles and do not always represent concrete manifestations within society. In other words just because any one individual can participate in activities of both codes, that does not mean that the codes do not exist; they are discursive constructions that writers have formulated as two opposing poles but do not restrict actual activity to one area.

The first chapter of this manuscript is an ahistorical study of some autobiographies of premodern China, including the earliest texts of their kinds. I do not try to show any historical progression or discuss these texts as representative of Chinese autobiography. Rather, I am looking back from the modern period to attempt to locate a division of represented existence into something similar to the codes I find in the modern period. I do indeed find such a polarization, with texts that privilege reference to social and physical structures on one hand, and those that are organized around reference to a detached literati life-style on the other. However, there is no hierarchy between these poles, leading me to believe that although the opposition is not of modern origin, the debasement of textual work that occurs in the twentieth century is in part the construction of an ideology of modernity. When I examine the modern criticism of one early writer, Tao Yuanming, I find that some critics have latched onto Tao's promotion of a literati life-style. Through constitution of Tao's life-style as an escapism that tries to act as a substitute for depiction of actual peasant life, these critics appropriate Tao's writing and reputation as a negative value in their creation of a valid modern ideology. Increasingly, "modern" appears to indicate an antitextual, antiliterary orientation.

Some colleagues and readers have objected to the inclusion of the first chapter, stating that not only is it ahistorical and thus can tell us little about the development of concepts of textuality, but it also establishes a theoretical framework that is not entirely relevant to the rest of my argument. While I recognize that my discussion does not establish development, the existence of two poles of textual strategy, impressionistic and circumstantial, is very relevant to modern critics' construction of a discourse which establishes two codes, one of positive action, materiality, and social relevance and another of negative textual work. Although I cannot claim the dichotomy as developing out of Chinese philosophical discourse, my work on premodern autobiographies indicates that there exists a tradition of texts which utilize referential strategies that correspond to the division I find in modern texts. Even more importantly, the lack of a positive/negative polarization among these texts shows that the widespread demotion of textual work is basically a modern phenomenon, something I have linked to an ideology of modernity.

In the second chapter I evaluate the period preceding the May Fourth Movement and leading up to it. The single event that immediately struck me as most significant in influencing literary authority was the 1905 abolition of the examination system. In the years preceding this event the debate over Chinese learning intensified a much older discussion that centered on the textual and literary focus of the examination. Reformers saw the examination as maintaining a link between textual learning and political power that worked against the establishment of a new modernity. To them the study of classical texts had not prepared Chinese scholars for their work as politicians; knowledgeable on poetry and philosophy but ignorant about military affairs, economics, science and technology, and geography, political figures had to be cut free from definition through their grasp of literature and textual scholarship. By the late Qing and early Republican era writers could not make use of the impressionistic autobiography without implying a connection to the newly disgraced literary and philosophic traditions of the past. In other words only autobiographies which recognized social and material reality in its most concrete form (names, places, institutions, detailed physical description) could be called modern; only they could assist the writer in establishing himself as someone who was not, as Hu Shi put it, delving into piles of rotten paper, but was oriented toward a nontextual "outside."

In chapter 2 I also deal with one of the most difficult challenges to my thesis: if from 1925 to 1935 literary and textual work is reconstructed as negative, and this reconstruction actually begins much earlier, why do some of the most famous critics as early as 1898 depict literature in glorious terms, as the salvation of the nation and the repository of the beautiful and the good? Isn't there a great deal of evidence to suggest that literature, at least Western-style fiction, was actually being elevated in the early modern period? If literature becomes an anti-ideology, why do writers continue to write at all? Why don't they become workers, revolutionaries, scientists, economists, or soldiers? Don't we actually see the opposite, with writers leaving fields in the military (Shen Congwen and Guo Moruo) and medicine (Guo Moruo and Lu Xun) to become writers?

My defense contains several prongs. First, even though I maintain that literary writing and scholarship lost social validity as an indicator of status and moral value when the examinations were attacked and finally abolished, this situation cannot be extended to mean that writers and critics instantly despised literature or that literature and scholarship meant nothing to anyone. In pinpointing the abolition of the examinations as the structural break in a system that previously had aligned textual mastery with political power, I mark it as a time when conditions were right for radical change. Criticism of the examination content as superliterary actually began much earlier, but as long as the system was intact and the content of the examination basically the same, the relationship between textual work and political power was maintained. Thus although it is true that after 1898 writers and critics romanticize and exalt literature and promote its social and moral value, I regard this elevation as evidence that literature's structural stability is being demolished. As I briefly discuss, when the practice of literary sponsorship was discontinued in the West, literature was romanticized; in modern China, even though literature was similarly exalted, conditions unique to China prevented an uninterrupted upward climb. Late Qing criticism of the excessively literary nature of Chinese studies and the opposition of Chinese textual work (literature and scholarship) with Western industrial and military strength had cast a shadow over the possibility of establishing textual work as a modern ideology.

Evidence from writers' autobiographies shows that at some level male writers participate in constructing the decline of literature and textual studies, but this does not indicate their desire to totally discard textual work. In their articles writers may delineate a negative realm for textual work, but that does not prevent them from writing about literature. Although critics and writers may indicate that texts do not possess the power they did during the time when the examination was in effect, and even that immersion in texts is harmful, that does not mean they will abandon their work. Writers theorize the possibilities of doing away with literature and replacing it with "productive" work, but clearly literature and textual studies still have a strong residual authority. Doubts and contradictions do not amount to wholesale disavowal; no ideology is unified and completely in control. When Zhou Shuren quits study to be a doctor, takes up writing as Lu Xun, and describes his switch as a move to help save the nation, I must admit he is placing great hope in literature. However, his hopes lessen as time goes on, and after 1925 Lu Xun becomes cynically critical of the power of writing.

However, perhaps the answers to the above issues are best dealt with as questions. After I interpreted the abolition of the examination system as cutting the connection between mastery of texts and political power, I was sure something must have happened to the status, role, and function of literature. When I looked at writers' autobiographies and essays, I found that a radical change was indeed underway. To those who believe the elevation of literature that occurred after 1898 (and continues to occur in some circles today) indicates nothing but the elevation of literature, I would ask: how can you explain the attacks on textual work and the opposing of textual work against the plainly more attractive options of physical or social work?

Another question could be raised about the choice of texts and the method of textual analysis. Wouldn't it be more appropriate to emphasize critical and theoretical texts rather than autobiographies? Isn't it in essays and articles that writers and critics truly lay out their views about textual work and its function within Chinese society? While I believe all texts are valuable and should be utilized without reference to their disciplinary category, it is in the autobiographies that I gained the most convincing evidence of a contradiction of authority within the works of writers and scholars. Investigation into critical texts and historical sources provided further evidence. On the contrary, if a study such as this were to rely only on what writers and critics expressed directly in their essays—if (to simplistically misrepresent a more sociological approach) I were to collect "positive" comments about literature and line them up against "negative" comments—it would be possible to miss the depth of the contradiction. The autobiographies, most of which were written from 1925 to 1935, provide evidence that during this period doubts about textual work were increasing and attempts to establish valid alternatives were underway. Investigation into earlier essays convinced me that this tendency was not limited to this period, but merely intensified a previous trend which was well into the process of questioning the validity of textual work. Therefore, while Lu Xun's autobiography alone seems to establish very little, in conjunction with his essays which posit revolutionary work as an opposition category to literature, and within the context of criticism directed against textual work that developed through the late Qing into the 1930s, it is revealing.

As I was completing this research, I could not help but consider the question of what has happened to the status of textual work in contemporary Chinese society. Although that question is beyond the scope of this study, it may be worthwhile to discuss it briefly. Surely the image of the old-style literary *wenren*, ensconced in his study without any interest in the actual conditions of society, has been attacked over and over since the 1920s, both overtly in articles and essays and covertly in literary policy. Leftist efforts to make certain that writers "immerse themselves in life" (*shenru shenghuo*) were initiated in the 1930s and took concrete form in Maoist literary policy. In asking writers to go out and live with peasants, workers, and soldiers, and in training these groups to produce their own writers, Mao tried to modify the distance between literary intellectuals and "the people." Nonetheless, the opposing categories of workers, peasants, and soldiers against literary intellectuals basically has remained unaltered, with the former exalted and the latter periodically criticized and demeaned. Even though this may appear to indicate that writers still possessed a great deal of potential power and thus inspire fear in authorities, other issues have clouded the dichotomy between the two codes I discuss in this manuscript.

Since 1949 a group of scientists and other intellectuals—lawyers, doctors, technicians—has emerged, and such people cannot easily enter the ranks of workers, peasants, and soldiers. At the same time they are not literary intellectuals. The term "intellectual" (*zhishifenzi*) now includes these new-style intellectuals whose work is worlds away from the majority of premodern *wenren*. China's expanding connections with other countries have changed the meaning of literary work; the possibilities of Nobel Prizes, travel abroad, and increased financial benefits are all altering the way literature works. The fact that Mao saw intellectuals as a group that could not only promote its own interests but also conceivably could snatch away his power does indeed show that they had a role that potentially overstepped the bounds Mao had delineated for them. But the new definition of "intellectual," which replaced the earlier *wenren,* also indicates we are working with a different set of issues. In premodern times the term *wenren* most basically meant someone with some degree of mastery over a set corpus of texts; that person may also be employed as a government official and have knowledge and skills in other areas. Modern society has no equivalent term. "Intellectual" can include a wide range of people from writers to scientists to doctors, and includes women as well as men. While the contemporary status of writers and textual work cannot be dealt with summarily, the addition of these people to the group that previously was called *wenren* could be regarded as a dilution; what used to be a definition based on textual mastery is no longer so, but includes a broader type of knowledge. In the early twentieth century writers and critics attacked the image of a writer or scholar "locked away" in a study without knowledge of politics and social affairs. By the 1980s the image is so clearly negative that it is not an ideal to anyone. More than anything else, this change represents a fundamental alteration in the role, status, and function of textual work within Chinese society.

This research also leads one to ponder over the evolution of leftist literary theory in China and wonder how it would appear if it were viewed only as an attempt to solve the problem of a perceived overdetermined textuality in intellectual life. While there are many reasons for the adoption of Marxist literary theories that are related to politics, economics, and military affairs, from the perspective offered by this research there are also compelling reasons for its rapid entrenchment in Chinese intellectual life that stem from the perception of the negative role of textual work within the larger category of significant, important, and high-status work. If writers and critics perceived intellectual discourse as overly textualized, a literary policy that deemphasized texts and replaced it with an emphasis on "immersion" into life, "reflection" of social affairs, and a clear political stance would go a long ways toward correcting the bias. Working under these strictures, literature would become closer to a type of material production. Scholarship, recreated as research into class structures and social conditions as reflected in texts, would be a far cry from the delving into rotten piles of paper that *kaozheng* implied to Hu Shi and others. Literary intellectuals may never be true workers, but as the contemporary term *naoli laodongzhe* (brain-strength workers; opposed to *tili laodongzhe*, body-strength workers) implies, their social role could be similar to that of the worker: a producer of valuable goods. Thus whereas it may be impossible to say that elite perception of literary and scholarly work as negatively textual stipulated the adoption of Marxist literary ideology, this research makes it clear that without denying the complex origin and effect of literary policy, it solves a problem specific to Chinese intellectual discourse.

Notes

Introduction

1   "Authority" is a critical term in the fields of literature, psychology, political science, and sociology. In literature the question of who is speaking, as indicated in the title of Welch D. Everman's *Who Says This?: The Authority of the Author, the Discourse, and the Reader,* Carbondale and Edwardsville: Southern Illinois University Press, 1988, is central to the determination of the authority in the text. Many contemporary critical texts question the primacy of the author in creating a text, substituting instead the reader and the act of reading, language as a referential system of signs, or cultural literary history, which allows meaning through links between emerging and past forms. Other articles and books which discuss literary authority include "The Notion of Literature," Tzvetan Todorov, *New Literary History* 5 (Autumn 1973); Michel Foucault, "What is an Author?" in *Textual Strategies,* ed. Josue V. Harari, Ithaca: Cornell University Press, 141–60; *Roland Barthes,* Roland Barthes, trans. Richard Howard, New York: Hill and Wang, 1977. My working definition of literary authority is broadly social and historical, focusing on the ways in which writing and scholarship are constructed and perceived by those whose primary work is textual and on what allows the text and its creators to maintain the ability to speak within Chinese society at a specific time.

2   What is autobiography in terms of the Chinese literary tradition? Autobiography has not been considered a genre by Chinese scholars, but in the last twenty years Western sinologists have become interested in concepts of the self in China. A pioneering study on autobiography by Wu Pei-yi, which has answered many questions on the history and form of Chinese autobiography, was published in 1989. Wu discusses the difficulty of defining autobiography clearly; for convenience's sake rather than out of any pressing desire to demarcate the limits of Chinese autobiography, I have used the following guidelines in my choice of what premodern texts to consider:

   1. Texts called *zizhuan* (autobiography), *zixu* (autobiographic note), or *zishu* (self-narration).

2. Texts called *zhuan* (biographies) and written by the subject in question.

3. Any *zixu* (self-written preface) that deals mostly with the author's life or identity.

4. Texts written in the first person that deal clearly with the author's life or identity.

In studying premodern autobiographies, I have chosen only those at the extreme ends of two poles of authority, and thus I do not claim the texts I discuss are representative of Chinese autobiography in general. See also Wu's discussion of the types of autobiographies available in premodern China in *The Confucian's Progress: Autobiographical Writings in Traditional China*, Princeton University Press, 1989. Wu would also include texts written by the author about the author, whether in the first person or not.

3 Most of the modern autobiographies I have read were written and published during the 1925–35 period; Guo Moruo's four-volume autobiography, however, contains some essays written in the 1940s. Although I find signs in intellectual intercourse that literary work is perceived negatively much before this period, I believe it is during this time that writers begin in earnest to posit literature and the writer adversely against other more "worthwhile" activities and roles. As Guo Moruo's text indicates, theorization about the function of writing in society continues much beyond 1935 and is still an active topic in Chinese literary circles today.

4 The texts that follow this pattern are written by Chinese male writers of the May Fourth generation. Although I have not made a study of women writer's autobiographies, in the texts that I read I suspect that a preoccupation with the function of writing and the writer is partially replaced by concern with gender and with what the category of "female" indicated in relation to writing. Therefore I use the terms "he" and "his" to refer specifically to male Chinese writers who are generally intellectuals living and working in cities which provided an eclectic, Western-influenced intellectual environment.

5 It is a "fundamental tenet" of American New Criticism and Continental Deconstructive Criticism that literary language is "non-referential," meaning that it "can be understood neither as the representation of an hupostasized author's intention nor as the representation of an external and prior 'reality.'" See Walter Benn Michaels, "The Interpreter's Self: Peirce on the Cartesian 'Subject,'" in *Georgia Review* 31 (Summer 1977), 383–402; p. 383. However, all language is referential to a certain signifying context; it is this context in which I locate differences. The issue of what or which references determine meaning in a text is crucial to a discussion of authority.

6 Without looking very far, two well-known examples from literature come to mind. In Lu Xun's "Ah Q zhengzhuan" [The true story of Ah Q] the narrator finds that Chinese literature lacks the form or title to allow him to write a biography of a commoner whose existence has never been recorded in any form—such as family records or even jail records—on paper. Lu Xun begins this story with a humorous and ironic description of the narrator's search for a proper literary form and title, questioning the traditional bounds of literary expression and the limited context of signification that is associated with biography proper. Emphasizing the wide gulf between the common person and the text, Lu Xun allows Ah Q a textual existence—a circle that serves as his signature on his confession and death warrant—only when he is about to be executed. Another example is Yu Dafu's "Chenlun" (Sinking), in which the protagonist, a Chinese student studying in Japan, contrasts an appealing escape into the romanticism of books and the old-style study replete with classical volumes with the realities of dealing with racism and his own degraded existence.

7 For example, Joanna Handlin's work on Lu Kun discusses the "general late Ming shift to an experiential outlook, that acknowledged a world of objective phenomena . . . [suggesting] why writings about statecraft gained respectability and attention during the late sixteenth and early seventeenth centuries" [215] and calls attention to the contrast between the themes of "personal experience, daily effort, and actual fact" against "bookish learning" which characterizes the writing of Ming scholar Lu Weiqi [197–98]. Lu Kun also warned his friend Yang Dongming against "lecturing and empty talk" as opposed to "statecraft and practicality" [75]. Handlin and other scholars have cited numerous other examples showing the "marked shift of emphasis from speculative philosophy to statecraft," which "required changes both in how scholar-officials regarded themselves and in what they perceived to be the most important bonds tying society together" [20]. See Joanna Handlin, *Action in Late Ming Thought: The Reorientation of Lu K'un and Other Scholar-Officials*, Berkeley: University of California Press, 1983. There is ample historical evidence that a change in the identity of the scholar-official was taking place at least from the Ming on.

8 See "Wenyi zhi shehui de shiming" [The social mission of literature], in *Wenyi lunji* [On literature], Shanghai: Guanghua shuju, 1932, 50–51.

9 See *Hu Shi wenxuan* [Selections from Hu Shi's writings], Taipei: Yuandong tushu gongsi, 1968, 214–15.

10 My use of autobiography is similar to what Janet Varner Gunn calls "the cultural act of a self reading." In other words I am approaching autobiography as the author's cultural act of "reading" what the self (of a writer or scholar) is or should be. See Janet Varner Gunn, *Autobiography: Towards a Poetics of Experience,* Philadelphia: University of Pennsylvania Press, 1982, 8.

11 Here the second element of "peasant" (*nongren*) in the Maoist triad of "worker, peasant, soldier" (*gong nong bing*) is lacking. Writers do not seriously attempt to establish an alternative identity as peasants because, I believe, this gesture (as opposed to the actual act of becoming a real peasant) is seen as part of the impressionistic, premodern literary tradition in which a disenfranchised writer, scholar, or official "retires" to life on the farm. Thus for early modern writers the category of "scholar turned peasant" is soiled with the flavor of the old-style literati and cannot function as an alternative to the same tradition. In his article "The Changing Concept of the Recluse in Chinese Literature" (*Harvard Journal of Asiatic Studies* 24 [1962–63], 234–47), Li Chi makes it clear that the concept of "recluse" is exclusively reserved for intellectuals and functions as an alternative to official service for the upright official/scholar. "Retirement" often means "to retire and engage in writing" [240] or to "indulge a love of natural scenery and poetry" [245], and although early recluses retired to a difficult life in the mountains, later adherents could retire to luxurious estates at the edge of the city or even remain in town and become "recluses in society" [241]. Mao Zedong later tried to recoup the value of the peasant role as an alternative to textual labor by insisting on more than a gesture from intellectuals; he asked them to participate in peasant labor and live as a peasant on an equal basis, as much as this was possible. For an example of the modern apprehension of the recluse tradition as a misleading and misrepresented aspect of traditional literati behavior, see *Wenxin*, by Ye Shaojun and Xia Mianzun (Shanghai: Kaiming shudian, 1933), which is discussed in chapters 1 and 3 of this book.

The category of "revolutionary" becomes, after 1949, an abstract concept which can be associated with or denied to the other categories.

12 Although both Lu Xun and Guo Moruo show similar concerns with textual work, they are recast as Communist heroes after 1949.

1 Referentiality and Authority

1 Other than Wu Pei-yi's book *The Confucian's Progress: Autobiographical Writings in Traditional China,* Princeton: Princeton University Press, 1989, other short texts include Yves Hervouet, "L'autobiographie dans la Chine traditionelle," in *Etudes d'Histoire et de Littérature chinoises offertes au Professeur Jaroslav Prusek,* Bibliothèque de l'Institut des Hautes Etudes Chinoises, vol. 24, Paris, 1976, 107–43; Robert L. Taylor, "The Centered Self: Religious Autobiography in the Neo-Confucian Tradition," *History of Religions* 17, nos. 3–4 (1978), 266–81; Stephen W. Durrant, "Self as the Intersection of Traditions: The Autobiographical Writings of Ssu-ma Ch'ien," *Journal of the American Oriental Society* 106, no. 1 (1986); Wolfgang Bauer, "Icherleven und Autobiographie in Alteren China," *Heidelberger Jahrbucher* 8 (1964), 12–40.

2 Here, the "context of referentiality" is the social, literary, or physical reality to which the word, sentence, or text refers. For example, the sentence "My father was a magistrate in the seventh district in Luoyang" contains referents to kinship relations and official position and situates the speaker in a relationship not only to his father, but also to social structures and institutions that indicate a powerful and wealthy status. Furthermore, the naming of an actual locale places the speaker within the realm of the "real," where names correspond to common usage and are part of an easily identifiable matrix of references to places. The "type of referent" means the arena to which the referent belongs: social relationships, official status and position, literary persona, etc.

3 The terms which I use to designate the premodern intellectual—scholar, writer, official, intellectual—are all aspects of the *wenren,* which often is translated as "scholar-official," "writer-official," or "literatus." *Wenren* actually means "writing-person," with *wen* more commonly associated with literary writing but taking on different connotations in different eras. No term should obscure the fact that until the twentieth century, in theory and most often in practice, government officials in China were deemed qualified for office because of their mastery of a large number of literary and philosophic texts and their skill with the written language—a social reality sanctioned by the examination system. In the twentieth century, officials may or may not be well trained in classical traditions, but even those whose educational background may not equal their premodern counterparts often make efforts to publicly link themselves with "literary writing" as a discourse signifying intellectual prowess and political power by making their calligraphy available for institutional signs (such as Mao Zedong's inscription *Beijing daxue* for the gateway into Beijing University), by publishing pictures of themselves with ancient books, by writing poetry in the classical style, or by making it publicly known that they still read and study classical texts.

4 See Wu's book *The Confucian's Progress* for many translations and analyses of autobiographies that lie outside the scope of this study.

5 Wu Pei-yi points out that the form of these autobiographies was modeled after the biography. However, the referents are very different. See Wu, ibid., 16.

6   See *Lidai zishuzhuan wenchao* [Self-narratives and autobiographies throughout the ages], ed. Guo Dengfeng, Shanghai: Shangwu shuju, 1937, vols. 1 and 2. There are nineteen "autobiographies appended to texts" listed in this collection. Some of the more well-known include Wang Chong's *Lunheng ziji* [Self-written notes to the *Lunheng*], Liu Xie's *Wenxin diaolong xuzhi* [Preface to the *Wenxin diaolong*], and Ge Hong's *Baopuzi zishu* [Self-written postface to the *Baopuzi*]. Chapter 70 of the *Shiji* has been fully translated by Burton Watson; all translations quoted here are his and referred to by page numbers in his text. Translations of the other autobiographies in this chapter are mine; page numbers refer to the Guo Dengfeng volume.

7   See the account of this incident in Burton Watson, *Grand Historian of China*, New York: Columbia University Press, 1958, and Sima Qian's own explanation in his letter to Ren An, trans. James R. Hightower, in Cyril Birch, *Anthology of Chinese Literature from Early Times to the Fourteenth Century*, vol. 1, 95–102. Translations in this chapter are Watson's, with page references to his text.

8   In his article "The End of Autobiography," Michael Sprinker calls attention to Freud's reference to *The Interpretation of Dreams* as the text a reader curious about the author should look into and calls it Freud's "true autobiography" [336]. The characteristic features of both the dream and the text on dreams are "superimposition, contiguity, juxtaposition, repetition" [340], and the resistance Freud identifies within dreams exists in his text as well [342]. See *Autobiography: Essays Theoretical and Critical*, ed. James Olney, Princeton University Press, 1980, 321–42. In *The Interpretation of Dreams* Freud characterizes the dream as "suppressed ideas" [72] and "psychical acts of dissumulation" [142]. Freud discusses the means by which complicated intellectual operations take place in dreams—how statements are confirmed or ridiculed, for example. The authority of Sima Qian's textual creation of self is obtained through his temporal juxtaposition with his father and line of ancestors, and spatial juxtaposition with rites, sacred texts, and the appearance of the emperor. The author's textual self is produced by juxtaposition with the authority-giving symbol of the father, which is hierarchy defined spatially, temporally, or in terms of power. These hierarchical symbols are one of the attributes of biography which the impressionistic autobiographies suppress. See *The Interpretation of Dreams*, in *The Complete Works of Sigmund Freud*, vol. 4, trans. James Strachey, London: Hogarth Press, 1900. See also Stephen A. Shapiro, "The Dark Continent of Literature: Autobiography," in *Comparative Literary Studies*, no. 5 (1968), 421–54. Shapiro describes autobiography as primarily "an art of juxtaposed perspectives" [437]. He also identifies superimposition, one of the dream mechanics analyzed by Freud, as a method of producing meaning in autobiography [440–41].

9   According to Stephen W. Durrant: "There is little sense of individuality here, little assertion of uniqueness. Rather, the self is a point at which various strands from the past intersect: in Ssu-ma's case, a family tradition of caring for historical records, a filial obligation, a conservative Confucian and a series of historical precedents wherein his own experience finds an echo of meaning. . . . Ssu-ma defines his existence not in substance, some inner core of private and personal meaning, but in a series of relationships to a tradition." "Self as the Intersection of Traditions," 39.

10 In his discussion of transmission (*shu*), Stephen W. Durrant emphasizes that Sima Qian means as much "to follow" as to transmit, establishing himself firmly in a "conservative" tradition following Confucius. Ibid., 38.

11 Stephen Shapiro characterizes autobiography as a recreation of struggle: "Men who had always felt at peace with themselves and the world around them would have no need to write autobiographies." See "The Dark Continent of Literature," 448.

The circumstantial autobiographies have in common the attempt to regain or rectify some aspect of the self and its authority that has been lost. Hundreds of years after Sima Qian, Guo Moruo implicitly recognizes the opposition of the transmission of moral and historical teachings against the reputation of a defiled body in his fictional renditions of a discussion between Sima Qian and Ren Shaoqing, in which Sima Qian defends the *Shiji:* "These have been the crystals of scholarship and morality—politics, the classical teachings, ritual, and music—since there was China. As time goes on my corporeal body can die or be chopped into pieces, but I believe this life in me can never die." See Guo Moruo, "Sima Qian fafen" [Sima Qian gets angry], in *Guo Moruo wenji* [Selected writings of Guo Moruo], Shanghai: Chunming Shudian, 1949, 32.

12 See Li Changzhi, *Sima Qian zhi renge yu fengge* [The character and style of Sima Qian], Hong Kong: Taiping shuju, 1963, 104–6, 231–40. The preface was written in 1947. Li shows that Sima Qian did much more than write down his version of history; Sima took pains to give his own opinion and express his ideas on politics and philosophy. Sima also included all kinds of occurrences within his definition of history, even raising the status of the commoner through his accounts. Li also claims that Sima Qian went from "broadness" to "depth," writing history that may not have "included" everything but got to the "soul" of human behavior. My thanks to Steve Durrant for pointing out this book to me. In another critical work Zhou Hulin claims that Sima Qian anticipated the "historical method" of the West. See *Sima Qian yu qi shixue* [Sima Qian and his historical study], Taipei: Wenxhizhe chubanshe, 1978, 281–90.

13 Wang Shuwen, an official and Hanlin scholar under De Zong of the Tang. Wang was involved in the episode of 805, which was an attempt to wrest power from the emperor De Zong and place it in the hands of the heir apparent, Shun Zong, whom Wang had known for some time. Wang formed plans for the future government and organized a group of supporters that included Liu Yuxi. In 805 Shun Zong's health was poor, and Wang could not gain supporters in the military. Another faction succeeded in placing Xian Zong on the throne, and Wang was executed in 806. See *The Cambridge History of China,* ed. Denis Twitchett and John Fairbank, Cambridge: Cambridge University Press, 1979, vol. 3, 601–4.

14 The text is called an "autobiography" and thus referred to by future scholars. For example, see Huang Zhonglun in *Tao Yuanming zuopin yanjiu* [A study of Tao Yuanming's work], Taipei: Bomier shudian, 1975 (originally 1969), 256–57.

15 *Tao Yuanming,* in Guo Dengfeng, ed., *Lidai,* 247. This is my translation. For a slightly different version, see *Tao Yuanming ji,* ed. Lu Xinli, Zhonghua shuju, 1979, 175–76. Annotated and discussed by Huang Zhonglun, ibid. Huang points out that although Tao initially used the phrase "five willows," after his time it was used in poetry by many writers, such as Li Bo, Bo Juyi, and Wang Anshi [256]. Wu Pei-yi also translates the entire text [*The Confucian's Progress,* 14], and it is also partially translated by James Hightower in *Tao Ch'ien,* London: Clarendon Press, 1970, 4, and completely translated by A. R. Davis, *T'ao Yuan-ming (A.D. 365–427): His Works and Their Meaning,* 2 vols., Cambridge: Cambridge University Press, 1983, vol. 2, 208–9. Wu Pei-yi identifies

the reference to Qian Lou as a comment from a disciple of Confucius quoted in the *Lienü zhuan* [Biographies of virtuous women] [14; note 1].

Wu Huai and Ge Tian refer to legendary emperors:

Wu Huai and Ge Tian are the *hao* of two legendary emperors. Wu Huai ruled by high moral standards, and the customs and lifestyle he represented were admired by all.

His method of controlling the world was to preserve life by means of the Way, and to calm transgression by means of morality. At that time the people of the world willingly ate his food, and were happy with his customs; they lived peacefully and respected his lifestyle. In their behavior and hearts was no good or evil. They lived until they got old and died without social intercourse.

Ge Tian ruled with great confidence and few words: "Ge Tian ruled the earth. In a high and lofty place, he built the statue of his power, so he got Ge Tian as his *hao*. His method of governing was to have great confidence and use few words, to do little, but let things happen by themselves. He seemed to float around, and no one could give him a name." Both referents indicate great independence and personal freedom. See *Cihai*, Taipei: Zhonghua shuju, 1972, vol. 1, 1834; vol. 2, 2487.

16 See Xiao Wangqing, *Tao Yuanming piping* [A critique of Tao Yuanming], Hong Kong: Taiping shuju, 1963, 5; originally published by Shanghai: Kaiming shudian, 1947. See also Zhong Youmin, ibid., 131ff., both for acknowledgment of the tendency of premodern and modern critics to see Tao as a literary aesthete and for his disagreement with that stance. Zhong sees Tao continuing and strengthening a tradition of "farmer-gentleman poetry" and even breaking through old stereotypes to provide new impetus for the genre [132–33]. The aesthetic, isolating flavor of Tao's poetry comes, according to Zhong, from the times, which favored Buddhism and mystical thought (*xuanxue*) over Confucianism. Such ideas entered Tao's thinking and merged with his respect for agriculture, producing his field and garden poetry [134]. Unlike other modern critics, Zhong claims Tao's field and garden poetry does not so much create a pastoral ideology as accurately reflect the life-style of the literatus who has left an official post and retired to the countryside [138].

17 See Guo Bogong, *Geyong ziran de liang da shihao* [Two great poets who praise nature], Taipei: Shangwu yinshua guan, 1964, 18.

18 See Gao Dapeng, *Tao shi xinlun* [New discussions on Tao Yuanming's poetry], Taipei: Shibao wenhua chuban shiye youxian gongsi, 1981; in particular the first chapter, "Tao shi zai wenxueshi shang suo banyan de juese yu diwei" [The status of and role played by Tao Yuanming's poetry in the history of literature].

19 In view of the opinion of twentieth-century critics, it is ironic that what was traditionally most valued in Tao Yuanming's poetry was its ability to seem totally "natural" (*ziran*) or "real" (*zhen*). For example, Qing critic Fang Dongshu [1772–1851] says "in reading Mister Tao's poetry, one can grasp the reality of a situation: the situation is real, the scene is real, feelings are real, and thoughts are real." See his *Zhaomei zhan yan*, ed. Wang Shaoying, Beijing: Renmin chubanshe, 1961, 61, quoted and translated in Pauline Yu, *The Reading of Imagery in the Chinese Poetic Tradition*, Princeton: Princeton University Press, 1987, 143. Yu points out that "Tao in his most distinctive poems confines himself to the level of the individual—his retirement, farm, and family—and in the most casual of circumstances" [143]; as we see by my following discussion, what

twentieth-century writers criticize in Tao is that his presentation of "reality" is so limited and biased as to subvert any possibility of a different "reality"—that of an actual individual peasant or of a variant social level—appearing in his poems.

20   Huang Zhonglun interprets these lines to mean "He has no particular affinity with his countrymen, so he does not know where he is from; he has no desire for fame, so he does not tell us his name." *Tao Yuanming*, 256.

21   Hans H. Frankel calls attention to the fact that "the association of wine with literary creation was a well-established tradition in the T'ang period." In this article Frankel emphasizes the importance of skill with letters in representations of Tang literati. See "T'ang Literati," in *Confucian Personalities*, ed. Arthur F. Wright and Denis Twitchett, Palo Alto: Stanford University Press, 1962, 65–83.

22   The creation of a strong persona that can function as a counter-orthodoxy means that reference to the social codes of ancestry, kinship, and official position must be suppressed; there is essentially no way the author can establish an identity within the confines of time and space if he seeks to transcend its traditional manifestations. In his discussion of *The Confessions of St. Augustine* William Spengemann discusses the divine form which is the basis of this path-breaking and widely imitated confession: "Because the divine form is the absolute ground of reality, and is in no way contingent upon its material, historical content, it is sufficient in itself." This divine form then determines Augustine's conversion, which "does not occur in time or space" [14]. Thus Augustine's revolutionary autobiography is an attempt to "re-collect" the events of his past life into an eternal form [27] and avoid entrapment in time. See William Spengemann, *The Forms of Autobiography: Episodes in the History of a Literary Genre*, New Haven: Yale University Press, 1980, 10. If Tao Yuanming were to use conventional biographical references to time, place, and ancestry, he could hardly avoid definition within the official tradition.

23   Wu Pei-yi feels that Tao's choice of the biographical form alone caused him and his imitators to adopt "for the self a guise too narrowly designed. What they achieved is not a portrait but a pose; they conceal more of themselves than they reveal" [*The Confucian's Progress*, 19]. Within my analysis it is precisely the establishment of this "pose" that allows Tao to set up an alternative literary mode against the official biography.

24   Therefore, one of the main assumptions of Western autobiography, that there exists a "substantial soul or self [which] precedes and governs individual experience and [which] may be discerned through that experience," is not applicable in this type of text or about any concept of "self" represented in Chinese texts. This assumption about autobiography is pointed out by William C. Spengemann, Roy Pascal, Elizabeth Bruss, and others. Spengemann claims that this basis in autobiography, unconscious or otherwise, has "enabled historical autobiographers to explain, philosophical autobiographers to search for, and poetic autobiographers to express, the absolute self behind their conditioned actions. . . . But for those who have shaped Hawthorne's conclusion [in *The Scarlet Letter*], the self is continually reshaped by efforts to explain, discover, or express it, [and] autobiography in the Augustinian sense is no longer possible" [Spengemann, 1980:167]. The lack of correspondence to this essentializing expectation has caused some (Zheng Zhenduo, for example) to conclude that there are no true Chinese autobiographies. See also Eugenio Donato, "The Ruins of Memory: Archeological

Fragments and Textual Artifacts?" in *Modern Language Notes* 93, no. 4 (May 1978), especially the section entitled "Autobiography and the Problem of the Subject."

25 Zhong Youmin mentions, but does not agree with, this modern approach to Tao Yuanming; he chides twentieth-century critics for unconsciously taking up the pre-modern formulation of Tao as a literary aesthete who reads poetry, enjoys the scenery, and does no actual physical labor. See *Tao Yuanming lunji* [Essays on Tao Yuanming], Changsha: Hunan renmin chubanshe, 1981, 131.

26 It is redundant but necessary to point out that I am not evaluating Tao's work and neither "believe" nor "disbelieve" the critics' claims. Rather, I find in twentieth-century criticism on Tao a tendency to see him as super-literary, which critics interpret within the bipolarity of literary against social, and I am analyzing his work with this modern bent in mind. Within modern discourse Tao becomes not only too literary, but also negatively so. For a good introduction to modern and contemporary (as well as earlier) research on Tao Yuanming, see Zhong Youmin, ibid. However, Zhong only mentions positive comments, avoiding the criticism of Tao as detached from social reality that I discuss in this chapter. See also Gao Dapeng, *Tao shi xinlun*, chap. 3 "Tao shi pingjia de lishi fazhan" [The historical development of criticism on Tao Yuanming's poetry]. The best collection of criticism on Tao Yuanming, starting with the earliest works and including modern texts through 1977 (but excluding texts from the People's Republic of China) is *Tao Yuanming yanjiu* [Research on Tao Yuanming], edited by the editorial board of Jiusi congshu, Taipei: Jiusi congshu, 1977.

27 I could find no retheorizations of Sima Qian that depicted him negatively. The most complete modern study of Sima Qian, the previously quoted *Sima Qian de renge yu fengge* [The personality and style of Sima Qian] valorizes him.

28 A. R. Davis comments:

> In many of the poems which can be dated with certainty in this later period of his life he writes of farming and his personal participation in it. The actuality need not be doubted, though it would be foolish to think of him as a peasant. Nevertheless, almost all Tao's references to farming, like his references to poverty, have symbolic values. The recluse, having rejected 'riches and honour' had to embrace an opposite 'poverty and humble position.' A scholar-gentleman who cast away his natural career of public office might find many ancient precedents for demoting himself from the first rank in society to the second rank of a farmer. Yet however indigent a member of the gentry Tao was at any point in the last two decades of his life, he remained an intimate of the officials of Xunyang. . . . He had reached a point of detachment where in Yan Yanzhi's words he 'disregarded affairs.' [9]

Twentieth-century critics deny that the "symbolic value" of Tao's reference to farming should supersede the reality of peasant life.

29 Cao Juren, *Wensi* [Literary thoughts], Hong Kong: Chuangken chubanshe, 1956. Writing in 1935, Lu Xun points out that although Tao Yuanming was a recluse, he still had slaves who waited on him, gardened for him, and did business for him, "otherwise, this old gentleman would not have any wine to drink or food to eat" and "would have starved to death long ago." See *Qie jie ting zawen erji; yinshi*, January 25, 1935; quoted in *Lu Xun lun Zhongguo gudian wenxue* [Lu Xun on classical Chinese literature], Fujian: Fujian renmin chubanshe, 1979, 87. In *Tao Yuanming*, however, while author

Liao Zhongan claims that Tao's associates were literati or officials, he insists that Tao worked the fields himself, eventually becoming used to a life of hard labor. See *Tao Yuanming,* Shanghai: Zhonghua shuju, 1965, 33–41. In *Tao Yuanming pinglun* [A critique of Tao Yuanming], Li Chendong claims modern (1956) abandonment of Tao as a model for textbooks because intellectuals erroneously brand him as "negative"; the reasons for his negativity, however, are different. When he promotes Tao's ideas, he writes, his friends state that although Tao was "poor," he had land and houses; if they were to follow his road, resign their positions, and "retire" to the country, they would have neither. See *Tao Yuanming pinglun,* Taipei: Zhonghua wenhua chuban shiye weiyuanhui, 1956, 155–60.

30   Other modern and contemporary critics have wrestled with the problem of accurately depicting the work of Tao and other field and garden poets, sometimes recognizing the romanticization of farm life but regarding it as positive. Zheng Qian first delimits the field by making a reasonable and accurate definition of *tianyuan shiren* (field and garden poet), thus avoiding recognition of the contradiction between Tao's romanticization of farm life and the hardship of true peasant existence:

> If you want to clearly see the nature of the field and garden poet, first you must realize that the so-called field and garden poetry is not merely text that lets you get lost in the pleasure of praising nature or wondering at the scenery. Many people think this is what field and garden poetry is, and that field and garden poets are just recluses who pass their days peacefully and happily; that is incorrect, or at least it is a very narrow viewpoint. True field and garden poets not only describe the environment of the countryside, but also the lives of the farmers; they cannot only write of the happiness of plowing, but also of the difficulties of farm life. The most important thing is personal experience. . . . But if a person is born and grows up on the farm, gets old and dies on the farm, living there an entire lifetime without leaving his home, and other than studying and plowing does nothing, this person may be able to write a few poems, but he will not become a poet, because the content of his life is too simple and impoverished. . . . So in all of history, none of those who are called field and garden poets have finished their lives as old peasants working on the farm. Rather, it is that in a certain period of their lives, in part of their works, there is the flavor of fields and gardens. . . . According to what I have said above, we must agree that Tao Yuanming is a field and garden poet.

See "Tao Yuanming yu tianyuan shiren" [Tao Yuanming and the field and garden poets], in *Tao Yuanming yanjiu,* vol. 2, 397–408; p. 397. Zhu Qian approaches Tao from a different angle, finding that his main strong point is that he "everywhere is close to human feeling" and "does not sing lofty tunes," making him both revolutionary in the context of twentieth-century literature and classical to the tradition of the *Shijing.* See "Tao Yuanming," in *Tao Yuanming yanjiu,* vol. 2, 358–76; p. 371, first printed in 1948 in *Shilun* [Discussions on poetry], chap. 13. Along the same lines, Liang Qichao praises Tao for avoiding the trap of seeking after material goods that his contemporaries had fallen into. See *Tao Yuanming,* Shangwu yinshuguan, 1923; see also "Tao Yuanming zhi wenyi ji qi pinge" [The art and style of Tao Yuanming], in *Tao Yuanming yanjiu,* vol. 2, 266–81. In short, modern critics find good and bad things to say about Tao, but their criticism and praise generally points to his avoidance of discussion of actual peasant life.

31 Other examples of impressionistic autobiographies are *Miaode xiansheng zhuan* [The biography of Master Marvelous Virtue] by Yuan Can (?–477), *Wuxin zi zhuan* [The biography of the one without a heart/mind] by Wang Ji (?–644), *Buli xiansheng zhuan* [The biography of Master Buli] by Lu Guimeng (?–881), and *Wudou xiangsheng zhuan* [The biography of Master Five Ladles], also by Wang Ji. Many more examples can be found in *Lidai zishu zhuanwen chao*. Editor Guo Dengfeng groups autobiographies and prefaces according to the circumstances of their printing or according to the overall conception of the work:

1. Independent, separate, self-written prefaces (18 texts).
2. Self-written prefaces included in other works (19).
3. Autobiographies (12).
4. Self-composed epitaphs (12).
5. Self-narrations in the style of letters (16).
6. Self-narrations in the style of elegy or for worship, miscellaneous recollections, and self-narrations included in illustrated texts (16).
7. Self-narrated appeals, disputes, and eulogies (24).

According to A. R. Davis, Tao Yuanming's *Wuliu xiansheng zhuan* is the prototype for these autobiographies, and Tao's text was imitated not only in later autobiographies, but also in poetry. See Davis, *T'ao Yuan-ming*, vol. 2, 209. Wu Pei-yi reaffirms these comments (*The Confucian's Progress*, 16–19).

32 These characters are invoked for their symbolic value. Qian Lou was a poor man of the state of Qi during the Spring and Autumn era who was famous for his ability to think of ways to fend off enemies of the country. Despite entreaties from King Wei of Qi, he refused to serve as an official. Bo Yi was a man of the Shang who starved to death hiding out in the mountains when he refused to serve the Zhou rulers. Yan Yuan was the most famous student of Confucius; he died early. Rong Qiqi, of the Spring and Autumn era, responded to Confucius's question as to why he was so happy by saying he was human, male, and had lived to age ninety.

33 This distinction has little to do with literary *value* or *style* as conferred by critics; many have assigned a high rating to Sima Qian's *Shiji*. For example, Zeng Xiuqi not only praises the *Shiji* as a literary treasure, but also points out the absurdity of delineating "literature" from "history" or "philosophy" and emphasizes the fictionality of some of Sima's narrative:

> All Chinese classical books, whether history or philosophy, have something of a literary nature; in compiling history, Sima Qian relied on the facts of history and established himself as an authority. He wanted to create a history that was his own, and purposely added his individual opinions when compiling history. His ability to evaluate history was profound, and he has special skills in literature (*wenxue*). Sometimes he even used more fabrication than fact; in order to write well, he would reverse the proper order between reality and fabrication. So Sima Qian's great work is not only important scholarship, a great work of history that organizes ancient culture, but also has become a famous literary work. It is a work literary people must study, and has greatly influenced literary history.

See Zeng Xiuqi, *Sima Qian sixiang tantao* [On Sima Qian's thought], Bingdong, Taiwan: Meihe chubanshe, 1976, 54–55.

34 Even a cursory examination of *Honglou meng* reveals two contrasting codes: "official,"

signifying in different characters a combination of the qualities of responsible, socially engaged, outward-looking, corrupt, and self-effacing, and litterateur, signifying playful, socially unaware or operating within an extremely limited and clearly demarcated social framework (for Jia Baoyu, the garden), self-indulgent, and creative. Elite women have only the option of litterateur, feminizing the literary when it is detached from the official; Jia Baoyu maintains his super-literary life-style until the end of the novel, when he takes the examinations and marries Xue Baochai. While officials such as Jia Zheng, Baoyu's father, write poetry and have a circle of poet friends, they do not participate in the poetry clubs and competitions of Baoyu and his female friends.

35 Wu Pei-yi points out that by the fourth century, eremitism was a well-established alternative to the life of government service. *The Confucian's Progress,* 16.

36 Many readers may wonder why I have not broached the subject of the Confucian/ Daoist dichotomy, which would seem to provide a simple and widely accepted explanation for the two textual selves I discuss, with Sima Qian and Liu Yuxi choosing to specify themselves as Confucians immersed in affairs, and Tao Yuanming and Bo Juyi as Taoists to some extent withdrawn from society and more interested in aesthetics. Partially this is because I am looking backward, trying to locate examples of the isolation of literary work that would help to explain how the *wenren* could become a *negatively* divided figure in the twentieth century. Although the Confucian/Daoist polarization would provide a native ideological environment for that split, this model would fail to underscore the significance of what I call the literary code, which is what is implicated in the twentieth-century devaluing of literature and writers.

2 Autobiographies of the Late Qing Dynasty and Political Implication

1 Benjamin A. Elman comments that in state schools "little actual teaching took place," as these schools eventually were "absorbed into the examination system," becoming "waystations for students to prepare on their own for civil service examinations." "Education" prepared one for the examination, and the examination content reflected "education." See Benjamin A. Elman, "Imperial Politics and Confucian Societies in Late Imperial China: The Hanlin and Donglin Academies," *Modern China* 15, no. 4 (October 1989), 379–418; pp. 381–82.

2 Y. C. Wang comments, however, that many late Ming and early Qing scholars "were adept with their hands," and some, such as Yan Yuan (1635–1704) and Li Gong (1659–1733), "went so far as to denounce book-learning in favor of practical training." See *Chinese Intellectuals and the West, 1872–1949,* Chapel Hill: University of North Carolina Press, 1966, 34. Such advocacy was a minority viewpoint, however, with most literati debates contained within letters and theories of letters. Nonetheless, Wang's comment shows that some elites theorize education within a dichotomy that places book learning and textual work against practical training. This is not to deny that textual work then again breaks down into other categories, such as moral philosophy (Ted Huters's [1987] translation of *yili*) and evidential research (*kaozheng*), or *wen* and *bi.*

3 It may seem contradictory for Zhang to emphasize the *shi* and *fu,* but it must be noted that the earliest traditions of commentary on these poetic genres insisted that they were

specifically historical and political, and some scholars subscribed to this interpretation through the Qing. The beginning of changes in this kind of criticism, which had been associated with the *Shijing* [Book of poetry] and the *Chuci* [Songs of Chu], came with the poetry of Tao Yuanming, whose extremely personal poems, while still using images that were "plausible elements from an actually perceived scene" [170], often did not lend themselves well to political implication. See Pauline Yu, *The Reading of Imagery in the Chinese Poetic Tradition,* Princeton: Princeton University Press, 1987, chaps. 1–3. Donald Holzman, however, insists that "even in the bucolic poetry of the greatest poets of them all, Tao Yuanming and Xie Lingyun," there is evident "a concern for politics, a yearning for participation in the life of the court at the center of the civilized world." See *Poetry and Politics: The Life and Works of Juan Chi,* Cambridge: Cambridge University Press, 1976, 7. Pauline Yu also points out that "Tang poets like Chen Ziang and Bo Juyi implicitly or explicitly collapsed the terms *bi* [comparison] and *xing* [stimulus] into one simply denoting political critique . . . eliminating their roots in imagery altogether," but that later scholars rejected Bo Juyi's "emphasis on a political function for a focus on the effects of subtlety and evocative openendedness" [211]. The dilution of the political meaning associated with *shi* could have been instrumental in the eventual conceptualization of poetry and other kinds of writing as super-literary and socially irrelevant.

4   In the rules of a late Qing study society; "Changde mingda xuehua zhangcheng," *Xiangxue xinbao* (1897–98), Taipei: Hualian chubanshe, 1966, 339. Quoted in Frederic Wakeman, "The Price of Autonomy: Intellectuals in Ming and Ch'ing Politics," *Daedalus* (Winter 1972), 63.

5   Johnson's language formulates the issue of text as a category, but he does not elaborate on this theme. In his general discussion on the emergence of *kaozheng* scholarship in the Qing, *From Philosophy to Philology: Intellectual and Social Aspects of Change in Late Imperial China* (Council on East Asian Studies, Harvard University, 1984), Benjamin A. Elman refers to aspects of Qing *wenren* existence of some relevance here. His discussion of the institutionalization of evidential research in the eighteenth century provides a history of the work of scholars who did *kaozheng*, such as Hu Shi; with this background it is easy to see that twentieth-century criticism of *kaozheng* is one component of an attack on Chinese letters. Such criticism focused on the extremely textual referentiality—scholarship referring back to another text, which refers to another text—that characterized *kaozheng*. Elman also refers to Sakai Tadao's research on printing in the sixteenth and seventeenth centuries and the growing environment of readily available books, which produced a "book-oriented atmosphere conducive to the development of evidential scholarship and interest in the practical arts" (Elman, ibid., 142; Sakai Tadao, "Shindai koshogaku no genryu," *Rekishi kyoiku* 5, no. 11 (1957), 30–34; and Sakai, "Confucianisms and Popular Educational Works," in *Self and Society in Ming Thought,* ed. William T. deBary, New York: Columbia University Press, 1970). Elman writes that literati book collecting, which became a passion in the Qing, set the stage for evidential research [143] and discusses the growth of family libraries, which flourished through the joint efforts of scholar-bibliophiles. Elman's comments on the large collections in Canton which were built by merchants working in the opium trade [150] shows that book collecting was an indicator of elite cultural status and desired even by those who had little interest in the books themselves.

6   The presence of money does not alone indicate status, but it is worth noting that the

amount of money coins issued during the Qing went from 71,663,900 *wen* in 1644 to 685,390,000 *wen* in 1734, at least revealing the money = value formula which would be part of the increased status of money to which Ho P'ing-ti refers became more, rather than less, common. See Yang Ruiliu, *Qingdai huobi jinrong shigao* [The history of coins in the Qing dynasty], Beijing: Sanlian shudian, 1962, 6–9.

7 Mau-sang Ng comments on May Fourth intellectuals and their alienation from society: These intellectuals chose to dissociate themselves from the family, which they perceived as rotten; the government, which they criticized as corrupt and oppressive; and traditional ties, which they objected to as an improper method for advancement. In the wake of their enlightenment, many found that they did not belong to any class in society, but were simply "men of letters" without a proper profession, a situation which left them adrift in isolation.
See *The Russian Hero in Modern Chinese Fiction,* Hong Kong: Chinese University Press, and New York: State University of New York Press, 1988, 2.

8 See Ping Wen Kuo, *The Chinese System of Public Education,* New York: Teachers College, Columbia University, 1915, 98–99.

9 Huters's work has been published in two articles: "From Writing to Literature: The Development of Late Qing Theories of Prose," *Harvard Journal of Asiatic Studies* 47, no. 1 (1987), 51–96; and "A New Way of Writing: The Possibilities for Literature in Late Qing China, 1895–1908," *Modern China* 14, no. 3 (July 1988), 243–76.

10 This discussion takes place with reference to Yu Ying-shih's article, "Some Preliminary Observations on the Rise of Ch'ing Confucian Intellectualism," *Tsing Hua Journal of Chinese Studies,* n.s. 11, nos. 1–2 (December 1975).

11 Many studies in the West refer to the elevation of fiction that was common in the writings of late Qing and May Fourth writers, but few make note of the evidence against it. A summary of the "elevation theory" is conveniently provided by Mau-sang Ng: "Since the late Qing, fiction had been considered by such leading writers as Liang Qichao to be the most effective instrument of social reform. This inspired a body of 'social novels' which formed an important part of the late Qing reform culture. Fiction was elevated to even greater heights by May Fourth reform writers. They saw fiction as capable of reflecting the moral fabric of society as well as transforming collective human consciousness." *The Russian Hero,* 4. In the writing of Liang Qichao, literature, in its heightened state, represents what he believes literary writing has accomplished in the West and the road he thinks it should take in China. C. T. Hsia notes that many late Qing scholars felt the novel could be instrumental in national reform. Liang Qichao advocated the idealistic political novel, but was contemptuous of traditional Chinese fiction, even *Shuihu zhuan* and *Honglou meng.* See "Yen Fu and Liang Ch'i-ch'ao as Advocates of New Fiction," in *Chinese Approaches to Literature From Confucius to Liang Ch'i-ch'ao,* ed. Adelle Rickett, Princeton: Princeton University Press, 1978, 221–57. May Fourth scholars and intellectuals eventually recouped vernacular fiction as more "progressive" than other kinds of traditional literature.

12 Although Huters's studies alone do not bear out this conclusion, I find that even in Huters's analysis, questioning literature's power even as it is elevated takes place in the texts of the more reform-minded rather than the culturally or politically conservative writers. Lu Xun claims a negative stance for writing in relationship to society, and Wang Guowei establishes an opposition between literary work and political activity. This

suspicion about literature embedded within the texts of these writers would seem to indicate that despite continued elevation of writing among both groups, to some extent deification of literature as a spiritual repository is becoming a conservative ideology. In the late 1920s and early 1930s politically progressive writers abandoned a definition of literature as a spiritual and cultural repository in favor of a new formulation of social relevance, thus lending credence to this interpretation.

13   In an apology for literature that was first published in 1935, Zheng Nong refers to the call for the abolition of literature and the social sciences that has been heard "for a long time" from the mouths of "scholars." See Zheng Nong, *Wenxue wenda ji* [Questions and answers on literature], Shanghai: Shenghuo shudian, 1937, 3.

14   Rosenheim writes:

> All satire is not only an attack; it is an attack upon *discernible, historically authentic particulars.* The "dupes" or victims of punitive satire are not mere fictions. They, or the objects which they represent, must be, or have been, plainly existent in the world of reality; they must, that is, possess genuine historic identity. The reader must be capable of pointing to the world of reality, past or present, and identifying the individual or group, institution, custom, belief, or idea which is under attack by the satirist.

See Edward W. Rosenheim, Jr., *Swift and the Satirist's Art,* Chicago: University of Chicago Press, 1963, 25.

15   In *Wenxue xunkan* [Literary thrice-monthly], no. 5 (June 20, 1921), translated by Perry Link in *Revolutionary Literature in China: An Anthology,* ed. John Berninghausen and Theodore Huters, White Plains, N.Y.: M. E. Sharpe, 1976, 18–19.

16   In this discussion Williams contrasts the "public" with the "people," which is a philosophical characterization that establishes an ideal reader who is different from the popular masses. The "people," thus constituted, are "one of the primary sources of the idea of Culture" [34]. Despite the fact that May Fourth writers wrote for a small intellectual elite, they increasingly came to regard the nonintellectual people as both their audience and the proper subject of their writing. Williams also discusses the "fusing into the common 'sphere of imaginative truth' of the two separate *arts,* or skills, of poetry and painting," which began to occur around 1815 [40]. Although I cannot say when the term *wenyi* [literature and the arts] came into common use, it may be during the first twenty or thirty years of this century, which would indicate the creation of a new category that is both essentialized and looking toward the "people."

17   Examples of writers and critics asking for a literature that distinguishes itself from a supposedly more artistic and less relevant past model are profuse in the early twentieth century. One is Zheng Zhenduo's short call to a "literature of blood and tears," *Literary Thrice-Monthly,* no. 6 (June 30, 1921):

> Don't we now need a literature of blood and a literature of tears more than works which are "stately and graceful" or which "sing to the wind and moan to the moon"? . . . The gunfire at Wuchang, rifle muzzles on the passenger coaches at the Xiaogan railway station, the bloodstains outside the Xinhua gate . . . have we forgotten? . . .
>
> Yet there are those who can somehow manage it: they rattle on about pure art, plagiarize a few bits of new terminology, and continually turn out vernacular Man-

  darin Duck and Butterfly style love stories and sentimental poems. . . . Fires of the revolution, burn, burn! Fire of youth, go ahead and burn!
  Translated by Perry Link in *Revolutionary Literature in China*, 19.

18 "Concrete learning" (*shixue*) is a term that has indicated different things when used by different people. In scholarship it referred to the ideas of the Cheng-Zhu school of principle, which emphasized both theory and action. "Concrete learning" was a goal of the New Text and Tongcheng scholars, who stressed moral principles. See Elman, *From Philosophy to Philology*, 234 and 243. Here, the opposition is of textual learning that has no external referent against learning (also textual) that has an external referent or learning that has some practical application.

19 I do not mean to imply that because they attacked past traditions, modern intellectuals completely did away with them or totally overturned the epistemological basis of "Chinese" thought in their own writings or in society at large.

20 Bao Xiaotian, *Chuanyinglou huiyilyu*, Hong Kong: Dahua chubanshe, 1971, 135, 145. Quoted and translated in Leo Ou-fan Lee and Andrew Nathan, "The Beginnings of Mass Culture: Journalism and Fiction in the Late Ch'ing and Beyond," in *Popular Culture in Imperial China*, ed. Evelyn Rawski, Berkeley: University of California Press, 1985, 364.

21 Liu Xinhuang classifies Yi Shunding as a late Qing poet who writes poetry in the style of the "late middle Tang." See "Qingmo minchu de wentan shulun" [On the literary circles of the late Qing and early Republic], *Xiandai Zhongguo wenxue shihua* [On the history of modern Chinese literature], ed. Liu Xinhuang, Taipei: Zhengzhong shuju, 1971, 1. Liu also notes that those participating in reform movements in the late Qing classified their poetry as "new style poetry" (*xinti shi*), but according to "old style poets," this new poetry was actually an evolution from Song poetry. Liu analyzes the poetic and prosodic style and political ideology of new- and old-style poets and essay writers, making a case for the identification between style and political intent. See pages 1–9.

22 See Chow Tse-tsung, *The May Fourth Movement*, Cambridge: Harvard University Press, 1964, 64–72, for an introduction to Lin Shu and his translations. See also Rey Chow, "Mandarin Ducks and Butterflies: Toward a Rewriting of Modern Chinese Literary History," Ph.D. dissertation, Stanford University, 1986, 72–78, for a discussion of the way in which traditional Chinese notions of love, gender, and kinship were introduced into translations of European fiction.

23 Aside from his vitriolic opposition to the new literature movement, there are other reasons why Lin Shu was regarded as a "conservative." At the end of his study *Tongchengpai wenxueshi* [The history of the Tongcheng school of literature] (Hong Kong: Longmen shudian, 1975), Ye Long devotes twelve pages to proving that Lin Shu was not a devotee of the Tongcheng school of classical writing. There are many facets of his argument, including a discussion of Lin's refutation of some of the Tongcheng tenets and his own claim that he was not of that school. More interesting, however, is Ye's raising of Hu Shi's claim, in "Zhongguo wushi nian lai zhi wenxue" [The last fifty years of Chinese literature], that Lin Shu associated with Tongcheng people [300]. While Hu Shi is generous in his praise of Lin Shu as an innovator in translation and a man of some literary genius, he still situates him within a very conservative school of classical writing, illustrating his own separation of intellectuals into categories based on social links. Ye Long points out that even though Lin Shu raised the banner of classical

writing, like the promoters of the modern literature movement, he wrote and advocated novels [312]. See Hu Shi, *Wencun* [Collected writings], 14 vols., Taipei: Yuandong tushu gongfi, 1953, vol. 2, 194–200; also Zhang Ronghui, *Qingdai tongchengpai wenxue zhi yanjiu* [Research on the Tongcheng school of literature in the Qing dynasty], chap. 5, "Lin Shu zhi guwen lilun" [Lin Shu's theories on classical writing], Taipei: Guoli zhengzhi daxue yanjiusuo, 1965, 217–24.

24   The line is annotated in *Peiwen yunfu* as coming from *Cui Xinming zhuan* [The biography of Cui Xinming] in the *Tang shu*. The description relates an exchange between Zheng Shiyi and Cui Xinming, in which the former requests to see some of Cui's poetry, especially that with the line "Maple leaves fall, the Wu River is cold" [feng luo wujiang leng]. The exchange takes place while both are in boats on the river. When Zheng finishes looking at the poetry, he comments: "What I have read does not equal what I have seen." He throws the manuscript into the water, and rows away. See vol. 5, p. 3727.3. Lin also claims to live in an area with many maple trees. However, especially in the context of this text, it seems possible that the "cold-red" refers to Lin's relationship with women. Translations in this chapter are my own unless otherwise noted; page numbers refer to the Guo Dengfeng volume, *Lidai zishuzhuan wenchao*, Shanghai: Shangwu shuju, 1937.

25   Incident here is quite different from incident in, for example, Proust, where one perception or incident can lead into a set of unconscious relationships; this incident is isolated and leads nowhere except to Lin's translation of *La Dame aux Camélias*.

26   Yi, *Ku an zhuan*, in Guo Dengfeng, ed., *Lidai*, 334–35. Yi's text is only slightly longer than the average impressionistic text I have studied. The approximate length of the autobiographies analyzed in the first two chapters is as follows:

Tao Yuanming	170 characters	Sima Qian	8,250 characters
Bo Juyi	900 characters	Liu Yuxi	1,000 characters
Lin Shu	300 characters	Liang Qichao	2,500 characters
Yi Shunding	425 characters	Wang Tao	3,000 characters

The impressionistic autobiography is much shorter than the circumstantial autobiography.

27   This is not to say that a circumstantial autobiography could not be written by a conservative; in that case, although the content of the text may express the author's rejection of the "new" intellectual definition, the structure of the text would not indicate alliance with the "past" as a uniquely Chinese ideology.

28   Cohen, *Between Tradition and Modernity*, Cambridge: Harvard University Press, 1974. Hao Chang comments that Wang Tao did not belong to the elite group of gentry-literati and thus was a "marginal" man lacking traditional respectability in the Chinese intellectual world whose voice would be "not often heard." See *Liang Ch'i-ch'ao and Intellectual Transition in China, 1890–1907*, Cambridge: Harvard University Press, 1971, 4.

29   *Wanguo gongbao*, no. 43 (August 1892), 12–13. Quoted and translated by Cohen, ibid., 166. Like many other reformers who criticized the examination system, Wang constructs it as a useless ritual that encourages super-literary study at the expense of "practical" matters.

30   For a brief discussion of the charges against Wang Tao, see Cohen, ibid., 44–56. Cohen feels the case against Wang is not conclusive but suggests that Wang Tao, having failed

in the examination and been unable to gain an appointment in an official position, made a "full transition to rebellion" [56].

31 Wang's insistence that the ancients did not write autobiographies shows both the lack of an established concept of autobiography (even though, as Wu Pei-yi's work has shown, autobiographies are plentiful) and the strength of the taboo against admitting that one is writing about the self.

32 According to Cai Yizhong, the "road of literary creation" that Liang Qichao took was that of Sima Qian and the *Shiji* in gaining an eclectic mastery of *baguwen,* the scholarship of the previous dynasties, record writing, and Buddhist terminology, and combining these into a unique style of his own. See *Zhongguo jin sanbainian wenxue mingzhu pingjia* [Evaluation of famous literary works of the last three hundred years in China], Taipei: Kaifang shucheng, 1983, 99.

33 Philip C. Huang, *Liang Ch'i-ch'ao and Modern Chinese Liberalism,* chap. 5, Seattle: University of Washington Press, 1972.

34 Andrew J. Nathan comments that Max Weber's distinctions between specialized "bureaucrats, professional politicians, and other professionals" are not valid for Liang and some other intellectual figures in the late Qing and early Republic, because they combine elements from each category. See *Peking Politics, 1918–1923: Factionalism and the Failure of Constitutionalism,* Berkeley: University of California Press, 1976, 16, note 42.

35 Liang had formed the Minzhudang (Democratic party) in 1912 and in 1913 amalgated this party with the Gonghedang (Republican party) and the Tongyidang (United party) to form the Jinbudang (Progressive party). For a summary of the Jinbudang platform, see Joseph R. Levenson, *Liang Ch'i-ch'ao and the Mind of Modern China,* Cambridge: Harvard University Press, 1965, 174–76.

36 See Zheng Pengyuan, *Liang Qichao yu minguo zhengzhi* [Liang Qichao and Republican government], Taipei: Shihuo chubanshe, 1978, 5, 43.

37 Wu Pei-yi points out a revolution in time scale in an autobiography by a Chan monk of the thirteenth century, in which the author describes a meeting that lasted three days in six hundred characters—over the length of a traditional biography (*The Confucian's Progress,* 83). Wu attributes this innovation to the influence of theater, which was just beginning to "capture both popular claim and literary attention" [84], and on the Buddhist sermon, and he marks this moment in narrative as something which "made possible, perhaps for the first time in Chinese history, a baring of the inner self" [83]. Wu also discusses the effectiveness of poet Li Qingzhao in using "random and seemingly insignificant details" [66], which also can affect the sense of time. The nineteenth-century *Fusheng liuji* [Chapters from a floating life] also depicts a day-by-day narration, but it was not printed until the twentieth century.

38 It was Hu Shi's plan to write a series of autobiographies at ten-year intervals, and Guo Moruo wrote his autobiography over a period of twenty years.

39 See Guo Moruo's quotes from his diaries and Hu Shi's references to his diaries in chapters 3–5 of this book. The use of diaries in Guo's text differs greatly from its use in an autobiography like that of Thoreau. Lyndon Shanley, in a study of the many versions Thoreau wrote before he pieced together the "final" *Walden,* comments that Thoreau actually condensed seven or eight years of revisions and made use of materials that went back to journal entries from April 1839, six years before Thoreau lived at Walden Pond.

Whereas Thoreau takes materials from his journal and revises them into the final text, Guo quotes directly from his diaries, authorizing past apprehension over present interpretation. See Lyndon Shanley, *The Making of Walden*, Chicago: University of Chicago Press, 1957, especially chapter 1.

40 See Chang, *Liang Ch'i-ch'ao*, 307; also Huang, *Liang Ch'i-chao*, 164.

41 An autobiography which occupies a rather special, unrepresentative position in the Qing tradition is *Fusheng liuji* [Six chapters of a floating life], written around 1810 by Shen Fu. Now only four of the original six chapters are still extant, although all of the titles have been preserved. This autobiography has been discussed in detail by Milena Doleželová-Velingerová and Lubomír Doležel in their article "An Early Chinese Confessional Prose: Shen Fu's *Six Chapters of a Floating Life*," *T'oung Pao* 58 (1972), 137–60. The authors point out the difficulty of "determining the genre of Shen Fu's work and placing it in historical trends of Chinese literature" [139]. They also discuss the "suppression of family motifs" and construct a table to illustrate the organization of the text by mood.

  The authors define autobiography as a "systematic depiction of the author's or narrator's life story and his personality development," or a text in which the "authors attempt an objective depiction of their spiritual development, respect chronology in the arrangement of events and use a sober, purely referential language" [152–53]. This definition would exclude short texts such as *Wuliu xiansheng zhuan*, which also eschew family motifs and language referential to kinship as well as a chronology or a temporal and spatial authority. However, in some respects Shen Fu authorizes his text in the conventions of the impressionistic text, avoiding reference to the power-bestowing structures of the socio-material world and invoking poverty and writing instead.

3   Shen Congwen and Ba Jin: Literary Authority Against the "World"

1 To repeat a comment of the introduction, I have investigated male writers who work in treaty ports or large cities. I am not convinced that the same contradiction exists for women writers, whose major concern seems to be gender related, focusing on the question of what the two categories of "woman" and "writer" mean when placed together.

  Eventually the choice between literature and action was more directly formulated; when "revolutionary" writers tried to create a "revolutionary" literature in the early 1930s, critics such as Su Wen (Du Heng) asserted that literature and revolutionary action dominated totally incongruous spheres:

  If you are truly a progressive fighter, you would no longer want literature.

  For revolutionaries, revolution is the most important; the literature of revolutionaries can only be action, which cannot be literature.

Quoted in Li Helin, *Jin ershinian Zhongguo wenyi sichao lun*, Hong Kong: Shenghuo shudian, 1947, 160–61.

2 The evaluation of writers' perception of the status of literary writing and writers in modern China is made difficult not only by the problems discussed thus far, but also by the comparison of the standing of letters in Chinese society with that of other societies. I assert that letters go down in status in modern Chinese society, but that status relative to other societies may still be very high. American writers who visit contemporary China

are often struck by the stature of writers and literature; at the same time I have been told by many high school and university students in Beijing that anyone who can will study in the sciences rather than the humanities. Mastery of literary and philosophical texts is no longer the primary indicator of elite status.

3 In *Xiaoshuo yuebao* 19, no. 10 (October 28, 1928), translated by Yu-shih Chen in "From Guling to Tokyo," in *Revolutionary Literature in China: An Anthology,* ed. John Berninghausen and Theodore Huters, White Plains, N.Y.: M. E. Sharpe, 1976.

4 The abolition of the examination system does not mean that literary writing *had* to be demoted in status within Chinese society; if another equally as powerful authority had developed to take its place, it is conceivable that literature could have maintained a conceptually and functionally high position. But neither the Marxism of the Communist party nor the liberalism/capitalism of the Nationalists after they went to Taiwan developed a powerful literary ideology with a social structure like the examination system to support it. Although Mao's Marxism theoretically maintained writers in a valuable social role, it also undermined their prestige by insisting on varying amounts of nonliterary work necessary to keep writers and scholars on a revolutionary track.

5 Unless otherwise stipulated, page references are to the 1949 edition of *Shen Congwen zizhuan* published by Kaiming shudian. This reference is to an afterword to his autobiography written in 1980. See *Shen Congwen wenji,* Hong Kong: Joint Publishing, 1985, vol. 11, 76–78; p. 77.

6 Jeffrey C. Kinkley calls attention to this attraction: "Later Shen Congwen liked to call himself a country person, but really he loved nothing more than the manufacturing processes he observed in town, from the extraction of tung oil to fireworks production" [27]. Kinkley also notes Shen's affection for water, his boredom with old-style school, his desire to become a soldier, and his eventual disillusion with that life, tracing the historical progress of Shen's life with great detail. See *The Odyssey of Shen Congwen,* Palo Alto: Stanford University Press, 1987.

7 Nieh Hua-ling notes Shen's record of "the stench of rotting flesh" [27] in the autobiography. See *Shen Ts'ung-wen,* New York: Twayne Publishers, 1972.

8 Wu Pei-yi notes the suppression of the father in the autobiography of the monk De-qing (1546–1623) and in the other autobiographies. *The Confucian's Progress,* 146.

9 In a Ph.D. dissertation that evaluates the *wen-wu* conflict in the stories of Lao She, Chen Wei-ming notes that "No matter how strong and positive an academic is, in Lao She's stories, he never fares well" [44]. Also, on the 1934 story "The Prescription": "The story clearly suggests that works of literature and criticism are ineffective as aids to cure society's ills" [91]. In "The New Emile," published in 1936, literature is also blamed for not having contributed toward the progress of society [95]. See "Pen or Sword: The Wen-Wu Conflict in the Stories of Lao She (1899–1966)," Ph.D. dissertation, Stanford University, 1984.

10 As discussed in the second volume of Guo's autobiography, *Moruo zizhuan,* 49–50.

11 In traditional literature, literati usually do not engage in physical labor or excel in military pursuits. Many famous heroes of fiction would, by modern Chinese or Western standards, be considered effete; Jia Baoyu is an excellent example. However, the word "effete" assigns a negative value to a quality generally presented as positive in premodern texts. It is in modern texts, where the literary loses its authoritative power, that the bookish intellectual often appears as weak and ineffectual.

12   Leo Ou-fan Lee notes that in *Xiangxing sanji* [Random sketches on a trip to Hunan], Shen Congwen betrays "a certain degree of alienation from the very environment to which he was emotionally attached." Shen cannot exert a personal impact on his environment and "has become an essentially passive, though empathetic, observer—a recipient of sentiment and action." I would argue that by this time (Shen made his return trip to Hunan in 1934 after an absence of eighteen years), Shen's representation of self has become codified as textually determined or, in other words, alienated from the alternatives of military work (in the autobiography) or immersion into local affairs (in *Xiangxing sanji*). See Lee, *Lu Xun and His Legacy,* Berkeley: University of California Press, 1985, 296.

13   Both articles collected in *Shen Congwen wenji* [The works of Shen Congwen], Hong Kong: Joint Publishing, 1985, vol. 12, 128–35, 166–71. Zheng Nong (*Wenxue wenda ji,* Shanghai: Shenghuo shudian, 1937) criticizes Shen for promoting a philosophy of "random writing" that has no goal or stance, claiming that it results in an elite art for entertainment purposes only [10].

14   Translations are my own, and page numbers refer to the 1958 edition published by Huitong shudian in Hong Kong.

15   It must be noted that I am discussing Ba Jin's construction of self and work *within the text.*

16   Nathan K. Mao notes: "This close and warm contact with the servants continued all the time Ba Jin was growing up, liberating him from his elders' rigid prejudices and making him appreciative of the virtues of the poor. Having been impressed by generous hearts among the poor and downtrodden during his childhood, he later became their passionate defender." See *Pa Chin,* New York: Twayne Publishers, 1978, 17.

17   Nathan K. Mao reports that Ba Jin
     worked compulsively day and night but had doubts about the effectiveness of his work as a weapon which would effect social change. In 1933 he declared that his writing had little impact on the masses and only wasted his energy and life; in a short story called Guangming [Light] a writer, presumably Ba Jin himself, wonders aloud: "Writing books—what's the use? it can only bring sorrow to mankind." . . . In short, during his most productive period, Ba Jin was deeply disturbed by inner discord and a search for his true self. He was haunted by his call for action by others, while he himself remained inactive, and by his gradual awareness of his own inability to change things.

     See Mao, ibid., 28–29. Ba Jin himself expresses ambivalence [or modesty] about being a writer throughout his life; in a 1980 talk in Japan, Ba Jin comments on his status and motives for writing:

     I am not a writer, but I have been writing for over fifty years. Each person approaches literature from a different route. Ever since I was small I enjoyed reading novels, sometimes even forgoing sleep and forgetting to eat. But this was not for the purpose of study, it was just to while away the time. Even in my wildest dreams I would never have imagined myself becoming a writer. I started writing novels only to find a way out.

     See "Wenxue shenghuo wushinian" [Fifty years of a literary life], in *Chuangzuo huiyi lu* [Recollections of literary creation], Hong Kong: Joint Publishing, 1981, 1–10; p. 1. On page 9 Ba Jin repeats his denial: "I am not a writer, I look on writing as only one part of my life." In this introduction Ba Jin also recounts his inadvertent slip into the "literary circles" of the time when his friends published one of his stories without his agreement. See pages 2–3.

18   Leo Ou-fan Lee observes that Ai Wu considered his southern travel an education about society and life and an "initiation into the real world." Lee criticizes Ai Wu for his didacticism in his 1935 *Nanxing ji* [Travels to the south], and for presenting his experience not aesthetically and philosophically, as Shen Congwen does, but from a "sociopolitical" and didactic perspective, but points out that this "social schooling" turned Ai Wu into a committed leftist. See Lee, *Lu Xun,* 1985, 301.

19   A similar view is presented by Cao Juren in his 1956 *Wensi* [Literary thoughts] when he writes that China is a nation that "worships writing" and insists on adding writing to paintings as if "painters must make use of poets to make up for their lack." See Cao Juren, *Wensi,* Hong Kong: Chuangken chubanshe, 1956, 103.

20   The opposition has some resonance in contemporary Western criticism, such as in the comments of Harold Bloom:

> What I understand least about the current academy, and the current literary scene of criticism, is this lust for social enlightenment; this extraordinary and, I believe, mindless movement toward proclaiming our way out of all introspections, our way out of guilt and sorrow, by proclaiming that the poet is a slumlord. . . . This is clap-trap. . . . If they wish to alleviate the sufferings of the exploited classes, let them live up to their pretensions, let them abandon the academy and go out there and work politically and economically and in a humanitarian spirit. They are the hypocrites: the so-called Marxist critics, and all of this rabblement that follows them now in the academies. They are the charlatans, they are the self-deceivers and the deceivers of others.

Consider also the response of Frank Lentricchia:

> You know, I love Harold, but that statement is so far off the wall that I don't know how to begin to respond to it. The poet *might* be a slum-lord: it's possible. The critic *might* be a hireling. But the point is not that they are or they are not. The point is how the poet's identity as a poet is constituted: what it bears upon; what it hides and doesn't hide. . . . Now, the other point that Harold makes is that if these people were authentic and humane they would get into the streets. Does this mean that Harold is suggesting that all those who remain in the academy—including himself—are not humane, are "charlatans"?

See Imre Salusinszky, *Criticism in Society,* New York: Methuen, 1987, 66, 193–94.

21   Teng and others, including Qu Qiubai, felt that modern literature after the May Fourth movement was in danger of again becoming elite and conservative, falling behind cultural and political trends. In his article "Gao yanjiu wenxue de qingnian" [To young people who study literature], Qu urges writers to go out and experience all aspects of life and move their writing from "literary revolution" to "revolutionary literature." The article is published in *Zhongguo qingnian,* November 17, 1923, and discussed by Paul G. Pickowicz in *Marxist Literary Thought in China: The Influence of Qu Qiubai,* Berkeley: University of California Press, 1981, 75. Pickowicz also points out that by mid-1924, Qu's "interest in the literary movement and in saving China by 'cultural means' had all but vanished," leaving him engrossed in political activities [80]. For another discussion of Zhong Dengxia and others as the purveyors of revolutionary

literature, see Fudan daxue Zhongwenxi: Xiandai wenxuezu xuesheng [Chinese Department, Fudan University: students of the modern literature group], *Zhongguo
xiandai wenxue shi: 1919–1942,* Chinese Department, Fudan University, n.d.

22   Translated by Arif Dirlik and quoted in his *The Origins of Chinese Communism,*
Oxford University Press, 1989, 188. In chapter 8, "May Fourth Radicalism at a
Crossroads: Study Societies, Communes, and the Search for Social Revolution," Dirlik
traces the Communists' emergence from study groups and immersion into work within
political society.

4   Hu Shi and Lu Xun: Writing, Identity, and Race

1   Before 1905 Zhang Shizhao was a progressive political activist who participated in the
founding of the Huaxing hui and worked against the Manchu dynasty. After studying in
Japan, an experience which radicalized many of his comrades, he believed that only
educational, not political reform, could modernize China, and he refused to join the
Tongmeng hui. He studied Western history in Hong Kong and, after returning to China
in 1911, supported the establishment of a constitutional government. In May 1914
Zhang founded his famous magazine, *Jiayan zazhi* [Tiger magazine], where he expounded on constitutional government and other political issues. By 1921 chaos in the
Chinese military and political arenas caused Zhang to doubt the possibility of a true
representative government in China, and he eventually criticized the parliamentary
system as a Western import suitable for industrialized nations, but not for agricultural
nations like China. Zhang served as minister of education and minister of justice under
Duan Qirui but was repeatedly attacked by students for his opposition to new cultural
and literary movements. Zhang was known for his excellent classical Chinese. See
Howard Boorman, ed., *Biographical Dictionary of Republican China,* New York:
Columbia University Press, 1968, vol. 1, 105–9.

2   For a good summary of the day-by-day events, see Ouyang Fanhai, *Lu Xun de shu* [The
books of Lu Xun], Guangzhou: Lianying chubanshe, 1949, 297–308. Ouyang discusses the conflicts between the students of the Women's Higher Normal School and
Beijing authorities which developed in 1924 and continued through 1926. Zhang
Shizhao was widely opposed by students for using police to enforce new education
measures, including the reorganization of Beijing colleges under the ministry of education, which would conduct all matriculation examinations.

3   See Ouyang Fanhai, ibid., 326.

4   Quoted in Wu Ying, ed., *Lu Xun wenlun xuan* [Selections from Lu Xun's essays],
Nanning: Guangxi renmin chubanshe, 1985, 4–5.

5   Jane P. Tompkins notes the same development: "After the French Revolution the study
of sensibility for its own sake turns into an effort to show that poetry's power over the
feelings can bind men together by appealing to their deepest human sympathies.
Wordsworth emphasizes the moral benefits of poetry both as a force for human
brotherhood and as a civilizing agency" [216]. Tompkins also points out that Wordsworth, however, felt that "poetry must operate at the most profound level of human
experience, rather than dissipate its force on any particular social issue" [216], in effect
depoliticizing the power of literature and removing its ability to function as an indicator

of specific historical circumstances; Shelley held a similar conception of poetry as "ahistorical," neither "produced by nor responsive to finite historical circumstances" [217]. See Tompkins, *Reader-Response Criticism,* Baltimore: Johns Hopkins University Press, 1980.

6 Lu Xun's earliest article on literature is his 1908 "On the Power of Mara Poetry" (discussed in chap. 2 of this manuscript and by Theodore Huters [1988], in which Lu Xun writes about the decline of Chinese literature and his own conception of the literary voice as supremely powerful.

7 The essays are "Geming shidai de wenxue" [Literature in a time of revolution], "Geming wenxue" [Revolutionary literature], "Wenxue he chuhan" [Literature and sweat], and "Wenyi he geming" [Literature and arts and revolution]. All are contained in *Lu Xun quanji* [The complete works of Lu Xun], Beijing: Renmin wenxue chubanshe, 1963 (originally published in 1956 in the People's Republic of China; previously in 1938 and 1941 by Lu Xun quanji chubanshe), vol. 3.

8 Ouyang Fanhai is trying to construe Lu Xun's immersion into classical studies and his statement against thinking of the future positively as reactions showing his hatred of Duan Qirui and Zhang Zuolin. See Ouyang Fanhai, *Lu Xun de Shu,* 353. In a late Cultural Revolution discussion of Lu Xun's writing, the unnamed author(s) claim that "After Lu Xun arrived in Xiamen, he was very concerned about the progress of the revolution, and profoundly worried about the fate and future of the nation." See *Lu Xun zawen de shehui lishi beijing* [The social and historical background of Lu Xun's essays], Beijing: Renmin chubanshe, 1974, 30.

9 The translations are my own; page numbers refer to the 1948 edition of *Lu Xun quanji* [The complete works of Lu Xun] published by Lu Xun xiansheng jinian weiyuanhui. *Zhaohua xishi* has also been translated by Yang Xianyi and Gladys Yang as *Dawn Blossoms Plucked at Dusk,* Beijing: Foreign Languages Press, 1976.

10 In his anthropological study of history and culture in a Taiwanese town, P. Steven Sanger discusses "a kind of tribal-level epistemology" in which the god mediates the boundary between insiders and outsiders or order and disorder. The inside/outside dichotomy, along with the "nested hierarchy" which constructs order among insiders, is reproduced in the structures of the autobiographies of Lu Xun, Guo Moruo, and Zhang Ziping (see chapter 5). All three fluctuate between functioning as insider and outsider in different contexts (Sanger's context-dependent boundary) until they arrive in Japan, where their absolute status as outsider is confirmed. In these three texts the authors all locate the self (as opposed to the god) as the site of mediation between inside and outside, prompting reflections on the new insights their trip out of China has provided. Basically, their absolute outsider status in Japan causes them to reevaluate the absolutely inside position of race, culture, and nationality. See P. Steven Sanger, *History and Magical Power in a Chinese Community,* Palo Alto: Stanford University Press, 1987, 157–59.

11 See "Cong baicaoyuan dao sanwei shuwu" [From hundred-plant garden to three-flavor study], in *Lu Xun zuopin jiangjie* [Explanation and discussion of the works of Lu Xun] (contributors: Sun Zhongtian, Zhang Fen, Fan Yeben, Wu Tianlin, Xiao Xinru, Gao Changchun), Jilin: Renmin chubanshe, 1979, 1–17.

12 Leo Ou-fan Lee comments on the oppositional nature of this section of the autobiography:

A long essay of this collection, "From the Hundred-Plant Garden to the Three-Flavored Study," gives a lyrical evocation of the two worlds of his childhood—the playful and fanciful world of the great tradition, symbolized by the garden, and the uninspiring world of the great tradition, typified by his tutor's study. He dramatizes his own preference for the former by contrasting the boring reading matter assigned by his tutor with a delightful book that the illiterate nurse has brought him—an illustrated edition of the *Shanhai jing* (Classic of Mountains and Seas).
See *Voices from the Iron House: A Study of Lu Xun*, Bloomington: Indiana University Press, 1987, 5.

In another autobiography by a writer of this era, *Lu Yin zizhuan* [The autobiography of Lu Yin], Lu Yin succinctly describes the frustration of her early education. Because she refuses to memorize texts, her mother locks her in a room which the author characterizes as a "jail." When locked in this jail, Lu Yin's ability to learn worsens, and when she is released, she takes refuge not in human society, which is tainted by the attitudes of her relatives toward her as a "stupid thing," but in the garden behind her house, where she takes as her companions the "insects in the dirt" [9–11]. Later Lu Yin amazes her mother and other relatives by learning to write letters in vernacular Chinese.

13 Hirokawa Sukehiro comments that it is a Chinese medical practice to draw from a concept rather than a reality; he quotes medical researcher Sugita Genpaku, who claims that in classical medical texts Dutch drawings are accurate, but not Chinese drawings. See *Natsume Soseki*, Tokyo: Shinshoosha, 1976, 95. As with the example of learning from texts rather than the bugs of the garden, Lu Xun implies a challenge to learning without reference to an "outside" reality.

14 Hirokawa discusses the distaste of Japanese students studying in America who find they are often taken to be Chinese. See page 92.

15 The many possible nuances of meaning are discussed by Hirokawa Sukehiro in chapter 2 of his book *Natsume Soseki*. This translation is the one favored by Yang Xianyi and Gladys Yang. Hirokawa's discussion, which covers the various possibilities of meaning in the way this sentence has been translated into Japanese, emphasizes Lu Xun's presentation of Tokyo, with its dancing Chinese students, as ultimately not very different from what he supposedly had left behind.

16 This incident is often thought to have been "fabricated" by Lu Xun, who may have decided to switch his efforts to literature because of poor performance in medical school. Leo Ou-fan Lee points out that according to Lu Xun's two brothers, there is much in *Zhaohua xishi* that is not entirely accurate. See Lee, *Voices from the Iron House*, 7. See also Zhou Xiaoshou [Zuoren], *Lu Xun xiaoshuoli de renwu* [The characters in Lu Xun's novels], Shanghai: Shanghai chubanshe, 1944, 220.

17 Although I have been advised that the concept of "race" is foreign to the Chinese and is not an appropriate translation of *minzu*, neither is the term "nation" sufficient; Lu Xun and Guo Moruo emphasize first the group (people, customs) composed of those who are Chinese, and then the nation (place, customs) composed of these people and their material environment. The emerging concept of nation as state is also included in differing degrees in their use of the word *minzu*.

18 See Ozaki Hideo, "Rojin to Nihon" [Lu Xun and Japan], in *Rojin to Gendai* [Lu Xun and the modern era], ed. Sasaki Kiichi and Kakeuchi Minoru, Tokyo: Keisoo shoboo, 1968, 29.

19 Translations are my own. Page numbers refer to the 1969 edition published in Taipei.

20 Liang Shi'i (1869–1933) was a government official and financier who worked to develop banking and railroads during the Beiyang period. In 1911 he was appointed vice president of the Board of Communications under Yuan Shikai. Three warrants for his arrest were issued. The first, in 1916, named him as a principal instigator in the monarchical plot. The second, in 1922, was ordered by Xu Shichang, who held him responsible for the Zhili-Fengdian war. The third, in 1928 by the Nationalists, was for working with Zhang Zuolin in Beijing. See Boorman, *Biographical Dictionary*, vol. 2, 354–57.

21 While it would be inaccurate to say that Hu does not discuss the content of what he thinks "modern literature" should be, the main focus of his literary ideology is in language reform. In his 1922 "Wenxue geming yundong" [The literary revolution movement], for example, Hu concentrates almost exclusively on the national, historical, and international significance of promoting vernacular literature. See Hu Shi, *Hu Shi wenxuan* [Selections from Hu Shi's writings], Taipei: Yuandong tushu gongsi, 1968, 212–30. In his epoch-setting article "Wenxue gailiang quyi" [Suggestions for literary reform] of 1917, Hu expounds his famous "eight don'ts" for literary writing. His first demand is for content, which he defines as emotions and thought, in literature; this is a clear if somewhat amorphous statement in favor of a literature of content. His second "don't" is to avoid imitating the ancients, a comment which pertains to both content and form but in Hu's discussion seems to focus on form. The idea of literary form being historically specific is strengthened in "Lishi de wenxue guannian lun" [On the concept of historical literature], written a few months after "Suggestions for literary reform." The fourth "don't" is not to write about suffering when one does not suffer; this is also a part-form part-content issue. All of the remaining "don'ts" concern language use. See Hu Shi, "Wenxue gailiang quyi" [Suggestions for literary reform], in *Zhongguo xin wenxue yundong shi ziliao* [Materials on the history of the new literature movement in China], ed. Zhang Ruoying, Shanghai: Guangming shuju, 1936 (first published in 1934), 27–39.

22 See *Zhongguo xiandai wenxue shi, 1919–1942* [History of modern Chinese literature, 1919–1942], Shanghai: Chinese Department, Fudan University, n.d., 65–69. This work is undated but is clearly from the Cultural Revolution era. The writers depict Hu Shi as concerned only with form:

> Not only does he have an erroneous, reactionary understanding of the "literary revolution," but his explanation of the revolution of poetry is also quite absurd. He thinks that the "great liberation of poetry" and the difference between old and new poetry is only in the difference between their styles and forms. In writing new poetry, all one must do is break through the five or seven word form, destroy tonality, discard rhyme, and get to the point where "you can say what you want." He pays no attention to whether the words that one says are worth saying.

See page 66.

23 Hu's studies of *Shuihu zhuan* (1920) and *Honglou meng* (1921), which cleared up many problems in dating and authorship, created great interest in vernacular novels among young intellectuals. For a brief discussion about some of the early controversies over

Hu's work, see Zhao Cong, *Wusi wentan diandi* [Bits and pieces on May Fourth literary circles], Hong Kong: Youlian chubanshe, 1964, 18–21.

24   Benjamin Elman discusses Hu Shi's critique of *kaozheng* that blames scholars for their literary focus and promotes textual evidence over experimentation. Elman calls Hu's concerns "overstated"; I suggest that Hu's writings are not so much overstated as part of a general early twentieth-century attempt to reinscribe Chinese learning as super-literary, and negatively so. See Benjamin A. Elman, *From Philosophy to Philology*, Cambridge: Council on East Asian Studies, Harvard University, 1984, 83–84.

25   As I noted in the introduction, my desire to glean references to Hu as an overly textual scholar is for the purpose of relating these criticisms to my thesis on the increasingly negative description of textual work rather than for any illumination on Hu himself, who participated in many kinds of political and scholarly endeavors.

26   The *Shuijing zhu* was written by Li Daoyuan (d. 527).

5   Guo Moruo: "China" versus China

1   See Jaroslav Prušek, "Subjectivism and Individualism in Modern Chinese Literature," in *The Lyric and the Epic*, ed. Leo Ou-fan Lee, Bloomington: Indiana University Press, 1980.

2   This is not to say that completely circumstantial autobiographies did not exist in the premodern era. Rather, it was necessary that the writer who wanted to be perceived as modern avoid the impressionistic form, which depicted a now undesirable stance that implied detachment from social affairs.

3   Here Zheng identifies those who engage in evidential research [*kaozheng*] or organization of the national heritage, two areas of work promoted by Hu Shi. He feels such scholars are best left alone "buried in piles of old books" (*Wenxue wenda ji*, Shanghai: Shenghuo shudian, 1937, 22).

4   Zheng has two essays which specifically target two groups previously excluded from any serious participation in "the literary." The first is soldiers; he answers a soldier's letter about the world view a soldier should have. The second is married women, who give up study and devote themselves, mistakenly in Zheng's view, to serving their husband and children. However, Zheng places these essays at the end of his book, making them the final two essays out of twenty-eight and implying a subordinate relationship.

5   See Guo Moruo, "Wenyi jia de juewu" [The awakening of a litterateur], *Xin wenxue yundongshi ziliao* [Materials on the history of modern literature], ed. Zhang Ruoying, Shanghai: Guangming shuju, 1936, 353–62; pp. 353–54.

6   See Guo Moruo, "Geming yu wenxue" [Revolution and literature], in *Xin wenxue yundongshi ziliao* [Materials on the history of modern literature], ed. Zhang Ruoying, Shanghai: Guangming shuju, 1936, 363–75; p. 363.

7   See Leo Ou-fan Lee, *The Romantic Generation of May Fourth Chinese Writers*, Cambridge: Harvard University Press, 1973, 180. Chapter 9 is on Guo Moruo.

8   Paul Pickowicz discusses Guo's transformation as taking place "well within the framework of romanticism," with "the proletarian romantics of 1928 merely replac[ing] the individualistic, transcendental, and 'bourgeois' romanticism of their early history with

a more explicitly political and socially directed romanticism." Guo and others in the Creation Society were still against the materialist conception of art which tied culture to economic conditions, favoring an idealist view that glorified the proletarian class and romantically construed literature as the vanguard of the revolution. See *Marxist Literary Thought in China: The Influence of Ch'u Ch'iu-pai*, Berkeley, University of California Press, 1981, 86–87.

9   See *Shaonian shidai*, 1–2. The texts I have used in this chapter are the 1979 edition of Guo Moruo's four-volume autobiography published by Renmin chubanshe in Beijing. In his *Zhongguo wenxue lunji* [Collections of discussions on Chinese literature], literary critic and historian Zheng Zhenduo writes that in China only short autobiographies existed in traditional literature, and there are no texts that can stand alone as a volume. See *Zhongguo wenxue lunji,* Shanghai: Kaiming Publishers, 1934, 37. Wu Pei-yi points out the abundance of autobiographical texts but the lack of an academic tradition that recognizes them as autobiographies. *The Confucian's Progress*, Preface.

10   Han Shizhong, 1089–1151, a military official who compiled a history of the Song dynasty. See *Sung Biographies,* ed. Hans Franke, Wiesbaden, 1976, vol. 1, 373–76. Han Xin, a Han dynasty general who wrote a text called *Bingfa* [Military methods].

11   Nomination as rectification was espoused by Confucius:

Zilu said: "The ruler of Wei has been waiting for you, in order with you to administer the government. What will you consider the first thing to be done?" The Master replied, "What is necessary is to rectify names."

"So, indeed!" said Zilu. "You are wide of the mark! Why must there be such rectification?" The Master said, "How uncultivated you are, Yu! A superior man, in regard to what he does not know, shows a cautious reserve. If names be not correct, language is not in accordance with the truth of things. If language is not in accordance with the truth of things, affairs cannot be carried on to success. When affairs cannot be carried on to success, proprieties and music will not flourish. When proprieties and music do not flourish, punishments will not be properly awarded. When punishments are not properly awarded, the people do not know how to move hand or foot. Therefore a superior man considers it necessary that the names he uses may be spoken appropriately, and also that what he speaks may be carried out appropriately. What the superior man requires, is just that in his words there may be nothing incorrect."

The assignment of a proper name is the basis upon which language may be employed, and this in turn regulates all of the affairs of the world. Proper nomination is the key to the rectification of the self (the road to the "superior man"), and improper nomination, such as the attribution of a name to something that it is not, perverts the rectifying power of nomination. See Confucius, *Lunyu*, trans. James Legge, Oxford: Clarendon Press, 1893–95, book 13, chap. 3, 263–64.

12   In the section of his book called "Zhengtong guannian yu caizi jia liumang" [Orthodox concepts and the hooligan plus the scholar], Shi Jian (Ma Bin) describes this contradictory nature of Guo's description of his early childhood as the "combination of the hooligan and the scholar":

When Guo Moruo was a young child, his family was both hooligan and landlord. It is without doubt that the generation before him had received some orthodox education and began to tire of and cast off the life of the hooligan . . . [but] the generation of Guo Moruo's father clearly could not completely change, so they decided to let their sons escape this circle. . . . The early education from hooligans that Guo received was not direct, as his father did not teach him this; but that is how his environment was, and its influence was subtle and persuasive, so naturally he was contaminated by the customs of the hooligans.

See *Guo Moruo pipan* [Criticism of Guo Moruo], Hong Kong: Yazhou chubanshe, 1954, 180–81.

13 Guo came from a nouveau riche family that was "trying to attain gentry status through the education of its sons." See David Todd Roy, *Guo Mo-jo: The Early Years*, Cambridge: Harvard University Press, 1971, 2. Shi Jian describes the social environment of Guo's early years in this way: "In this period of transition, intellectuals have two roads: one is to study actively, and seek to change society by becoming a revolutionary; the other is to live with the sorrow of being unable to understand society, and find a way to numb oneself through the good life and self-enjoyment. From the beginning, Guo Moruo received orthodox education, but there was no way the Chinese classics and histories could change with the times." Ibid., 182.

14 Mothers are frequently the early agents of education in the lives of their sons (see Guo Moruo, Shen Congwen, Hu Shi), providing a positive approach to learning before it comes under the negative auspices of father/authority and society. In contrast is the relationship of the woman writer Lu Yin with her mother, who does not nourish her with study but rather functions as a schoolmaster, locking her in her room to "learn." Women, of course, were the indirect beneficiaries of their sons' education, since their status was dependent on their sons' success in the examination.

Even the warlord Feng Yuxiang wrote a two-volume autobiography entitled *Wode dushu shenghuo* [My life of study], Shanghai: Zuojia shuwu, 1947, with the purpose, he writes, of showing that in China it is more difficult for a poor man to study than to ascend to heaven [vol. 1, 4].

15 Writing in 1926 on his ideas about literature, Liu Bannong also brings up the problem of punctuation and separation of sentences and paragraphs. Whereas he supports the separation of essays into paragraphs to assist the reader in locating certain sentences or phrases which he or she wishes to investigate further, he believes the additions of periods will only restrict meaning. See Liu Bannong, "Wo zhi wenxue gailiang guan" [My ideas on literary reform], in Zhang Ruoying, *Xin wenxue yundong shi ziliao* [Materials on the history of the new literature movement], Shanghai: Guangming shuju, 1936, 63–77; pp. 75–76.

16 Liao Jiping (originally Liao Dengting, also known as Liao Ping) was a scholar of the Gongyang school of classical interpretation and supported the *jinwen* [new text] versions of the Chinese classics. He attained the *jinshi* degree in 1881 and headed the *Guoxueyuan* [Academy of Chinese studies] in Chengdu. Liao was a disciple of Wang Kaiyun in the 1880s and expressed his controversial theories in *Jingu xue kao* [On the new text and the ancient learning]. The Gongyang school held that the officially recognized *guwen* [old text] versions of the classics were inauthentic and the *jinwen* versions of the Former Han were authentic. Liao claimed that the *Zuozhuan* was a forgery by Liu Zin. Liao criticized Kang Youwei for stealing his ideas and demanded acknowledgment; whereas Kang admitted that he had been influenced by Liao's theories, he denied that he had plagiarized them. See Howard Boorman, *Biographical Dictionary*, vol. 2, 367–68; Hao Chang, *Liang Ch'i-ch'ao and Intellectual Transition in*

China, 1890–1907, 25; and Joseph Levenson, "Liao Ping and the Confucian Departure from History," in *Confucian Personalities*, ed. Arthur F. Wright and Denis Twitchett, Palo Alto: Stanford University Press, 1962, 317–25.

17   There are many other examples of unconventional use of names in the first part of Guo's autobiography. A teacher who asks students to read over inscriptions to find references to the selling of dog meat is called "Mr. Dogmeat" [*Gourou xiansheng*] [Guo, I, 106]. The students with whom Guo associates have a secret code name, *fenfei*, they use to refer to their nocturnal escapades, and a group of wild students is called "the eight great planets" [*ba da xingxing*]. These names are almost all secret or mysterious in the referent's lack of knowledge of the name or in the generation of the name through a secret or mysterious process.

18   There are some well known exceptions, such as Liao Ping, who refused appointment as a magistrate, choosing to remain in Sichuan so he could be near his parents. He taught in provincial schools before taking up his position in Chengdu.

19   Cen Chunxuan, 1861–1933, was a Qing official and rival of Yuan Shikai. He played a leading role in the anti-Yuan campaigns of 1915–16 and later joined the southern military government at Canton, serving as head of this government from 1918 to 1919. See Boorman, *Biographical Dictionary*, vol. 1, 305–8. Duanfang, 1861–1911, was the part-Manchu governor of Hubei from 1901–4 who became superintendent of the Guangzhou-Hanzhou-Chengdu Railway. See Boorman, ibid., vol. 2, 780–82.

20   Guo Moruo provides many examples of voyeurism as the motivation for passive participation. The conflicts between bandits and home protection units inevitably brings out people to watch, regardless of the danger [I, 275]. The marriage ceremony, another example, is surrounded by people wishing to watch what is going on [I, 280]. In the political and military world student leaders admit that their attendance at political meetings is merely to see what is happening [I, 224], and students go out to the city wall to see what is going on with the soldiers [I, 179]. Emphasis on *kan renao* devalues the motivation behind any specific action, implying that a political meeting, to which one supposedly would go in order to assist in the improvement of the political situation, is no different from a fight in the street. If voyeurism is a motive, all action taken by the individual is morally suspect. Most of this first volume of Guo Moruo's autobiography consists of descriptions of scenes or episodes where he is either a passive observer or someone being acted upon by others. The culmination of this passivity is his marriage, where Guo becomes a direct victim of this system for the first time.

21   As Guo describes his marriage ceremony, he twice refers to the "outside" world, and defensively qualifies his explanations of Sichuan customs by first writing that he does not know what the traditions of other places are like [Guo, I, 275, 285]. His apology for Sichuan against other unidentified traditions foreshadows confrontation with foreign elements that Guo will meet when he leaves Sichuan and to which he refers at the end of "Heimao."

22   These terms come from Spencer's *Study of Sociology* and were used by Yan Fu in his translation of that text. See Roy, *Kuo Mo-jo: The Early Years*, 52.

23   Organization based on the concept of total and unit is evident in *Zhang Ziping zizhuan* [The autobiography of Zhang Ziping], Shanghai: Diyi chubanshe, 1934. The first paragraph reads:

My home is Mei County in Guangdong. In the early Qing, it was called Jia-ying Province. Jiaying Province is a department formerly ruled by the provin-cial government, and it has four counties under its jurisdiction. But on its own, it also has jurisdiction over a considerable area of regions. After the Xinhai Revolu-tion, the regions under its direct jurisdiction were changed into county regions. Speaking accurately, Jiaying Province and Mie County cannot be lumped together, because the area of the present-day Mei is only a small part of the previous Jiaying Province.

Outside the east gate of Mei City, over thirty *li* away, there is a small county village called San Keng Yue, which belongs to Dongxiang Ward of the thirty-six wards. It is in this San Keng Yue—a half-country, half-city village—that I was born [2].

Like Guo, Zhang Ziping follows a general movement outward, from the family home to a series of schools, each farther away, to a large city, and finally to a foreign country.

24   In *Guo Moruo de wenxue daolu* [The literary road of Guo Moruo], Tianjin renmin chubanshe, 1981, 23, Huang Houxing comments:

But this was an era that had abandoned literature. All young people with ideals and qualifications took the road of "solid occupations to save the country" or "science to save the country." It was as if the ancient "spiritual civilization" of China could be supplemented by the "material civilization" of the West. . . . In this kind of environ-ment, even Guo Moruo, who had liked literature since he was a child, went along and looked down on literature. "Although the true nature of poetry occasionally lifted the mask of my fear, I refused it, as I had no desire to know it further." He did not continue to explore the "true spirit" of poetry; the "awakening of poetry" was killed in infancy as its sprouts broke through the ground.

The internal quote is from Guo Moruo, "Wode zuo shi de jingguo" [What I went through in writing poetry], in *Guo Moruo wenji*, Beijing: Renmin wenxue chubanshe, 1963, vol. II, 138–39.

25   This term appears later as a criticism of Guo by the poet Xu Zhimo. Guo internalizes the criticisms of others in his continual ironic reference to himself as a vandal who cries worthless tears.

26   Even though many students left, many returned quickly, and Chinese students con-tinued to study in Japan up until the 1930s.

27   In this context of international invasion and the violation of Chinese territory, as Guo discusses the formation of the literary group and his study of medicine in Japan, he mentions the dissection of a corpse, a Japanese girl with name attached to the body on a tag, in one of his classes. This incident, he writes, caused him to think up his first short story. It depicts a man who keeps the corpse of a girl in ice, raping it at his desire. The story was rejected by the magazine *Dongfang* [The east] [Guo, II, 49–50].

28   Guo Moruo insists that his autobiography is history or historical material [Guo, II, 2]. The only time Guo claims that the episode in question is not history is when he is defending himself against Lu Xun's attacks. Under this disavowal, however, is his frantic insistence that we accept his version of the "facts" [Guo, II, 28]. Only when he worries that the reader may question his "history" does he deny that it is such and claim it as his own personal interpretation.

29   Guo defends himself in several passages in these two chapters:

    A. Upon hearing from Tian Han that Zheng Boqi was not impressed with Guo when Zheng visited him in Japan [Guo, II, 61].

    B. When Xu Zhimo criticizes him as a superficial person whose tears are as worthless as a woman's [Guo, II, 95].

    C. When he is criticized in *Wenxue xunkan* (Literary tri-monthly) as an "indiscriminate translator" [Guo, II, 126].

    D. When Hu Shi criticizes him as "shallow, boring, and unaware of it" and "just out of school" [Guo, II, 141].

    E. When Liu Bannong criticizes him for "calling himself a poet like Goethe" [Guo, II, 197].

    F. When Zeng Qi criticizes him for following the "red" economic line [Guo, II, 223].

    G. When Lin Kui criticizes him for his play *Wu dikang zhuyi zhe* [Passive resistors] [Guo, II, 245].

Guo cites far fewer instances of praise. He admits that it is Lu Xun's criticism which prompts him to write "Chuangzao shinian," but this instance is only paradigmatic of all the criticism which forms a partial background to his negative transmission of the self.

30 See Roy, *Kuo Mo-jo,* 170, note 15.

31 At the beginning of the last section of "Continuation," Guo comments ironically on the way lecturers use language at the time, utilizing short sentences, slogans, and totally lacking in the analysis which they claim could put people to sleep [Guo, II, 230–34]. He states that instead of teaching people how to think, this method of lecturing discourages them from thinking. Language is corrupted and degraded in an opium den in the form of poetry riddles upon which participants bet. In this environment language is for the purpose of entertainment and profit [Guo, II, 236–38]. Third, Guo claims that the new terms of the era, such as *jingji* (economics) and *langman* (romantic), only cause misunderstanding. The other terms used with regularity in literary parlance, such as "genius," "poet," "slogan," and "foreign *bagu* (*yang bagu*), have, writes Guo, the power to kill.

32 The issues of race, negativity, and writing are again neatly tied together in a recent short story by Liu Daren ("Fengjing jiu ceng an," [Familiar scenes relearned], *Qishi niandai* [The seventies], April 1983, 88–95). The narrator of the story is a Chinese-American cancer specialist who is invited back to China, where he lived as a child, on a medical tour. His main fantasy is that he can be reunited with his "Fourth Uncle" (*sijiu,* a homonym for the "four olds," or old habits, old ways of thinking, old ideas, and old relationships, all criticized during the Cultural Revolution), not really a relative but a special friend of the family from his youth. When the family left China for Taiwan in 1949, Fourth Uncle prepared to follow, but was stopped by an unfavorable divination off a Chinese character. This is the first instance of the author depicting writing as symbolically powerful. Fourth Uncle, the narrator recalls, was an accomplished calligrapher who loved to write characters [91].

    When the narrator arrives in China, he finds he cannot communicate with Fourth Uncle, who simply refuses to talk of his experiences of the last thirty years. Language is no longer a tool of communication; Fourth Uncle can only repeat a few empty sentences. The narrator leaves disappointed, but arranges for Fourth Uncle to come and live with his family in the United States. Only when the narrator's children ask about the strange marks on their great-uncle's body does his nephew discover that his uncle was

tortured during the Cultural Revolution. After six months in America, Fourth Uncle decides to return to China.

When the narrator's family went to Taiwan in 1949, his father organized a study and calligraphy group, but eventually they stop meeting, as contemporary society in Taiwan does not seem to nourish such activity. The symbolic use of writing as a means to maintain and extend cultural identity cannot survive outside the physical confines of China. When the narrator comes of age and takes up residence in America, he also loses part of his language and cultural identity, as his wife and children, although ethnically Chinese, cannot speak the language.

Fourth Uncle's job in China is to use his fine calligraphy to write out political slogans—a context that degrades the art of writing but retains the symbolic power of writing lost outside China, in Taiwan and America. Fourth Uncle has accepted both his torture and his continued voluntary existence in the nation that tortured him and, in contrast to those who have left China, continues to exist as a symbol of racial and linguistic integrity. See Wendy Larson, "Writing and the Writer in the Works of Liu Daren," *Proceedings of the 1986 Summer Workshop for Gifted Teachers of Chinese and Russian,* ed. Albert Leong and Wendy Larson, Eugene: University of Oregon, 1987, 59–63.

33 Depending on the interpretation of the character *lai* in "Gui qu lai," the title could mean "Returning Going Coming" or "Returning Going."

34 Guo also comments on his desire to immortalize the spirit of a friend who died along the way and appeals to the reader to take over the burden of his memory [III, 3], turning this section of his text into a type of memorial quite common in premodern China.

35 Ironically, Guo Moruo gets his first taste of "proletarian" literature when he reads *Zhuzai ji* [The record of a coolie], a story written by a coolie who had been exploited in America. I have not been able to locate this story. Jack London's writing astonishes him: "Many Chinese students went to America or France, but none of them wrote about workers [Guo, I, 38]. These books he identifies as the catalysts in his eventual conversion to Marxism and to proletarian literature. However, Guo Moruo does not become enlightened about the Chinese laborer through direct experience, but through a *text* written by a victim of mistreatment in another country.

36 Even though he comes to doubt the value of literature, it is during the 1930s that Guo establishes his reputation as a classical scholar, publishing *Jiaguwenzi yanjiu* [Research on tortoise shell characters], *Jin wen yu shi zhi yu* [Further interpretations on bronze inscriptions], and *Yin Zhou qingtong qi ming wen yanjiu* [Inscriptions on copper instruments of the Shang and Zhou dynasties], all in 1931, and following up with *Jin wen congkao* [Investigations into inscriptions on bronze] in 1932 and *Gudai mingke huikao* [Studies in ancient inscriptions] in 1933.

37 "K" for Kuo, the Wade-Giles romanization of Guo's last name.

38 Guo has trouble recasting his work with Chiang Kai-shek as revolutionary. He again uses the term "vandal," which was used by Lu Xun to criticize him and his literary friends, to reproach his enemies. He calls Chiang Kai-shek a vandal [III, 122, 135], and the "Three Principles ('-isms') of the People" have turned into "vandal-ism" under Chiang's guidance [III, 129]. In "Qing kan jinri de Jiang Jieshi" and in "Tuoli Jiang Jieshi yihou," Guo goes to great lengths to discredit the Nationalist party leader. In the

late 1920s Guo worked in the Nationalist party under Chiang's supervision, and in this text he attempts to present himself as a double agent working for the revolutionary forces at an early date [III, 126–29]. At the same time, however, he attaches great importance to his discussions with Chiang, often quoting them in full and even implying that Chiang regards him in a special light and feels he is indispensable [III, 126, 146]. Although he writes that he merely "went along with him [Chiang]," Guo becomes a secret political section chairman and calls himself a "private prostitute" [III, 147–48].

39 The term *zuoguan* can refer to being an officer in the military or being a civilian official in the government. As I have previously discussed, in the first volume of his text Guo indicts government officials as corrupt, inefficient, and anachronistic. In *Wode shaonian shidai* Mr. Chen tries for decades to pass the exam and become an official and is finally killed by a concubine when he succeeds. Guo's brother sees his idealistic hopes of saving the country vanish after he becomes an official.

40 Zhang Fagui (1896–1980) was a Cantonese military official commander of the Twelfth Division and later was in the Fourth Army. Zhang worked for Chiang Kai-shek initially but later opposed Chiang's connection with Wang Jingwei.

41 One reader pointed out that "gui qu lai" may mean either "returning, going, coming," or "returning, going," with "lai" functioning as a particle; another reader wrote that "gui qu lai" means "the return" or "returning," without any separate meaning assigned to "qu" or "lai." Previous usage would seem to indicate that the interpretation "the return" is correct (Tao Yuanming's poem *Gui qu lai ci*, for example, is usually translated as "the return"), but since there is dissent among native speakers, I translated each word. The main significance of "returning" and its implication is the same in all translations.

42 For comment on the inaccuracy of some of the facts in *Hongpo qu*, see Sima Changfeng, "*Hongpo qu* li de chaqu" [The tune of *Hongpo qu*], *Nanbei ji*, no. 33 (February 16, 1973), 64–65. The article has a picture of Guo with the caption: "When Zhu De was on the long march, Guo Moruo was hiding in Japan." See also Sima Changfeng, "Guo Moruo de *Hongpo qu*" [The *Hongpo qu* of Guo Moruo], *Nanbei ji*, December 16, 1972, 50–52.

43 Guo uses the character *yi*, which usually refers to something left because of death, three times.

44 Chen Wei-ming claims that it is only during wartime that Lao She's stories became more affirmative of *wen*, or writing and writers. "Pen or Sword: The Wen-Wu Conflict in the Stories of Lao She (1899–1966)," Ph.D. dissertation, Stanford University, 1984, 95. In other words, when literature has a clear goal, either propagandistic or commemorative, it is "useful."

Works Cited

Ayers, William. *Chang Chih-tung and Educational Reform in China*. Cambridge: Harvard University Press, 1971.

Ba Jin. *Ba Jin zizhuan* [The autobiography of Ba Jin]. Shanghai: Diyi chubanshe, 1934; Hong Kong: Zili chubanshe, 1956.

Ba Jin. "Wenxue shenghuo wushinian" [Fifty years of a literary life]. In *Chuangzuo huiyi lu* [Recollections of literary creation], 1–10. Hong Kong: Joint Publishing, 1981.

Bao Xiaotian. *Chuanyinglou huiyilu*. Hong Kong: Dahua chubanshe, 1971.

Berninghausen, John, and Theodore Huters. *Revolutionary Literature in China: An Anthology*. White Plains, N.Y.: M. E. Sharpe, 1976.

Birch, Cyril. *Anthology of Chinese Literature*. Vols. 1 and 2. New York: Grove Press, 1965.

Beijing daxue, Beijing shifan daxue, Zhongwenxi jiaoshi tongxue [The students and teachers of the Chinese departments of Beijing University and Beijing Shifan University]. *Tao Yuanming yanjiu ziliao huibian* [Collection of edited materials on the research of Tao Yuanming]. Beijing: Zhonghua shuju, 1962.

Boorman, Howard, ed. *Biographical Dictionary of Republican China*. New York: Columbia University Press, 1968.

Borthwick, Sally. *Education and Social Change in China: The Beginnings of the Modern Era*. Stanford: Hoover Institute, Stanford University, 1983.

Cao Juren, *Wensi* [Literary thoughts]. Hong Kong: Chuangken chubanshe, 1956.

Chang, Hao. *Liang Ch'i-ch'ao and Intellectual Transition in China, 1890–1907*. Cambridge: Harvard University Press, 1971.

Chen, Wei-ming. "Pen or Sword: The Wen-Wu Conflict in the Stories of Lao She (1899–1966)." Ph.D. dissertation, Stanford University, 1984.

Chou Min-chih. *Hu Shih and Intellectual Choice in Modern China*. Ann Arbor: University of Michigan Press, 1984.

Chow, Rey. "Mandarin Ducks and Butterflies: Toward a Rewriting of Modern Chinese Literary History." Ph.D. dissertation, Stanford University, 1986.

Chow Tse-tsung. *The May Fourth Movement*. Cambridge: Harvard University Press, 1964.

Confucius. *Lunyu* [The analects]. 3 vols. Trans. James Legge. Oxford: Clarendon Press, 1893–95.

Davis, A. R. *T'ao Yuan-ming (A.D. 365–427): His Works and Their Meaning*. Vols. 1 and 2. Cambridge: Cambridge University Press, 1983.

Dirlik, Arif. *The Origins of Chinese Communism*. New York: Oxford University Press, 1989.

Doleželová-Velingerová, Milena, and Doležel, Lubomír. "An Early Chinese Confessional Prose: Shen Fu's *Six Chapters of a Floating Life*." *T'oung Pao* 58 (1972), 137–60.

Donato, Eugenio. "The Ruins of Memory: Archeological Fragments and Textual Artifacts?" *Modern Language Notes* 93, no. 4 (May 1978).

Elman, Benjamin A. *From Philosophy to Philology: Intellectual and Social Aspects of Change in Late Imperial China*. Cambridge: Council on East Asian Studies, Harvard University, 1984.

———. "Imperial Politics and Confucian Societies in Late Imperial China: The Hanlin and Donglin Academies." *Modern China* 15, no. 4 (October 1989), 379–418.

Feng Yuxiang. *Wo de dushu shenghuo* [My life of study]. Dongqing: Sanhu tushu she, 1940; part of the volume was also republished by Shanghai: Zuojia shuwu, 1947.

Franke, Wolfgang. *The Reform and Abolition of the Traditional Chinese Examination System*. Cambridge: Harvard University Press, 1960.

Frankel, Hans H. "T'ang Literati." In *Confucian Personalities*, ed. Arthur F. Wright and Denis Twitchett, 65–83. Palo Alto: Stanford University Press, 1962.

Fudan daxue Zhongwenxi: Xiandai wenxuezu xuesheng [Chinese Department, Fudan University: students of the modern literature group]. *Zhongguo xiandai wenxue shi: 1919–1942*, [History of modern Chinese literature: 1919–1942]. Chinese Department, Fudan University, n.d.

Gao Dapeng. *Tao shi xinlun* [New discussions on Tao Yuanming's poetry]. Taipei: Shibao wenhua chuban shiye youxian gongsi, 1981.

Grieder, Jerome B. *Hu Shih and the Chinese Renaissance: Liberalism in the Chinese Revolution*. Cambridge: Harvard University Press, 1970.

Gunn, Janet Varner. *Autobiography: Towards a Poetics of Experience*. Philadelphia: University of Pennsylvania Press, 1982.

Guo Dengfeng, ed. *Lidai zishuzhuan wenchao* [Self-narratives and autobiographies throughout the ages]. Vols. 1 and 2. Shanghai: Shangwu shuju, 1937. Includes 114 authors and 140 works.

Guo Moruo. *Geming chunqiu*. 2 vols. Shanghai: Xin wenyi chubanshe, 1956, 1957.

———. "Geming yu wenxue" [Revolution and literature]. In *Xin wenxue yundongshi ziliao* [Materials on the history of modern literature], ed. Zhang Ruoying. Shanghai: Guangming shuju, 1936.

———. *Moruo zizhuan* [The autobiography of Guo Moruo]. Vols. 1–4. Beijing: Renmin chubanshe, 1979.

———. *Shaonian shidai*. Shanghai: Haiyan shudian, 1947.

———. "Sima Qian fafen" [Sima Qian gets angry]. In *Guo Moruo wenji* [An anthology of Guo Moruo's writings]. Shanghai: Chunming shudian, 1949.

———. "Wenxue yu shehui" [Literature and society]. In *Guo Moruo wenji* [The works of Guo Moruo], vol. 17, 326–28. Beijing: Renmin wenxue chubanshe, 1963.

———. "Wenyi jia de juewu" [The awakening of a litterateur]. In *Xin wenxue yundongshi ziliao* [Materials on the history of modern literature], ed. Zhang Ruoying. Shanghai: Guangming shuju, 1936.

———. "Wo zuo shi de jingguo" [What I went through in writing poetry]. In *Guo Moruo wenji*, vol. 2. Beijing: Renmin wenxue chubanshe, 1963.

Handlin, Joanna. *Action in Ming Thought: The Reorientation of Lu K'un and Other Scholar-Officials.* Berkeley: University of California Press, 1983.

Hegel, Robert E., and Hessney, Richard C. *Expressions of Self in Chinese Literature.* New York: Columbia University Press, 1985.

Hightower, James. *T'ao Ch'ien.* London: Clarendon Press, 1970.

Hirokawa Sukehiro. *Natsume Soseki.* Tokyo: Shinshoosha, 1976.

Ho, Ping-ti. *The Ladder of Success in Imperial China: Aspects of Social Mobility, 1368– 1911.* New York: Columbia University Press, 1962.

Holzman, Donald. *Poetry and Politics: The Life and Works of Juan Chi.* Cambridge: Cambridge University Press, 1976.

Hsia, C. T. "Yen Fu and Liang Ch'i-chao as Advocates of New Fiction." In *Chinese Approaches to Literature From Confucius to Liang Ch'i-chao,* ed. Adelle Rickett. Princeton: Princeton University Press, 1978.

Hu Shi. *Hu Shi wenxuan* [Selections from Hu Shi's writings]. Taipei: Yuandong tushu gongsi, 1968.

———. *Sishi zishu* [Self-narration at forty]. Shanghai: Yadong tushu gongsi, 1933; Taipei: Yuandong tushu gongsi, 1969.

———. "Wenxue gailiang quyi" [Suggestions for literary reform]. In *Zhongguo xin wenxue yundong shi ziliao* [Materials on the history of the new literature movement in China], ed. Zhang Ruoying. Shanghai: Guangming shuju, 1936 (first published in 1934).

———. "Zai tantan zhengli guogu" [Another discussion of the organization of the national past]. In *Guoxue yandu fa lunji* [Collection of discussions on research methodology in Chinese studies], ed. Hu Shi and Liang Qichao, 33–37. Taipei: Mutong wenshi zongshi, 1974.

———. "Zhixue de fangfa yu cailiao" [Methodology and materials in research]. In Hu Shi and Liang Qichao, *Guoxue yandu fa lunji* [Collection of discussions on research methodology in Chinese studies], 161–72. Taipei: Mutong wenshi zongshi, 1974.

Hu Shi and Liang Qichao. *Guoxue yandu fa lunji* [Collection of discussions on research methodology in Chinese studies]. Taipei: Mutong wenshi zongshi, 1974.

Huang, Philip. *Liang Ch'i-ch'ao and Modern Chinese Liberalism.* Seattle: University of Washington Press, 1972.

Huang Houxing. *Guo Moruo de wenxue daolu* [The literary road of Guo Moruo]. Tianjin: Tianjin renmin chubanshe, 1981.

Huang Zhongkun. *Tao Yuanming zuopin yanjiu* [A study of Tao Yuanming's work]. Taipei: Bomier shudian, 1975 (originally 1969).

Huters, Theodore. "From Writing to Literature: The Development of Late Qing Theories of Prose." *Harvard Journal of Asiatic Studies* 47, no. 1 (1987), 51–96.

———. "A New Way of Writing: The Possibilities for Literature in Late Qing China, 1895– 1908." *Modern China* 14, no. 3 (July 1988), 243–76.

Jian Shi [Ma Bin]. *Guo Moruo pipan* [Criticism of Guo Moruo]. Hong Kong: Yazhou chubanshe, 1954.

Jin Yingxi. "Hu Shi de zhixue fangfa he qi fandong benzhi" [Hu Shi's research methods and their reactionary nature]. In *Hu Shi sixiang pipan* [Criticism of Hu Shi's thought], vol. 3, 258–67. Beijing: Sanlian shudian, 1955.

Johnson, David. "Communication, Class, and Consciousness in Late Imperial China." In *Popular Culture in Imperial China,* ed. Evelyn Rawski, 34–72. Berkeley: University of California Press, 1985.

Judd, Ellen R. "Prelude to the 'Yan'an Talks': Problems in Transforming a Literary Intelligentsia." *Modern China* 11, no. 3 (July 1985), 377–408.

Kinkley, Jeffrey C. *The Odyssey of Shen Congwen.* Stanford: Stanford University Press, 1987.

Larson, Wendy. "Writing and the Writer in the Works of Liu Daren." In *Proceedings: Summer 1986 Intensive Workshop in Chinese and Russian,* ed. Albert Leong and Wendy Larson, 59–63. Eugene: University of Oregon, 1987.

Lee, Leo Ou-fan. *Lu Xun and His Legacy.* Berkeley: University of California Press, 1985.

———. *The Romantic Generation of May Fourth Chinese Writers.* Cambridge: Harvard University Press, 1973.

———. *Voices from the Iron House: A Study of Lu Xun.* Bloomington: Indiana University Press, 1987.

Lee, Leo Ou-fan, and Andrew Nathan. "The Beginnings of Mass Culture: Journalism and Fiction in the Late Ch'ing and Beyond." In *Popular Culture in Imperial China,* ed. Evelyn Rawski, 360–95. Berkeley: University of California Press, 1985.

Levenson, Joseph. "Liao Ping and the Confucian Departure from History." In *Confucian Personalities,* ed. Arthur F. Wright and Denis Twitchett, 317–26. Palo Alto: Stanford University Press, 1962.

Li Changzhi. *Sima Qian zhi renge yu fengge* [The character and style of Sima Qian]. Hong Kong: Taiping shuju, 1963.

Li Chendong. *Tao Yuanming pinglun.* Taipei: Zhonghua wenhua chuban shiye weiyuanhui, 1956.

Li Da. *Hu Shi fandong sixiang pipan* [A critique of Hu Shi's reactionary thought]. Hankou: Hubei renmin chubanshe, 1955.

Liang Qichao. *Tao Yuanming.* Shanghai: Shangwu yinshuguan, 1923.

———. *Sanshi zishu* [Autobiography at thirty]. In *Lidai zixuzhuan wenchao,* ed. Guo Dengfeng, 91–101. Shanghai: Shangwu shuju, 1937.

Liao Zhongan. *Tao Yuanming.* Shanghai: Zhonghua shuju, 1965.

Lin Shu. *Lenghongsheng zhuan* [The biography of the cold-red master]. In *Lidai zixuzhuan wenchao,* ed. Guo Dengfeng, 330–32. Shanghai: Shangwu shuju, 1937.

Liu Bannong. "Wo zhi wenxue gailiang guan" [My ideas on literary reform]. In *Xin wenxue yundong shi ziliao* [Materials on the history of the new literature movement], ed. Zhang Ruoying. Shanghai: Guangming shuju, 1936.

Liu Daren. "Fengjing jiu ceng an" [Familiar scenes relearned]. *Qishi niandai* (April 1983), 88–95.

Liu Xinhuang, ed. "Qingmo minchu de wentan shulun" [On the literary circles of the late Qing and early Republic]. In *Xiandai Zhongguo wenxue shihua* [On the history of modern Chinese literature]. Taipei: Zhengzhong shuju, 1971.

Lu Xinli, ed. *Tao Yuanming ji* [A collection of Tao Yuanming's works]. Beijing: Zhonghua shuju, 1979.

Lu Xun. "Geming shidai de wenxue" [Literature in a period of revolution]. In *Eryiji.*

Shanghai: Beixin shuju, 1928. Also found in *Lu Xun quanji* [The complete works of Lu Xun], vol. 3. Beijing: Renmin wenxue chubanshe, 1963.

———. *Lu Xun quanji* [The complete works of Lu Xun], edited by the editorial board of Lu Xun xiansheng jinian weiyuanhui. Shanghai: Lu Xun quanji chubanshe, 1938.

———. "Wenyi yu zhengzhi de qitu" [The diverging roads of literature and politics]. In *Lu Xun quanji* [The complete works of Lu Xun], vol. 7. Beijing: Renmin chubanshe, 1981.

———. *Zhaohua xishi* [Morning blossoms picked at dusk]. Beijing: Beixin shuju, 1933. Other published versions include Dalian: Lu Xun quanji chubanshe, 1947, and Hong Kong: Sanlian shudian, 1958 (annotated).

Lu Yin. *Lu Yin zizhuan* [The autobiography of Lu Yin]. Shanghai: Diyi chubanshe, 1934.

Mao, Nathan K. *Pa Chin.* Boston: Twayne Publishers, 1978.

Michaels, Walter Benn. "The Interpreter's Self: Peirce on the Cartesian 'Subject.'" *Georgia Review* 31 (Summer 1977), 383–402.

Nieh Hua-ling. *Shen Ts'ung-wen.* New York: Twayne Publishers, 1972.

Ng, Mau-sang. *The Russian Hero in Modern Chinese Fiction.* Hong Kong: Chinese University Press, and New York: State University of New York Press, 1988.

Olney, James, ed. *Autobiography: Essays Theoretical and Critical.* Princeton: Princeton University Press, 1980.

Ouyang Fanhai. *Lu Xun de shu* [The books of Lu Xun]. Guangzhou: Lianying chubanshe, 1949.

Ozaki Hideo. "Rojin to Nihon" [Lu Xun and Japan]. In *Rojin to Gendai* [Lu Xun and the modern era], ed. Sasaki Kiichi. Tokyo: Keisoo shoboo, 1968.

Pickowicz, Paul G. *Marxist Literary Thought in China: The Influence of Qu Qiubai.* Berkeley: University of California Press, 1981.

Průšek, Jaroslav. *The Lyrical and the Epic,* ed. Leo Ou-fan Lee. Bloomington: Indiana University Press, 1980.

Rosenheim, Edward. "The Satiric Spectrum." In *Satire: Modern Essays in Criticism: From Formalism to Post-Structuralism.* Baltimore: Johns Hopkins University Press, 1980.

Roy, David Todd. *Kuo Mo-jo: The Early Years.* Cambridge: Harvard University Press, 1971.

Salusinszky, Imre. *Criticism in Society.* New York: Methuen, 1987.

Sanger, P. Steven. *History and Magical Power in a Chinese Community.* Palo Alto: Stanford University Press, 1987.

Shanley, Lyndon. *The Making of Walden.* Chicago: University of Chicago Press, 1957.

Shapiro, Stephen A. "The Dark Continent of Literature: Autobiography." *Comparative Literary Studies,* no. 5 (1968), 421–54.

Shen Congwen. "*Congwen zizhuan* fuji" [Afterword to *The Autobiography of Shen Congwen*]. In *Shen Congwen wenji* [Selections of essays by Shen Congwen], vol. 11. Hong Kong: Joint Publishing, 1985, 76–78.

———. *Shen Congwen zizhuan* [The autobiography of Shen Congwen]. Shanghai: Zhongyang shudian, 1943; Shanghai: Kaiming shudian, 1949. Also published as *Congwen zizhuan,* Hong Kong: Wenli chubanshe, 1960. Republished in *Shen Congwen sanwen xuan* [Selections from the essays of Shen Congwen], 1–118, Beijing: Renmin wenxue chubanshe, 1982.

———. "Xiaoshuo yu shehui" [Fiction and society]. In *Shen Congwen wenji,* vol. 12, 128–35. Hong Kong: Joint Publishing, 1985.

―――. "Xin wenren yu xin wenxue" [New literati and new literature]. In *Shen Congwen wenji*, vol. 12, 166–71. Hong Kong: Joint Publishing, 1985.

Shen Fu. *Fusheng liuji* [Six chapters of a floating life]. Beijing: Renmin chubanshe, 1980.

Shi Jian [Ma Bin]. *Guo Moruo pipan* [Criticism of Guo Moruo]. Hong Kong: Yazhou chubanshe, 1954.

Sima Changfeng. "Guo Moruo de *Hongpo qu*" [Guo Moruo's *Song of the Rushing Waves*]. *Nanbeiji* (February 16, 1972), 50–52.

―――. "*Hongpo qu* li de chaqu" [The tune of *Song of the Rushing Waves*]. *Nanbeiji*, no. 33 (February 16, 1973), 64–65.

Sima Qian. *Taishigong zixu* [The self-written preface of the grand historian]. In *Lidai zixuzhuan wenchao*, ed. Guo Dengfeng, 101–36. Shanghai: Shangwu shuju, 1937.

Spengemann, William. *The Forms of Autobiography: Episodes in the History of a Literature*. New Haven: Yale University Press, 1980.

Sprinker, Michael. "The End of Autobiography." In *Autobiography: Essays Theoretical and Critical*, ed. James Olney. Princeton: Princeton University Press, 1980.

Sun Dingguo. "Pipan Hu Shi zhexue sixiang de fandong shizhi" [A critique of the reactionary nature of Hu Shi's philosophical thought]. In *Hu Shi sixiang pipan* [Criticism of Hu Shi's thought], new ed., vol. 1, 126–78. Beijing: Sanlian shudian, 1955.

Sun Zhongtian, Zhang Fen, Fan Yeben, Wu Tianlin, Xiao Xinru, and Gao Changchun. *Lu Xun zuopin jiangjie* [Explanation and discussion of the works of Lu Xun]. Jilin: Renmin chubanshe, 1979.

Tao Yuanming. *Wuliu xiansheng zhuan* [The biography of Master Five Willows]. In *Lidai zixuzhuan wenchao*, ed. Guo Dengfeng, 247–48. Shanghai: Shangwu shuju, 1937.

Tao Yuanming yanjiu [Research on Tao Yuanming], edited by the editorial board of Jiusi congshu. 2 vols. Taipei: Jiusi congshu, 1977.

Tompkins, Jane P., ed. *Reader-Response Criticism: From Formalism to Post-Structuralism*. Baltimore: Johns Hopkins University Press, 1980.

Wakeman, Frederic. "The Price of Autonomy: Intellectuals in Ming and Ch'ing Politics." *Daedalus* (Winter 1972), 35–70.

Wang Huanxi. *Zhongguo wenxue jingyao shumu* [A catalog of essentials in Chinese literature]. Beijing: Jianshe tushuguan, 1930.

Wang Tao. *Miyuan laomin zizhuan* [The autobiography of the old one of Mi yuan]. In *Lidai zixuzhuan wenchao*, ed. Guo Dengfeng, 315–27. Shanghai: Shangwu shuju.

Watson, Burton. *Ssu-ma Ch'ien, Grand Historian of China*. New York: Columbia University Press, 1958.

Williams, Raymond. *Culture and Society: 1780–1950*. New York: Columbia University Press, 1983.

Wu, Pei-yi. *The Confucian's Progress: Autobiographical Writings in Traditional China*. Princeton: Princeton University Press, 1989.

Wu Tianlin. "Cong baicaoyuan dao sanwei shuwu" [From the garden of a hundred plants to three-flavor study]. In *Lu Xun zuopin jiangjie* (contributors: Sun Zhongtian, Zhang Fen, Fan Yeben, Wu Tianlin, Xiao Xinru, Gao Changchun), new ed. Jilin: Renmin chubanshe, 1979.

Wu Ying, ed. *Lu Xun wenlun xuan* [Selections from Lu Xun's essays]. Nanning: Guangxi renmin chubanshe, 1985.

Xiao Wangqing. *Tao Yuanming piping* [A critique of Tao Yuanming], 5. Hong Kong: Taiping shuju, 1963. Originally published by Shanghai: Kaiming shudian, 1947.

Yi Shunding. *Ku an zhuan* [The autobiography of the crying bowl]. In *Lidai zixuzhuan wenchao*, ed. Guo Dengfeng, 332–34. Shanghai: Shangwu shuju, 1937.

Yu, Pauline. *The Reading of Imagery in the Chinese Poetic Tradition*. Princeton: Princeton University Press, 1987.

Yu Ying-shih. "Some Preliminary Observations on the Rise of Ch'ing Confucian Intellectualism," *Tsing Hua Journal of Chinese Studies* 11, nos. 1–2 (December 1975).

Zhang Ziping. *Zhang Ziping zizhuan* [The autobiography of Zhang Ziping]. Shanghai: Diyi chubanshe, 1934.

Zhao Cong. *Wusi wentan diandi* [Bits and pieces on May Fourth literary circles]. Hong Kong: Youlian chubanshe, 1964.

Zheng Nong. *Wenxue wenda ji* [Questions and answers on literature]. Shanghai: Shenghuo shudian, 1937 (first published in 1935).

Zheng Pengyuan. *Liang Qichao yu minguo zhengzhi* [Liang Qichao and Republican government]. Taipei: Shihuo chubanshe, 1978.

Zheng Qian. "Tao Yuanming yu tianyuan shiren" [Tao Yuanming and the field and garden poets]. In *Tao Yuanming yanjiu* [Research on Tao Yuanming], vol. 1, 397–408. Taipei: Jiusi chubanshe, 1977.

Zheng Zhenduo. *Zhongguo wenxue lunji* [Collection of discussions on Chinese literature]. Shanghai: Kaiming chubanshe, 1934.

Zhong Youmin. *Tao Yuanming lunji* [Essays on Tao Yuanming]. Changsha: Hunan renmin chubanshe, 1981.

Zhou Hulin. *Sima Qian yu qi shixue* [Sima Qian and his historical study]. Taipei: Wenxizhe chubanshe, 1978.

Zhou Xiashou [Zuoren]. *Lu Xun xiaoshuoli de renwu* [The characters in Lu Xun's novels]. Shanghai: Shanghai chubanshe, 1944.

Zhu Qian. "Tao Yuanming." In *Tao Yuanming yanjiu* [Research on Tao Yuanming], vol. 1. Taipei: Jiusi chubanshe, 1977.

Index

Agriculture: Liang Qichao and, 21; Tao Yuanming and, 20

Ai Wu, 80–81, 84

Alternatives: aesthetics and Tao Yuanming as, 23; authority and, 47, 61; of Japan, 97–99; of labor, 46, 79; to literature or scholarship, 87; of military work, 79; orthodoxy and Tao Yuanming as, 19–24; of politics, 132; to social involvement, 54; to textual work, 2, 8; within literature, 141–46; to writing, 46

Authority, 161 n.1; autobiography and, 8; contradiction in, 4; impressionistic, 4; literary, 1, 4, 5; Liu Yuxi and, 18; negative, 24, 93; of phenomena, 60; Sima Qian and, 15; social, 3; socio-material, 2, 4, 5, 74; textual, 5, 46, 61–62, 74–76

Autobiography: authority and, 8; Chinese, 11, 119–20, 161 n.2, 178 n.31; circumstantial, 3, 11–12, 18, 22, 56, 58, 113, 121, 154, 166 n.11, 177 n.26; deconstruction and, 126; as historical enterprise, 102–3; impressionistic, 3, 5, 7, 11–12, 27–28, 47, 50, 154, 171 n.31, 177 n.26; modern, 155–56; Western, 119–20, 168 n.24

Ba Jin, 61, 76–80, 85, 93, 146, 153–54; alternative of labor and, 76–77, 80; books and, 78–80; childhood and, 76–78; China as concept and, 78–79; father and, 77; homosexuality and, 78; orthodoxy and, 76, 79; writing and, 78–79

Ba Jin zizhuan, 61, 76–80

Biography, Chinese, 2; Liu Yuxi and, 19; orthodoxy and, 58; Tao Yuanming and, 20, 22

Bo Juyi, 26–28, 50; Buddhism and, 27; impressionistic autobiography and, 26, 28; myth and, 28; nomination and, 27–28; as poor, 27

Books: Ba Jin and, 146; book-learning and, 172 n.2; collecting of, 82, 173 n.5; as dry and dull, 71; as hazardous, 78–80; Hu Shi and, 105; impoverishment by, 82; as life, 70; Lu Xun and, 94–98; versus material production, 67–69; as useless, 115; as world, 81; versus the world, 70–71

Cai Yuanpei, 48, 80, 84, 137

Calligraphy: the examination system and, 45; race and, 192–93 n.32; as useless, 143; *Xin Qingnian* and, 85

Cao Juren, 26, 182 n.19

Castration: Li Ling case and, 16; Sima Qian and, 13–16; writing and, 16

Chen Duxiu, 48, 84

Chen Xiying, 88–89
Childhood and prechildhood: Ba Jin and, 76–78; bizarre events in, 66, 69, 94–96, 119–21, 126–27; Guo Moruo and, 120–24; Hu Shi and, 104; Lu Xun and, 94–96; Shen Congwen and, 67–70
China: as a concept, 76, 78–79, 93–94, 119; versus Japan, 98–101, 144–46; as a land of writing, 82–83; as negative, 98–99, 127, 130–37, 146; as poor, 149–51; as weak, 145–46
Class, social: Ba Jin and, 76–80; laboring and, 80, 85; orthodoxy and, 122
Codes: of action, 154–55; alternative, 154–55; literary, 3, 5, 12, 24–26, 61–62; of text, 154–55
Cohen, Paul A., 52–53
Conservatism, 5; circumstantial stance and, 177 n.27; impressionistic stance and, 51; Lin Shu and, 48, 176 n.23
Contradiction, 61–62; in autobiography, 8; Guo Moruo and, 117; of literature and revolution, 117; of self and work, 85; Wang Tao and, 55; of *wen* and *wu*, 72; of world and text, 71
Creation Society, 59, 93; Guo Moruo and, 132
Culture, 150; literature and, 64, 137; versus the market, 42–44; as national, 98; traditional Chinese, 63

Davis, A. R., 19–20
Diaries: in circumstantial autobiographies, 58
Dirlik, Arif, 84–85
Dream of the Red Chamber, 110, 171–72 n.34

Educational system: Chinese, 124; the examination system and, 34–35, 44–46; fathers and, 69, 96; versus the garden, 96–97; Guo Moruo and, 121, 124–28; as infrastructure, 59; Lu Xun and, 95–97; versus material phenomena, 69–71; mothers and, 69, 189 n.14; as a new world, 74; as orthodoxy, 70; as positive, 104–5; Shen Congwen and, 69–71; Wang Tao and, 53
Examination system, 6, 7, 31–35, 43–44, 121, 155; education and, 44–46; as link between literature and politics, 63–65; Liu Yuxi and, 17; mothers and, 69; Wang Tao and, 52; Zhang Zhidong and, 33–34

Gao Dapeng, 20
Geming chungiu, 137–46
Guo Bogong, 20
Guo Moruo, 6, 59, 79, 99, 109, 113–53, 162 n.3, 164 n.12, 178 nn.38–39; bizarre motifs and, 69; China as a concept and, 113, 127, 130–37, 144–46; as forced to write, 5; language and, 135; literature and, 114–16, 131–38, 141; Marxism and, 59, 116, 118; nation and, 131–37; Qu Yuan and, 118, 148, 150–51; race and, 118–19, 137–38, 145–46; rejection of *wenren* and, 116; revolution and, 117; science and, 135; sexuality and, 125–26; Sima Qian and, 166 n.11; textual work and, 118
Guo Shaoyu, 36–37

Hirakawa Sukehiro, 99
Homosexuality: Ba Jin and, 78
Hongpo qu, 146–52
Hu Shi, 6, 48, 59, 87–88, 101–12, 120, 140, 153–54, 138 nn.38–39; critique of Chinese scholarship and, 106–10; national past and, 106–9; negative textual work and, 5; as overly textual, 9, 110–12; People's Republic of China critique of, 110–12; rotten paper and, 101, 108; science and, 107–9
Huters, Theodore, 35–40

Intellectuals, 9, 132; as enlightened individuals, 45; the examination system and, 34; Lin Shu and, 48; post-1949, 158–59; rank and, 139–41; Tao Yuanming and, 26; workers, peasants, and soldiers and, 148

Japan, 140; as alternative, 97–99, 130–31, 144; racism and, 133–34
Jin Yingxi, 110–11

Kan renao: as passive observation, 74–75; as voyeurism, 190 n.20
Kingston, Maxine Hong, 126–27
Ku an zhuan, 50–51
Kuo, Ping Wen, 34–35

Labor and work, manual or physical, 46, 60, 61, 76, 80–84, 146, 153; adulation of, 85; as code, 154; as important, 84; versus literature, 92; as practical, 63; as sacred, 80; theory of, 84–85; as vital, 73
Labor and work, textual or literary, 2, 59, 61, 64; as code, 154–55; as deficient, 25, 65; demeaning of, 3, 4, 162; the examination system and, 65; as harmful to the nation, 88, 110, 112; Hu Shi and, 9, 106–12; as impractical, 63; as killing, 80; in the late Qing, 35–40; as negative, 4, 5, 71, 110–12, 153–60; versus other work, 10, 11, 25, 28, 62, 113, 118, 153; versus military work, 65–67, 72–74; overdetermined, 109–10; as passive, 74–75; privileging of, 74; reality and, 40; as scholarship, 102, 106–10; versus social involvement and, 38–39, 116, 132, 153; as valuable, 114–16. See also Literature; Writing
Language: dead, 105; disorder and, 135; national, 98; as negative, 192 n.31; poverty of, 68; punctuation of, 107, 189 n.15; versus reality, 68, 128
Leng hong sheng zhuan, 49–50
Li Da, 111
Liang Qichao, 6, 50, 52, 55–58, 123; circumstantial stance and, 58; marital prowess and, 56; new citizen and, 64; as reformer, 55–56; as revolutionary, 55–56; Shiji and, 57; as wenren, 55; writing and, 57
Lin Shu, 47–50, 52, 54, 57; conservatism and, 48; courtesans and, 49; impres-

sionistic stance and, 48–50; intellectuals and, 48; poverty of, 49; transmission and, 49
Literati: as effete, 18 n.11; as false, 75; modern ideology and, 24–26, 114; Tao Yuanming and, 21–26; Wang Tao and, 52
Literature: as a central discourse, 38, 44; as cure, 136; disorder and, 135; essentialization of, 41–43; the examination system and, 44; form of, 106; history and, 103–4; leisure and, 91–92; living, 106; Lu Xun and, 39; nation and, 131–33; national weakness and, 90–92; negativity and, 39; versus physical work, 82–84; political ideology and, 76; as Qing category of knowledge, 37; Qing theories of, 38–40; race and, 138; versus reality, 84; as repository of culture, 64; versus revolution, 87–93, 139; revolutionary, 117, 132–33; as science, 135; as social labor, 141; and social role, 90–92; as socially significant, 134–35; as useless, 87; as valuable, 114–16. See also Labor and work, textual or literary; Writing
Liu Daren, 192–93 n.32
Liu E, 62–63
Liu Yuxi, 17–19, 54–55; circumstantial stance and, 18; examinations and, 17; Sima Qian and, 18; textual authority and, 18; Wang Shuwen and, 18–19
Lu Yin, 185 n.12, 189 n.14
Lu Xun, 79, 87–101, 104, 109, 119–20, 132, 135, 146, 153–54, 156–58, 162 n.6, 164 n.12; attack on education, 5; bizarre motifs and, 69; childhood and, 94–97; education and, 95–101; Japan and, 97–101; literature versus revolution and, 87–88, 89–93; on literature versus work, 92; on Mara poetry, 39; nation and, 93, 98–101; on race, 93, 101; on scholarship, 88–89; Zhang Shizhao and, 88

Mao Dun, 64–65

Mao Zedong, 148, 151–52, 158–59, 180 n.4

Marxism, 47, 152; Guo Moruo and, 59, 116, 118; Hu Shi and, 106–112; literary theory and, 159–60, 182 n.20; Mao Zedong and, 180 n.4

Material production: death and, 68–69; as distinct from writing, 2, 67–69; literature and, 114; versus literature, 92; water and, 67–69

May Fourth, 59–60, 113, 152, 162 n.4, 174 n.11; era, 1, 43–45; intellectuals, 46, 62; as labor-learning experience, 85; modernity and, 120, 155

Memory: Lu Xun and, 100; Shen Congwen and, 66; Tao Yuanming and, 24

Mi yuan laomin zizhuan, 53–55

Military work, 159; versus Chinese traditions, 47, 52; as code and mystique, 66, 154; foreign, 46, 130, 156; versus literary work, 44, 46, 60, 65–67, 72–74, 84, 139, 153–60; martial prowess and, 56; moral authority and, 129; organization and, 46; as reality, 79, in text, 95

Modernity, 1, 7; circumstantial texts and, 61–65; education and, 125; the examination system and, 31–35, 40; ideology of text and, 8, 12, 154–56; as ideology, 8, 120; internal production of, 5; literary, 1; nation and, 133; self and, 137; the recluse-literatus and, 24–26

Monuments, 149–52; Nanjing and, 150; Tolstoy and, 149

Moruo zizhuan, 119–52

Mythologizing: Hu Shi and, 104; of literature, 64; Lu Xun and, 94–96; self and, 28; Tao Yuanming and, 20

Nation, 88, 150; internalization of, 131–37; literature and, 90–92; national past and, 106–10; nationalism and, 56; negative authority and, 93, 98–101, 119, 136; race and, 138, 145–46; railway and mining rights, 46; Zhang Ziping and, 145–46

National essence, 43

Nomination: Bo Juyi and, 27–28; false, 121, 127; figural, 28; proper, 54; Tao Yuanming and, 22

Orthodoxy: bankruptcy of, 124–27; biography and, 58; childhood and, 121–24; counter-orthodoxy and, 168 n.22; the examination systems and, 32; Liu Yuxi and, 19; myth and, 119–21; Tao Yuanming and, 9, 19–35; teachers and, 126; tradition and, 29

Others: power of, 73, 79, 154

Ouyang Fanhai, 92–93

Ozaki Hideo, 99

Passivity, 74, 81, 129; of Chinese, 99–101

Peasants, 148, 158, 163 n.11; Tao Yuanming and, 20, 25–26, 155

Phenomena, material: authority of, 60; bizarre, 69, as real education, 71; Sima Qian and, 14

Poetry, 155; the examination system and, 33, 45; Guo Moruo and, 117–18, 124, 151; as punishment, 124; workplace, 84

Poverty: Bo Juyi and, 27; China and, 149–51; of language, 68; Lin Shu and, 49; modern critique of, 25; Tao Yuanming and, 23–24; of teachers, 125; Yi Shunding and, 51

Qingnian shidai, 80–81

Qu Yuan, 118, 148, 150–51

Race, 88, 150; commoners and, 137; disillusionment with the Chinese, 136; nation and, 138, 145–46; negative authority and, 93, 98–101, 119, 192–93 n.32; and prostitutes, 137; as reformist ideology, 56; soldiers and, 137; writing and, 134, 136

Realism: critical, 152; European, 47; social, 65, 152

Reality: broader, 63; versus language, 68, 128; versus literature, 84; manual labor

as, 85; of military work, 79, 85; opposed to reclusivity, 21; as peasant life, 26; social work as, 85

Recluse, 163 n.11; Tao Yuanming as, 20–21

Rectification: Bo Juyi and, 28; of self, 15; Sima Qian and, 15; of time, 15

Referentiality, 11–12; context of, 3, 24, 29, 113, 164 n.2; literary, 8, 26; referential language and, 17, 24; socio-material, 8; Tao Yuanming and, 22, 24–26; textual work and, 61

Reform: Liang Qichao and, 55; for modern writers, 63; Wang Tao and, 52

Return: as act, 99–101; nation and, 144–48

Revolution, 9, 61, 64, 146; versus books, 105; as code, 154–55; versus the individual, 141; literature and, 117; versus literature, 87–93, 139, 153; as medicine, 134, 136; rank and, 139; as ritual, 129; writing and, 65

Rosenheim, Edward, 40–41

Sanshi zishu, 56–59

Satire, 40–41

Scholarship, 87; as anti-revolutionary, 89; versus banditry, 124; Chinese, 102, 106, 110; conservatives and, 88–89; as evidential or experimental, 108; as *kaozheng* or *yanjiu*, 9, 111, 160, 173 n.5, 187 n.3; as negative, 106–10, 156; as overdetermined, 109–10; versus social movements, 105; *Woman Warrior* and, 127

Science: as cure, 136; versus textual work, 5, 6, 87–88, 106, 112, 155; examination system and, 33, 45, 52; social, and literature, 114–15, 135; Western, 153

Self, 62; knowledge, 57; as lost, 62–63; romanticized, 142; Western, 168 n.24

Sexuality, 125–26, 129; classical texts and, 126

Shaonian shidai, 119–31

Shen Congwen, 4, 61, 65–76, 79–80, 85, 93, 104, 135, 140–41, 153, 156; on books, 67–68, 70–72; death and, 68; education of, 71–76; literary metaphor and, 83; military versus literary and, 65–67, 72–76; on the material, 67–69; 71; passivity and, 74–76; reality versus language and, 68; orthodoxy and, 70; as soldier, 69, 72–76; textual authority and, 74–76; water, and, 67–68

Shen Congwen zizhuan, 61, 65–76

Shen Fu, 179 n.41

Shiji, 13–17, 54, 57

Sima Qian, 13–17, 54–55; castration and, 13–16; Liu Yuxi and, 18; orthodox ideology and, 14; rectification and, 15; Sima Tan and, 13–15; as transmitter, 13–16; 49–50; writing and, 16

Soldiers, 9, 67, 69, 73–74, 163 n.11; as common, 140; Guo Moruo and, 118, 139–41; uncultured, 137

State, the, 45–46

Statecraft: letters and, 37

Sun Dingguo, 110

Tao Yuanming, 19–26, 50; agricultural life and, 20–26; as alternative, 20–24; biography and, 22; circumstantial stance and, 22; as literati ideal, 21; modern ideology and, 24–26; nomination and, 22; orthodoxy and, 20–23; peasants and, 25–26; poverty and, 23–24; transmission and, 24; twentieth-century appropriation of, 20–21, 24–26; as recluse, 20–26; in *Wenxin*, 25–26; writing and, 22–25

Teaching, 45, 97, 125, 127–28; as negative, 126–28

Tompkins, Jane P., 40–41, 183 n.5

Tongcheng school, 36–37

Transmission: Sima Qian and, 15–16, 165 n.10; Tao Yuanming and, 24; teachers and, 126

Wakeman, Frederick, 45–46

Wang Guowei, 38–40

Wang Shuwen, 18–19
Wang Tao, 47, 50–55; alternative life and, 54; educational system and, 53; examination system and, 52–53; literati and, 52; nomination and, 54; as reformer, 52–53; science and, 52; Taiping rebellion and, 53–54
Watson, Burton, 13
Wenren, 12, 47; Liang Qichao and, 55; as premodern category, 63, 116, 158–59, 164 n.3; Qing theories of, 36–37; splitting of, 25, 172 n.36
Wensi, 26, 182 n.19
Wenxin, 25–26, 81–84, 163 n.11
Williams, Raymond, 42–43
Woman Warrior, 126–27
Workers, 9, 60, 82–84, 142, 158, 163 n.11; body strength, 160; brain strength, 160; intellectuals and, 142–43; revolutionary, 143
World: as book, 81; versus books, 70–71; versus text, 65
Writing, 4, 146; alternatives to, 46; castration and, 16; commemorative, 151–53; as dead libraries, 136–37; as distinct from material production, 2, 67–69; examination system and, 33; as hazardous, 78–79; as indicator, 47; versus manual labor, 76, 82–84; as negative, 2, 60, 63–65, 152, 192–93 n.32; race and, 134, 137; redefinition of, 8; as riddles, 137;

as self-knowledge, 57; as sick, 144; Sima Qian and, 16; Tao Yuanming and, 22–23; textual authority and, 43; as tool of action, 83; as toxin, 133–34, 137; as valid, 148; for workers, peasants, and soldiers, 148. *See also* Labor and work, textual or literary; Literature
Wuliu xiansheng zhuan, 19–24
Wu Tianlin, 96–97

Xia Mianzun, 81, 163 n.11
Xiao Wangqing, 20
Xin Qingnian, 84–85

Yan'an, 151
Ye Shaojun, 25, 41–44, 81, 163 n.11
Yi Shunding, 47, 50–52, 54, 57; circumstantial stance and, 50; conservatism and, 51; essentialism and, 51; impressionistic stance and, 50; poverty and, 51
Yu Dafu, 134, 162 n.6

Zhang Shizhao, 88, 183 n.1
Zhang Zhidong, 33–34
Zhang Ziping, 145–46, 190 n.23
Zhang Ziping zizhuan, 145–46
Zhaohua xishi, 89, 92–101, 119
Zheng Nong, 114–16, 175 n.13
Zi Liuzi zizhuan, 17–19
Zuiyin xiansheng zhuan, 26–28

Wendy Larson is Associate Professor of Chinese Language
and Literature at the University of Oregon. She has
published a translation of a novel by the contemporary
writer Wang Meng, *Bolshevik Salute: A Modernist Chinese
Novel,* and is working on a book on women and writing in
modern China. Her research interests include feminism,
literary and cultural theory, and modern Chinese
literature.

Library of Congress Cataloging-in-Publication Data
Larson, Wendy
Literary authority and the modern Chinese writer:
Ambivalence and autobiography / Wendy Larson
ISBN 0-8223-1113-5
1. Authors, Chinese—20th century—Biography.
2. Chinese literature—20th century—History and
criticism.
PL2277.L563   1991
895.1'09005—dc20
[B]   90-27835 CIP